01-15

On the Path to Enlightenment

Translated from the Tibetan
with the collaboration of
CHRISTIAN BRUYAT
of the
Padmakara Translation
Group

English translation by
CHARLES HASTINGS

On the Path to
ENLIGHTENMENT

Heart Advice from the Great Tibetan Masters

MATTHIEU RICARD

Shambhala
BOSTON & LONDON
2013

Shambhala Publications, Inc.
Horticultural Hall
300 Massachusetts Avenue
Boston, Massachusetts 02115
www.shambhala.com

ENGLISH EDITION © 2013 SHAMBHALA PUBLICATIONS, INC.

This is an abridged edition and English translation of
Chemins spirituels: Petit anthologie des plus beaux textes tibétains
© NiL Editions, 2010, Paris.

9 8 7 6 5 4 3 2

Printed in the United States of America

♾ This edition is printed on acid-free paper that meets
the American National Standards Institute z39.48 Standard.
♻ This book is printed on 30% postconsumer recycled paper.
For more information please visit www.shambhala.com.

Distributed in the United States by Penguin Random House LLC
and in Canada by Random House of Canada Ltd

Designed by Michael Russem

Library of Congress Cataloging-in-Publication Data
Chemins spirituels. English. Selections
On the path to enlightenment: heart advice from the great Tibetan
masters / Matthieu Ricard; translated from the Tibetan with the
collaboration of Christian Bruyat of the Padmakara Translation
Group; English translation by Charles Hastings.—First Edition.
pages cm.
ISBN 978-1-61180-039-5 (pbk.)
1. Spiritual life—Buddhism—Quotations, maxims, etc. 2.
Buddhism—Tibet Region—Quotations, maxims, etc. I. Ricard,
Matthieu, editor of compilation, translator, writer of added
commentary. II. Title.
BQ7775.C49213 2013
294.3'444—dc23
2013000270

To Taklung Tsetrul, Pema Wangyal Rinpoche,
with great respect and gratitude

What we call "mind" is a very curious phenomenon. Sometimes it is rigid and resistant to any change. It can also become very flexible as long as we make constant efforts to transform it and convince ourselves, through reflection, that this change is not only possible but essential. To do so, wishes or prayers are not enough. We need to use reason based on experience. One should not expect this transformation to happen overnight, as our old habits will resist any rapid solution.

HIS HOLINESS
THE FOURTEENTH DALAI LAMA

Contents

Preface

These few drops taken from the vast ocean of Tibetan Buddhist literature are not intended to be a definitive anthology. They are simply a compilation of the most inspiring texts that I have had the privilege to read over the years. I chose them for their clarity and for the authenticity of their authors.

I wanted the passages quoted in this book to represent as wide a range as possible of the different spiritual traditions of Tibet. On several occasions, I have drawn from sources that I found particularly clear and refreshing, especially those of the masters that I have had the good fortune to meet and who so perfectly represent traditions that have been preserved intact to this day. My choice has also included the words of the Buddha himself, as well as certain teachings of the great Indian Buddhist masters often quoted in Tibetan literature.

This is a "small" anthology since it does not pretend to be exhaustive, if only because of my limited knowledge. But I hope that, like a drop of honey, which, despite its small size, has all the flavor of the jar from which it is taken, this collection will contain the essence of the Buddhist path, especially in its most practical aspect, the use of every moment of existence to progress toward enlightenment.

In Bhutan in 1981, the great Tibetan spiritual master Dilgo Khyentse Rinpoche (1910–91) gave the transmission of the *Treasury of Spiritual Instructions (Gdams ngag mdzod)*, which lasted for two months. In this thirteen-volume collection, Jamgön Kongtrul, one of the greatest masters of the nineteenth century, brought together the pith instructions of what are known as the Eight Great Chariots of the Accomplishment Lineage. The eight chariots are the main transmission lineages of Buddhist teachings that flourished in Tibet: Nyingma, Geluk-Kadam, Sakya, Kagyu, Shangpa Kagyu, Kalachakra, Orgyen Nyendrub, and Chö-Shiche (see the appendix for more on these lineages).

One evening, after the teachings, Khyentse Rinpoche said to me, "When we come to appreciate the depth of the view of the eight great traditions and also see that they all lead to the same goal without contradicting each other, we think 'Only ignorance can lead us to adopt a sectarian attitude'." So, to illustrate the words of Khyentse Rinpoche, I made the wish to translate a selection of texts from all of these schools. This little anthology is the modest fulfillment of that aspiration.

I translated many of the texts in the collection myself during the thirty-five years that I have spent in the East. Those from other sources are referenced in the sources section. Sometimes I went back to the Tibetan and modified the first translation.

According to tradition of the Padmakara Translation Group,* of which I am a member, the translations were checked with the original Tibetan by another translator, in this case, my friend Christian Bruyat, who also modified the translation of many texts. While doing the English translation, Charles Hastings not only improved the flow of the presentation but again checked some important passages against the Tibetan original and made a number of improvements.

Preliminary versions of this anthology benefited from sugges-

---

* Padmakara was founded over thirty years ago to translate the great texts of Tibetan Buddhist literature as accurately as possible and publish them so as to make them accessible to Western audiences.

tions by Carisse Busquet, Madeleine Tréhin, Yahne Le Toumelin, and other members of the Padmakara Translation Group.

We are very grateful to the Tsadra Foundation for its support to the Padmakara Translation Group for the revision of the French translation.

Introduction

Buddhism is essentially a way of knowledge that leads to liberation from suffering. The awakening in which it culminates is both a wisdom based on an accurate understanding of reality and a freedom from the disturbing emotions and obscurations caused by ignorance. The practice of Buddhism does not require us to give up what is good in our life, but to abandon the causes of suffering, to which we are often attached to the point of addiction. So studying the Buddhist teachings does not mean overloading the mind with a lot of information. We just need to master the specific knowledge that will enable us to get free from samsara, the cycle of lives conditioned by ignorance and pain.

The Buddhist path is structured so that it takes into account the gradual nature of inner transformation. Each step leads naturally to the next. It is like building a house: you cannot put the roof on without having laid the foundation, raised the walls, and installed the timbers.

Certain factors will help this transformation. The most important is to realize that one already possesses the potential for transformation, what Buddhism calls "buddha-nature," or literally "the embryo of buddhahood." Then comes the inspiration aroused by meeting an authentic spiritual master, followed by an enthusiastic determination to cultivate altruism, compassion, and the other essential qualities that the master exemplifies, and finally, the perseverance that is indispensable to achieve any real change.

I

The reflections, meditations, and spiritual exercises that we use along the way make use of the body, speech, and mind, but ultimately it is the mind that we must transform to put an end to our own suffering and that of all beings. That is why the Buddha said,

> Without doing any harmful act,
> Abundantly perform beneficial acts.
> Completely tame your mind.
> That is the Buddha's teaching.

Where can we start? To truly set out in a meaningful way on the road to transformation, we have to first take a close look at ourselves. "What am I doing with my life? What have been my priorities until now? What can I do with the time I have left to live?" Of course these thoughts only make sense if we feel that change is both desirable and possible. "Can I say that nothing needs to be improved in my life and the world around me? Is that change possible?" It is up to us to decide.

The next question is in what direction we want to change. "If I try to climb the social ladder, to become rich or have more pleasure, am I really sure that these things, if I can achieve them, will bring real fulfillment?" At this crossroads, where we are asking what our goals should really be, we need to be honest with ourselves and not satisfied with superficial answers.

The answer that Buddhism provides is that our human life is extremely precious; the disillusionment that comes over us at times does not mean that life is not worth living. However, we have not yet clearly identified what it is that makes it meaningful.

"The question is not whether life has a meaning, but how each of us can give it one," says the Dalai Lama.

Our extremely precious existence is even more so when we enjoy all our physical and mental faculties, have the freedom to choose what we do, and use those conditions to release the potential for transformation that is within us. Time is running out. Accidents, sickness, and, inevitably, death can occur without warning. Hence there is an emphasis on diligence.

This anthology reflects the different stages of the spiritual journey according to the Tibetan Buddhist tradition, which is founded on the original Buddhism of India. First come four topics for contemplation that transform our worldview and turn our mind toward spiritual practice. The first of these reflections concerns the extraordinary potential of human existence. The second invites us to observe the transient nature of everything in general and life in particular, so as to encourage us to make the best use of the limited time available. The third is the law of the cause and effect of actions. If we want to end suffering and achieve enlightenment, as with any other goal, we need to go about it in the right way. There are things to be done and others to be avoided because each of our actions inevitably affects both ourselves and the outside world. This reflection helps us to understand the consequences of our behavior and the conclusions we can draw from that understanding. The fourth contemplation concerns the defects of samsara, which means conditioned existence characterized by ignorance and suffering. These four topics of contemplation help us to distinguish between the actions, words, and thoughts that need to be cultivated and those that will bring us unhappiness or simply waste our time.

The teachings of the great Buddhist masters are not random recipes. They are real guides that spring from the living experience of experts in the spiritual path, who possess extraordinary knowledge and understand clearly the mechanisms that produce happiness and suffering.

Once we have explored these four themes, we will discuss the concept of "taking refuge." This does not mean invoking the protection of occult and mysterious powers but relying on the teachings that lead to enlightenment, which means true knowledge of mind and the nature of reality. It is that knowledge that can free us from suffering. At first, it is essential to rely on beings that already have that wisdom and illustrate it by their actions. Their perfect representative is the Buddha.

Then come the teachings on altruism and compassion, which are the heart of the path. What is the point of freeing yourself from suffering when those around you continue to suffer? Such a limited approach would be doomed to failure because our joys and sorrows are inevitably linked to those of others. In other words, we all have to cross "the ocean of suffering" together.

Before starting a journey, it is essential to equip oneself with the things one needs to reach one's destination and deal with the obstacles that will inevitably arise on the way. It is the same with the spiritual adventure. We must first get rid of the mental poisons that prevent our mind from evolving and second generate the "merit," or positive energy, that will provide the necessary momentum for the process of interior growth.

We also need the invaluable assistance of spiritual friends and especially a qualified master who, by the power of his own experience and great kindness, will be able to untiringly show us the way.

The best gift that a spiritual teacher can give is to show us the nature of our own mind so that we can recognize it. Generally, what is called "mind" or "consciousness" seems to be a mass of thoughts related to perceptions, emotions, memories, and imagination. But behind that curtain of thoughts, can we discern the fundamental component of the mind? Can we see the pure awareness of the present moment that underlies all mental activity? What the great meditators that we quote in this anthology have to say will help us to recognize the essential nature of mind and master the thoughts and emotions that, until now, have endlessly followed, one after the other, and kept us in a state of confusion.

Then we will see, as explained by the sages of the past, how it is essential to allot periods of time in which we can fully concentrate on the process of inner transformation.

We will see what practices are involved, either for the hermit who withdraws temporarily from the world or for the practitioner who pursues his or her spiritual journey in the context of everyday life. We will see how both must learn to perceive the world more clearly and develop ever-expanding love and compassion for all beings. We will see what kind of view, meditation, and action they practice to accomplish their goal for themselves and for others.

Finally we will include advice for avoiding the traps such as laziness, pride, and uncontrolled passions that the demon of ego is sure to lay in our path. Often, out of humility, this advice is presented in the form of reprimands addressed to the author himself. They provide valuable tools to enable us to progress without hindrance.

We have prefaced each chapter of the collection with a few sentences of introduction, to provide a small bridge between the reader and the texts whose vocabulary and style are not necessarily familiar to everyone.

May these few treasures we have inherited from the Tibetan Buddhist sages of the past allow us to make the best use of our own wealth, the extraordinary potential of human existence!

PART ONE

Turning the Mind
to the Spiritual Path

CHAPTER I

The Value of Human Existence

The first step for someone who aspires to follow the spiritual path is to understand how precious this human life is. Used wisely, it offers a unique opportunity to actualize the potential for enlightenment that is within us all, yet it is very easy to neglect or squander. According to Buddhism, of all possible life forms that we may take in the round of existences, being born as a human is highly unusual. It is compared to enjoying a banquet after centuries of famine.

One reason why this life is so precious is that all beings have within them what is called "tathagatagarbha" in Sanskrit, the essence of, or potential for, buddhahood, which is the fundamental nature of all conscious beings. That nature, temporarily obscured by confusion and disturbing emotions, is like a treasure buried within us. The purpose of practicing the Buddhist path, or "Dharma," is to remove those obscurations. We are not trying to "manufacture" the state of buddhahood but simply to reveal what is already there since we cannot add to or subtract from that nature, which is the very basis of our mind. The qualities acquired on the way to enlightenment are not fabricated. They reflect the gradual reactivation of our nature, like the brilliance of a jewel covered in mud that is revealed gradually as the dirt is removed.*

* Some scholars of Buddhism have a slightly different view and consider that the *tathagatagarbha*, or essence of buddhahood, is not fully present in every being but develops through the practice of the path, like a seed that matures and eventually gives fruit, in this case buddhahood.

Shabkar Tsogdruk Rangdröl

A sailor should cross the ocean if he has a boat; a general should defeat the enemy if he has an army; a poor man should milk the "cow of plenty"* if it is within his reach; a traveler who wants to go to distant lands should pursue his journey if he has an excellent horse. As for you, who have a precious human life for the moment and have received instructions from a spiritual master, the embodiment of all the buddhas of the three times,† think with joy and enthusiasm of traveling the great path of the supreme Dharma and getting ever closer to the ultimate goal: enlightenment and liberation.

Shechen Gyaltsap

We now have a precious human life, through which we have met an authentic spiritual master, received profound teachings, and are on the path to liberation. However, if, like an explorer who returns empty-handed from an island covered with treasure, we just enjoy this inestimably valuable life for some time without bringing back the gem of the sublime Dharma, our journey will have been useless. And if, caught up in the activities of daily life, we neglect the liberating instructions, we will have possessed this invaluable human existence but gained nothing from it.

The implementation of the Buddha's teaching, the Dharma, mostly takes place in the mind. The mind relies on the body, and the relationship between the two is rarely perfect. If you are lucky enough not to be affected by diseases of body and mind, if you are

---

* In Buddhist mythology, it is called an "inexhaustible cow udder"; it is the symbol of abundance and the fulfillment of any aspiration.

† The buddhas of the past, present, and future. According to Mahayana Buddhism, 1,001 buddhas have appeared or will appear during our era, or *kalpa*, which represents the duration of a particular universe. Shakyamuni Buddha, born about 2,500 years ago, is said to be the fourth of its buddhas.

not bound to the service of anyone and thus enjoy all the freedom necessary for spiritual practice, seize this opportunity without further delay and devote all your energy to the supreme path.

Dilgo Khyentse Rinpoche

Ask yourself how many of the billions of inhabitants of this planet realize how rare it is to have been born a human being.* How many of those who realize this think of using that chance to practice the Dharma? How many of these actually start to practice? How many of those who start continue to practice? How many of those who continue attain ultimate realization? The number of those who attain ultimate realization is like the number of stars you can see at daybreak compared to the number you can see on a clear night.

We need to be born a human being, as this is the only state of existence in which there is enough suffering to give us an acute desire to be free from samsara, yet not so much suffering that we no longer have the opportunity to free ourselves through the practice of Dharma. If we do not make use of the precious opportunity of a human existence, we cannot but go downward, like a stone rolling down a hill.

Jamgön Kongtrul Lodrö Thayé

Getting butter from milk is only possible because milk already contains cream. No one ever made butter by churning water. The prospector looks for gold in rocks and not in wood chips. Likewise, the quest for perfect enlightenment only makes sense

* The author is saying that even if they seem to be extremely numerous, they only represent an infinitesimal fraction of the sentient beings populating all the different realms of existence. A human life is thus extremely rare compared to all the other possibilities.

because buddha-nature is already present in every being. Without that nature, all efforts would be futile.

Shechen Gyaltsap

You might ask: "If the nature of buddhahood is in me, why can't I perceive it right away?" It is because, like gold hidden in its matrix, that nature is hidden by the tendencies we have accumulated since time immemorial, tendencies that have themselves been created by mental poisons and then reinforced by the actions that those disturbances have produced. It says in *The Praise of the Ultimate Dimension*, "The brilliance of the sapphire is always there, ready to manifest, but does not appear while the sapphire remains embedded in its matrix. The ultimate dimension is immaculate but remains hidden under the thick veil of confusion. Its brightness cannot manifest in samsara, the world of suffering, but is revealed in nirvana, the state beyond suffering."*

You might also wonder if it is possible that all beings, even dogs or pigs, have deep in their consciousness the many qualities of buddhahood, such as the "ten strengths." Those qualities are in fact present in the potential for enlightenment of all living beings; the fundamental nature of consciousness and its attributes cannot be separated, just as fire cannot be separated from heat. But these qualities are not manifest. It is like a sword whose sharpness remains invisible while the blade is in its sheath, or like a mirror, which has the capacity to reflect shapes and colors but not while it remains in darkness.

The qualities of enlightenment are inherent in consciousness but can remain invisible for a long time. The ultimate nature of mind, emptiness endowed with the qualities of supreme enlight-

---

* *Praise of the Ultimate Dimension* (Skt. *dharmadhatustava*, Tib. *chos dbyings bstod pa*), composed by Nagarjuna.

enment, is always present in us but remains latent until we recognize it and become familiar with it. It is not enough to intellectually understand the nature of mind. We have to get rid of the veils that obscure it, and the best way to do so is to generate the bodhichitta, the "mind of enlightenment," which is the supreme intention to achieve enlightenment for the benefit of all beings. That is the only way to discover true enlightenment or, in other words, to become buddha.

Jigme Khyentse Rinpoche

ADVICE FOR A BASKET WEAVER

Some people say they have no purpose in life, yet they definitely have at least one: they want to be happy, just like all beings. We all want to be happy. This feeling is the basic and fundamental sign that we have a potential within us, a richness to be exploited. No one, deep down inside, really wants to suffer. Even if a masochist says he likes to suffer, it is only because it gives him pleasure.

To feel responsible for our loved ones is commendable, but we have the ability to open our mind and accept the responsibility for infinite beings. Why limit our deep sense of tenderness to a few people, when we can extend it to all beings? Moreover, with respect to our friends and relatives, we should offer them something really useful that we can be proud of when we die. It is not enough to make them happy by taking them on a cruise, for example. What would that really do for them? If they have a problem, it might entertain them for a while, but in most cases, they will take their problems with them wherever you take them. If they have a broken heart, if their boyfriend or girlfriend has left them, or if someone has upset them, they will go over and over their bitterness on the ship, and it will still be there after the cruise has ended. We have much better things to do to help those around us.

Think about it. What would we like to pass on to our children? A good image of ourselves, so they see us as being better than we really are? What's the point? Or material goods? That would be handing them a heap of problems. They will squabble over our wealth after our death, and even if we share it with them in our lifetime, some of them will think themselves hard done by and envy what the others have received. They can get material comfort by other means, by working, for example. Our presence? Whether we like it or not, they will be separated from us when we die. At that time, their grief will not bring us back to life and will do them no good.

But we could also leave them an inspiration, a vision that is meaningful and that can give them confidence in every moment of their lives. Of course, to be able to do that, we need to get some confidence ourselves, to develop an inner certainty. It is obvious that this feeling can only come from our mind, so it is high time we did something about it.

Since we were born, we have let our mind do what it likes, like a spoiled child, and we have to admit that nothing really positive has come of it. To take control of it is indispensable. That is something worth spending time on, even if it is just a little bit each day.

So we had better think again and use our common sense. If we let our mind mistreat us so that we spend our lives suffering and making others suffer around us, that's a sign of a lack of common sense. The thoughts and words that come from a disturbed state of mind can be considered "negative." Instead of complaining about our fate, if we cultivate altruism and compassion, so that those "positive" states of mind improve our well-being and that of others, that shows that we do have common sense.

The underlying sense of uneasiness that we have now is actually a good thing: it is the expression of our sensitivity. Those who go through life without feeling ill at ease are unconscious. The uneasy feeling caused by our awareness holds tremendous potential for transformation. It is a treasure of energy that we can grasp with both hands and use to build something better. Indifference doesn't lead anywhere.

If you think that the whole world is your enemy, imagine that you are a basket weaver, and you have a huge pile of reeds. To make baskets, you have to weave them in the right way. Similarly, faced with the challenges you encounter, you have to weave an inner basket big enough to hold all the ups and downs of life without them overwhelming you. In short, you need to take care of your mind wisely.

Minling Terchen Gyurme Dorje

Advice to ease the pain of the noble lady named Sönam Paldrön,
a native of Ukpa Lung.

Namo guru ratnaya!
Homage to the masters and the Three Jewels!*

My mind closely united
With that of the immensely good Teacher,
I beg him to rain on us
The shower of his blessings
So that all painful circumstances
May be spontaneously liberated in great bliss.

The alternation of thoughts
Of happiness and suffering, desire and aversion,
Is nothing more than the play

---

* The Three Jewels: The Buddha; his teaching, the Dharma; and the community of practitioners, the Sangha.

Of luminous emptiness and mind.*
Without altering whatever arises,
Look at its nature,
And you will perceive it as great bliss.

While you have this human existence,
Apply yourself wholly to practice the supreme Dharma.
The thousand things to be done will never end.
They are vain distractions, devoid of substance.
Forsake them all completely!

When you have subdued an opponent,
A thousand more are still to be overcome.
Instead, crush your negative emotions,†
Which are the enemies dwelling in your mind.

Family and friends may get along,
But discord easily arises.
Those who are dear to us in this life
Are also causes of torment.

It may be that you become rich,
But you will have a hard time being satisfied.
Be able to cut the knot of greed.
That is what really matters.

---

* This refers to the fact that, as will be explained in other texts, the mind is not a truly existent entity. However, it is not a mere nothingness but has the "luminous" quality of consciousness.

† Attachment, aversion, ignorance, pride, and jealousy (Tib. *nyon mongs*, Skt. *klesha*). These mental states arise from fundamental ignorance of the nature of mind and the phenomenal world. They disturb the mind and are the source of negative actions, which lead to suffering.

When you are betrayed by those you trusted,
Let your heart rely on the unfailing Three Jewels!

When you are in despair after the loss of a beloved child,
Clearly understand the ultimate nature of your affliction,
And rest, mind free and open
In the space of indescribable luminous emptiness.

It is absurd to maintain attachment and hatred
Toward beings of the six realms
Who have all been our parents.
Realize that they are all equal.
Is this not in itself a great liberation, a great happiness?

All happy or unhappy situations
Are the essence of mind itself, free of mental fabrications,
Like rainbows that do not alter the sky.
Leave everything in vast space free from attachment!

Shechen Gyaltsap

When heat, moisture, and fertile soil come together, you do whatever you can to sow grain. When you discover a deposit of gold
or silver, you do whatever you can to exploit it. When the crops
are ready in autumn, you do whatever you can to harvest them.
When you have an escort to accompany you on a dangerous path,
you redouble your energy. When you have labor and assistants,
you accomplish your tasks. Now that you have a precious human
life free of all impediments and endowed with all favorable conditions, apply yourself unrelentingly to spiritual practice!

Think well that there is no time left to sleep or even to pause
for breath and exert yourself without interruption. Whatever you
do—walking, eating, sitting, and so forth—abandon laziness,

indolence, apathy, negligence, and distraction. Master the habitual patterns that make you resist any change in your body, speech, and mind, even in the most insignificant activities. Once you have embarked on the path of liberation, it is inappropriate to behave in an ordinary way: observe your mind all the time with vigilance and lucidity. If you have committed a negative act, regret it and promise never to do it again. Be glad if you have committed none.

Give yourself up to spiritual practice, whether formal or not, with the enthusiasm of a starving person ready to swallow any kind of food. By taking care not to neglect even the simplest positive action while not losing sight of the illusory nature of all things, travel the path of the double accumulation of merit and wisdom, the path that delights the conquerors, and also encourage others to do the same. To devote yourself day and night to the practice of the teachings, and thus trace your path to happy future lives, is the way to give your life a real meaning.

CHAPTER 2

Reflections on
Impermanence and Death

Death does not wait to see
what has been done or is still to be done.
SHANTIDEVA

Every moment of our lives has tremendous value. Yet we let the time go by, like gold dust running through our fingers. What is sadder than coming to the end of one's life empty-handed? We need to be aware that every second of our life is inestimably precious and have the intelligence to decide to make the best use of it for our own good and the good of others. First of all, we need to get rid of the illusion of believing that we have "our whole life ahead of us." This life passes like a dream that can be interrupted at any time. We should take care of what is really essential without further delay so as not to be filled with regret at the hour of our death. It is never too early to develop our inner qualities.

We can see the ephemeral nature of all things before us in two ways: gross impermanence—the changing seasons, the erosion of the mountains, the aging of the body, the fluctuations of our emotions—and subtle impermanence, which takes place in the smallest conceivable unit of time. At each infinitesimal instant, all that seems to exist in a sustainable way inexorably changes. It is because of this subtle impermanence that Buddhism compares the world to a dream or an illusion, an ungraspable constant flux.

The thought of death should always be present in a practitioner's mind. However it should not be morbid or depressing but serve as an encouragement to use every minute of life to complete the interior transformation to which one aspires. We tend to say, "First I will take care of my current business and finish all my projects, and when that's all done, I'll see more clearly and be able to devote myself to spiritual life." But thinking like that is fooling ourselves in the worst way, for not only will our death inevitably come, but the timing, causes, and circumstances that will bring it about are utterly unpredictable. All the situations of everyday life, even the simple acts of walking, eating, or sleeping can suddenly turn into a cause of death. That is something that a sincere practitioner should always keep in mind. In Tibet, hermits who light their fire in the morning train themselves to think that they may no longer be there the next day to light another. They even consider that they are lucky to be able to breathe in again each time they breathe out. The thought of death and impermanence is a spur to encourage them each day to pursue their spiritual practice.

Nagarjuna

With all its many risks, this life endures
No more than windblown bubbles in a stream.
How marvelous to breathe in and out again,
To fall asleep and then awake refreshed.

Padmasambhava

As a river rushes to the sea,
As the sun and moon glide across the mountains
    of the west,
As days and nights, hours and moments flee,
Life flows away, inexorably.

Dilgo Khyentse Rinpoche

Just as every single thing is always moving inexorably closer to its ultimate dissolution, so also your own life, like a burning butter-lamp, will soon be consumed. It would be foolish to think that you can first finish all your work and then retire to spend the later stages of your life practicing the Dharma. Can you be certain that you will live that long? Does death not strike the young as well as the old? No matter what you are doing, therefore, remember death and keep your mind focused on the Dharma....

A hunted criminal never has a tranquil moment. He is always alert, urgently devising a thousand schemes to escape the punishment that awaits him. You will never find him drawing plans for his future house. How can you rest when death threatens to strike at any moment? From now on, your sole recourse must be the practice of Dharma. There is no other way to turn death into something favorable....

There is a right time for everything. Farmers know when the time has come to plow, to sow, or to harvest, and they never fail to do each job when it is necessary. Now that you are in full possession of your faculties, have met a teacher, and have received his instructions, will you let the field of liberation lie uncultivated?...

Most people, thinking of the future, make a lot of plans—but the future they plan for is only the very few years of this life. This is very shortsighted; we have such a long way to go in lives to come. Death is just the threshold, which we have to cross alone, aided only by our faith in the teacher and the Three Jewels and by our confidence in the practice. Relatives, friends, power, wealth, and whatever else we have become so used to relying on will simply no longer be there. So if you waste your life now on endless minor tasks, you can be sure that at the time of death you will weep with regret and be stricken with intense anxiety, like a thief who has just been thrown into jail and anxiously anticipates his punishment.

A person might find himself with nothing to eat, no clothes to wear, and no house to live in; but if his mind is filled with faith in his teacher and the Three Jewels, that person will both live and die with his heart always joyful and confident.

Padmasambhava

This life passes as quickly as autumn clouds;
Family and friends are like passers-by in a market;
The demon of death approaches like twilight's shadows;
What the future holds is like a translucent fish in cloudy
    waters;
Life's experiences are like last night's dreams;
The pleasures of the senses, like an imaginary party.
Meaningless activities are like waves
lapping on the surface of the water.

Dilgo Khyentse Rinpoche

Nothing ever stands still; from moment to moment everything is changing. In spring, seeds send out shoots; in summer, the shoots grow into leaves, stems, and flowers; in autumn, the grain ripens and is harvested; and in winter, the earth is again prepared to receive next year's crop. As the moon waxes and wanes over the course of a day, everything undergoes incessant change. Noon might see a thousand people singing and dancing in a fairground, yet dusk finds the whole place silent and empty. In the meantime, each one of those revelers will have slipped a few hours closer to death.

Shechen Gyaltsap

Amidst the fleeting clouds of illusion
Dances the lightning flash of life.
Can you say that tomorrow you will not be dead?
So practice the Dharma.

Gunthang Tenpai Drönmé

The turquoise dancing water
With a perpetual murmur of waves,
When imprisoned beneath the cage of winter ice,
Is like a girl crying for help with muffled voice.

Joyful fields of flowers humming with bees
When attacked by morning frost in autumn
Become a deserted ghostly plain.
They wail in agony before the hail's onslaught.

The white and the black rats, day and night
In turn consume life's fragile straw.
We too step every instant
Ever closer to the enemy, death.

When aged parents mourn their young son's death,
Their bodies shaking and bent as bows,
Their hair white as conch shell,
Who can maintain that the old die first?

Tennyi Lingpa

A MEDITATION ON IMPERMANENCE

Imagine that you are in an unknown place: you don't know where
you have come from or where you are going. There is a gloomy

rocky valley facing north and the black soil is littered with red-dish ruins. You see no trace of human presence, but you hear the deafening roar of a waterfall tumbling down the dark and stony mountain. Fragile screes scar the slopes where the wind howls in the brush, and wild animals jostle for the corpses they shred; the yelping of jackals mixes with the cawing of crows and hooting of owls. Rocky peaks hatch the sky, the wind whistles, the sun is about to disappear behind the mountains, and the shadows darken.

Lost without a companion or guide, you do not know where to go. You lament in the depths of despair, "Poor me, where am I? I am lost. Where are my children, my parents, my possessions, my country? This is terrible!"

Distraught, you start to walk, but you soon stumble and fall into a ravine. During your fall, your right hand manages to grab a large clump of grass protruding from a rock. Trembling, sus-pended in mid-air, you hang on with the energy of desperation. Below, you can only see a bottomless abyss, and above, only the huge cliff, soaring skyward, smooth as a mirror. The wind whips your ears. To the right of the tuft of grass, a white mouse emerges from a crack in the wall. It bites off a bit of grass and carries it away. On the left is a black mouse, which also chops off a blade of grass before disappearing. Both mice continue their activity, each in turn, and the tuft of grass is gradually getting smaller.*

With no way to stop them, and terrified of dying, you lament, "Alas! My last hour has come!" But there is no one to hear your cries for help. "Before, I didn't think I would have to die, and I neglected my Dharma practice. I didn't imagine meeting my death so quickly, and suddenly here it is before me. I will never see my children, my friends, my property, or my country again. Thinking

* The white mouse and the black mouse represent the alternation of days and nights during which our lives run out.

only of accumulating wealth, I didn't bother about accumulating virtue, and now I have to leave everything behind and go alone to an unknown destination. It's terrifying! How can I escape my plight? Do I have any chance at all to get out of this?"

Then your spiritual master appears in the sky. Upon a lotus and moon disc, adorned with the six bone ornaments, sounding his bell and playing his little drum,* he dances majestically in space.

"Unhappy one!" he exclaims. "Being subject to the impermanence of all things, you will soon be gone. The seasons pass, and all beings, friends, and enemies alike, grow old and eventually die. Even youth declines, a little more, day by day, month by month. There is no way to postpone death, but if you think you might have a chance, look at the situation you are in and immediately, without delay, arouse fervent devotion and listen respectfully to the words of your teacher!"

At these words, you cry: "Alas! I'm already on the verge of death, and I bitterly regret not having trained my mind. Whether I die or survive, I place all my trust in the teacher and the Three Jewels. They are compassionate. May they free me from the abyss of the circle of lives! O master, you who embody all the Three Jewels in one, I place myself in your hands!"

When you invoke your master from the depths of your being with intense devotion, from his heart a ray of light springs forth and touches your own heart, just as the tuft of grass on which your life was hanging finally gives way. The rays pull you from the precipice, and you find yourself in the pure buddhafield of Great Bliss. From your heart flow infinite rays of light that guide all

---

* These objects are symbols that visually remind the disciple of certain qualities: the lotus (which is rooted in the mud but flowers above the water) symbolizes being present in the ordinary world without being affected by its defects; the moon disc represents compassion; the six bone ornaments symbolize the six transcendent virtues; the bell, wisdom; and the small drum, great bliss.

beings of the three spheres of samsara without exception to that same pure land.

Meditate thus, cultivating intense compassion.

Shakyamuni Buddha

Like a shooting star, a mirage, a flame,
An optical illusion, dewdrops, bubbles in water,
A dream, a lightning-flash, and a cloud:
Thus consider all composite things.

The Seventh Dalai Lama, Kelsang Gyatso

When comes the time to carry
The load of life through death's door,
One can take neither relatives, friends,
Servants, nor possessions.
Attached mind is instinctual mind:
Abandon attachment.

Godragpa Sonam Gyaltsen

Body impermanent like spring mist;
Mind insubstantial like empty sky;
Thoughts unestablished like breezes in space.
Think about these three points over and over.

Gampopa

In the beginning, you should be pursued by the fear of birth and death, like a deer escaping from a trap. In the middle, you should have nothing to regret, even if you die at this moment, like a peasant who has worked his land with care. In the end, you should be happy, like someone who has completed an immense task. . . .

The most important thing to know is that there is no time to lose, as if an arrow had hit a vital spot in your body.

Milarepa

Fearing death, I went into the mountains.
Through meditating on the uncertainty of when it will come,
I conquered the immortal bastion of the unchanging.
Now, my fear of death is long gone!

Jigme Lingpa

Tormented by the summer's heat, beings sigh with pleasure
In the clear light of the autumn moon.
They do not think, and it does not alarm them,
That a hundred of their days have passed away.

Patrul Rinpoche

*This story about Patrul Rinpoche was told to the author
by Nyoshul Khen Rinpoche.*

THE MEETING OF PATRUL RINPOCHE
AND CHÖYING RANGDRÖL

One day, Patrul Rinpoche, the famous wandering hermit of the nineteenth century, accompanied by his friend Pema Dorje, decided to go to the monastery of Kathok. He slowly walked along the shore of Black Lake, reached the glaciers of the Rampart of Thromgo and then a sacred mountain, one of whose sides is a sheer cliff known as Queen of the Fierce Rock.

On its lonely but blessed slopes lived a great meditator named

Chöying Rangdröl, who had spent most of his life in retreat. He had not studied much, but he had reached the final stage of the contemplative path of the Great Perfection. For warm clothing, he wore only a worn-out sheepskin over a simple tunic with the collar and hem sewn inside out. He had never traveled, having remained day and night sitting on his mat, absorbed in deep meditation.

Upon arrival, Patrul Rinpoche prostrated three times before the hermit and asked him to deliver the teachings of the *Essence of Luminous Space*, according to the spiritual lineage of the patriarchs of the monastery of Kathok.

The first day Chöying Rangdröl folded his hands on his heart, recited a few verses of the teaching, and then repeated the first verse slowly three times:

> "Alas!
> It is difficult to bring together the freedoms
>   and favorable conditions
> Conducive to the realization of enlightenment."

Tears rolled down his cheeks. Patrul Rinpoche also began to cry, and Chöying Rangdröl remained silent for a moment. That was the day's teaching.

The next day Chöying Rangdröl taught in the same way, without recourse to texts, but drawing directly on his personal experience. Here are the words he uttered:

> "The life of beings rushes by like a mountain waterfall!"

He folded his hands again and, weeping, continued after a pause:

> "Do not waste the favorable conditions and
>   freedoms that you have been granted;
> Do not let your life be spent in vain!"

At that point, Pema Dorje said to himself, "How amazing! Look at Patrul Rinpoche, a master who knows all the teachings perfectly, receiving instructions as basic as that! Yet, at the mere mention of the rarity of a human existence, master and disciple both began to cry. I can't believe it!"

CHAPTER 3

From Seed to Fruit, or the Law of Cause and Effect

When an act is committed, whatever it is, we can expect that sooner or later it will produce an effect. So if one wishes to overcome suffering, it makes sense to perform certain acts and avoid others. The law of causality is the foundation of the Buddha's teaching. He said,

> Without doing any harmful act,
> Abundantly perform beneficial acts.
> Completely tame your mind.
> That is the Buddha's teaching.

All phenomena arise from the combination of an infinity of causes and conditions in constant flux. Like a rainbow that appears when the sunlight hits a patch of rain and vanishes when one of the factors contributing to its formation disappears, phenomena occur only through interdependent circumstances and are, therefore, devoid of independent and permanent existence.

Phenomena mutually influence each other in a constant dynamic and creative process, and nothing arises arbitrarily: the law of causality is inexorable.

Karma, which refers to both actions and their effects, is a particular aspect of that law of causality. It is what determines our share of happiness and suffering. In other words, what we

31

experience now is the consequence of our past behavior, and we are the architects of our future lives.

From this perspective, our destiny is not dependent on an external power, such as divine will, for example. It is the fruit of our actions. We reap what we sow, and nothing and no one forces a person to be reborn in a certain way, apart from the power of his or her own actions.

"Actions" refers not only to physical actions but also words and thoughts. Actions can be beneficial, neutral, or harmful. Good and evil are not absolute values. Conduct is considered "good" or "bad" depending on the altruistic or malicious intention behind it and the consequences it produces in terms of the happiness or unhappiness of ourselves and others. Every moment of our lives, we reap the consequences of our past and shape our future through newly produced thoughts, words, and deeds. They are like seeds that, once sown, will produce the corresponding beneficial or harmful fruit.

From this perspective, sufferings for which we are apparently not responsible—the harm that others do us, or diseases, or natural disasters—are due neither to God's will nor to ineluctable fate, nor to pure chance. They originate ultimately from our own actions. This idea may seem disconcerting to a Westerner, especially when applied to an innocent person who is suffering, or a thoroughly good person whose life is a series of tragedies. We need to understand that, according to Buddhism, every being is the result of a complex set of causes and conditions, good and bad seeds sown in the past, and it is this combination of multiple factors that unfolds gradually, each in its own time, in the course of our lives. Simply being aware of this makes us more responsible in our attitude. For example, it prevents us from blaming others for unpleasant things that happen to us.

Not to rail and rebel against what befalls us by the nature of things is not being fatalistic. We can always make the best of a difficult situation, whatever it might be. And it is up to us to decide what we should do or not do in order to lay the foundations for our future happiness and cease to create suffering for ourselves.

When we have understood that our harmful actions are the source of all suffering for ourselves and others and that our beneficial actions are the source of happiness, we can choose how to act with discernment. As it is said, "If one keeps one's hand in the fire, there is no point in hoping not to be burnt." In conclusion, we do not collect a "reward" or a "punishment": what happens to us simply obeys the law of causality.

Shantideva

Beings long to free themselves from misery,
But misery itself they race to catch.
They long for joy, but in their ignorance,
Destroy it, as they would a hated enemy.

Jetsün Mingyur Paldrön

If you want to totally free yourself from suffering, it is important to distinguish what to do from what not to do since you cannot hope to taste the fruit of beneficial actions that you have not done, nor escape the consequences of your own harmful actions. After death, you will follow the course traced by your actions, good and bad. Now that you have a choice between two paths, one that leads up and one that leads down, do not act in a way opposed to your deepest wishes. Practice all possible beneficial actions, even the smallest. Doesn't the accumulation of little drops end up filling a large jar? Use them as a supreme remedy because they are the origin of all good qualities.

Do not do any harmful act, even the most insignificant. Just as a tiny spark fanned by the wind can rapidly burn a mountain of dry grass, a single bout of violent anger can destroy a mountain of merit. Avoid any harmful conduct like poison, understanding that it is the cause of all your suffering, and also transform neutral actions into positive ones.*

Finally, if you understand that even your good deeds are, like everything else, devoid of ultimate reality, they will also help you to get free from cyclic existence. And just as when we harvest grain, we also obtain straw, you will know temporary happiness as well as ultimate liberation. So how can you not be diligent!

Dilgo Khyentse Rinpoche

The great master Padmasambhava said,

Even if my view is higher than the sky,
The attention I pay to my actions and their effects is finer than flour.

When your realization of the emptiness of all phenomena becomes as vast as the sky, your confidence in the law of causality of actions will grow proportionately, and you will become aware of the real significance of your conduct. In fact, relative truth is inseparable from absolute truth. The profound realization of the empty nature of all things has never led anyone to believe that positive actions do not create happiness and negative actions do not cause suffering.

* Neutral actions that are neither good nor bad in themselves, such as washing, walking, and dressing, for instance, can be transformed into beneficial acts if we accompany them with a positive thought. When washing, for example, we can consider that we are purifying our negative karma along with that of all beings.

The Fourteenth Dalai Lama, Tenzin Gyatso

The mind is malleable: it is capable of change. So we need to learn to see how we can transform it. We need to identify the ways to achieve that transformation and put them into action. Samsara, the circle of existences, and nirvana, the state beyond it, are not like geographical locations far from one another. They are two states of mind. Samsara is a deviation from knowledge, a distorted vision of reality that makes the mind the slave of negative emotions, while nirvana is a state of inner freedom, free of any conceptual and emotional obstacles.

All things, including nirvana, arise from causes and conditions. To find happiness, it is indispensable to have a correct view of the nature of mind and the world. Someone who has a wrong view about that nature cannot transform themselves to attain liberation. What is meant by "right view" is not faith or believing in a particular dogma but a clear understanding that is reached through thoroughly examining reality. This kind of examination will refute the belief in the independent existence of things, which is the root of our distorted vision of the world, and replace it with the right view.

Acquiring the right view implies a recognition that the nature of buddhahood is the essence of our own mind, our fundamental cognitive ability, luminous* and pure without confusion. It also involves identifying the factors that keep us from perceiving that nature, so that it becomes possible for us to remove them.

Kangyur Rinpoche

Just as a little salt—a few fractions of a measure—can make a small amount of water taste salty but cannot change a huge river

* "Luminous" here refers to the clarity and lucidity of the fundamental nature of consciousness that is not obscured by the veils of ignorance and mental constructs.

like the Ganges, know that, in the same way, even a small negative action can harm someone whose positive deeds are weak but cannot harm anyone who has frequently performed immensely positive actions, vast in scope. So we should try to perform powerful positive actions repeatedly on a vast scale.

CHAPTER 4

The Inherent Unsatisfactoriness of the World Conditioned by Ignorance

What we call "happiness" is generally a source of suffering. We might long for wealth, power, and glory, or succumb to the obsessive quest for pleasure, imagining that those things will bring us happiness. In our daily life, things appear to us as "pleasant" or "unpleasant" and people as "good" or "bad," and we believe that those qualities or defects are inherent. And what we call "I," the one who experiences all this, seems to be real and concrete. Yet there is a big difference between the way things appear to us and the way they actually are.

We attribute a continual existence to transient phenomena and a solid reality to our mental constructs. But what appear to us to be autonomous entities are in fact an infinite network of interdependencies in constant flux. This mistake leads to powerful reflexes of attachment and rejection that in turn lead to frustration and suffering.

In his first teaching, the Buddha spoke of what is known as the "four noble truths": the truth of suffering that inexorably permeates the world conditioned by ignorance; the truth of the cause of suffering—mental confusion, negative emotions and actions with their inevitable results (or karma); the truth of cessation, which is the possibility of putting an end to suffering; and the truth of the path that leads to that cessation. "Suffering" is a broad term that includes all forms of dissatisfaction and painful experiences such as birth, aging, sickness, and death, being confronted with enemies, losing loved ones, and so on.

The Buddha distinguishes three kinds of suffering: visible suffering, the suffering of change, and the universal suffering that is inherent in all phenomena composed of elements that come together momentarily and are transient by nature. Visible suffering is evident everywhere: illness, death, war, natural disasters, and so forth. The suffering of change is the suffering latent in the various pleasures that seem to last but sooner or later turn into their opposites. The fleeting experience of pleasure is dependent upon circumstance, on a specific location or moment in time. It is unstable by nature, and the sensation it evokes soon becomes neutral or even unpleasant. Likewise, when repeated, it may grow insipid or even lead to disgust; savoring a delicious meal is a source of genuine pleasure, but we are indifferent to it once we've had our fill and would sicken of it if we were to continue eating.

Pleasure is exhausted by usage, like a candle consuming itself. It is almost always linked to an activity and naturally leads to lassitude by dint of being repeated. Listening to beautiful music requires a focus of attention that, minimal as it is, cannot be maintained indefinitely. Were we forced to listen for days on end, it would become unbearable. This type of pain can occur at any moment of our lives, but we never think of it that way. We are fascinated by the mirage of appearances and forget that beings and things are constantly changing.

Finally, universal suffering is the most difficult to detect because it is concomitant with the blindness of our mind and is constantly renewing itself as long as we are in the grip of ignorance and attachment to the ego. It stems from the fact that we have not grasped what we need to do to avoid suffering. This confusion and the tendencies associated with it lead us to perpetuate the very actions that are at the root of our troubles. To dispel this suffering, it is necessary to wake up from the sleep of ignorance and understand the mechanisms of happiness and suffering.

The Fourteenth Dalai Lama, Tenzin Gyatso

There are two types of suffering: physical suffering caused by disease, hunger, and other problems often beyond our control, and mental suffering such as fear, grief, and so forth. In many cases, we can bear or overcome physical suffering through the power of the mind. But when it comes to mental suffering, we cannot relieve it just by acting on the body since the ultimate responsibility for suffering and also for happiness lies with the mind.

When we think continually about "I! I! I!" and only talk about ourselves, we considerably reduce the size of the world that we want to be ours. The events that occur in the narrow sphere of selfishness affect us deeply and will certainly disturb our inner peace. The situation is very different when we feel primarily concerned with others and bear in mind that they are so numerous that, in comparison, our own personal concerns are negligible. If on top of that our desire is to remove their suffering, we will not get discouraged. It will give us more courage and determination, in contrast to self-pity, which depresses us and reduces our courage.

Asanga

Drinking, dancing, singing, and the pleasures of the flesh never fully satisfy. There are several reasons for this. First, those pleasures do not satisfy both the body and mind. Second, they depend on external circumstances over which we never have complete control, and as such are not always immediately available whenever and wherever we want them. They are also of no help in developing the "seven supreme riches"—faith, discipline,

generosity, and so on. Nor can we take what produces those pleasures with us at the time of death and in future lives. Also pleasures
are not in themselves an ultimate goal. Moreover, the very process
of enjoyment is such that it necessarily disappears sooner or later,
like a match consumed by its flame, and the slightest adverse circumstance may also bring it to an end. The benefit produced by
those pleasures, far from providing complete satisfaction, creates
ever more intense desire. On reflection, pleasures are the cause of
great frustration and repeated suffering. They can only increase
our torments, just as scratching a wound momentarily seems to
relieve the itch, when in reality it aggravates the wound and leads
to worse discomfort in the future.

However, the happiness provided by the Dharma is quite different. It permeates the body and mind at all times and in all circumstances. The more we taste it, the deeper is our satisfaction.
No enemy and no event can take it away from us, and its benefits
continue into our future lives. That is why it is an ultimate goal to
achieve. The path of Dharma dispels all suffering. It leads to true
happiness and the total disappearance of all disturbing emotions
and harmful behavior.

Dilgo Khyentse Rinpoche

Ordinary enjoyments are pleasurable in the beginning, but as
time goes on, they become an increasing source of torment. If you
wrap a strip of wet leather around your wrist, it is fine at first, but
as the leather dries and shrinks, it tightens painfully. What a relief
it is to cut it away with a knife! . . .

Once you have understood the union of emptiness and the
dependent arising of phenomena, you will see clearly how deluded
and deceiving the ways of the world really are, and, like an old man
forced to play children's games, you will find them very tiresome.
When you have realized the utter foolishness of spending your

life attached to friends and scheming to subdue your enemies and competitors, you will find it tedious.

Once you have been struck by the pointlessness of letting yourself be forever influenced and conditioned by your habitual tendencies, you will become sick of it. . . . That will inspire you to strive towards liberation—and by striving for it, you will attain it. Samsara will never just disappear on its own. You have to want to get rid of it actively yourself.

Dilgo Khyentse Rinpoche

The function of the sense-consciousnesses is simply to perceive their corresponding objects—forms, sounds, smells, and the rest—without adding anything. But the mind then elaborates on these perceptions, thinking, "This is beautiful," "That is ugly," "This might harm me," "That will bring me pleasure." It is not the form of the external object, nor the eye, nor the visual consciousness that produces these subjective elaborations, which in the end lead to the accumulation of karma; it is the mind.

A beautiful object has no intrinsic quality that is good for the mind, nor an ugly object any intrinsic power to harm it. Beautiful and ugly are just projections of the mind. The ability to cause happiness or suffering is not a property of the outer object itself. For example, the sight of a particular individual can cause happiness to one person and suffering to another. It is the mind that attributes such qualities to the perceived object.

The Seventh Dalai Lama, Kelsang Gyatso

If there is a way to become free from misery,
One should use each moment to achieve it.
Only the fool wants more pain:
A melancholy scene, knowingly eating poison.

The Fourteenth Dalai Lama, Tenzin Gyatso

Buddhism essentially consists of two things: the view, which means a definitive understanding of the interdependence of all things, and action, which can be loosely defined as nonviolence. But if one were to summarize the Buddha's teaching in one word, we would have to say that it is universal interdependence, of which nonviolence is a natural consequence. Since we are all dependent on each other and all other beings want to be happy and not suffer, just as I do, my personal happiness and suffering are inextricably linked with those of others.

This nonviolence does not mean weakness or passivity. It is the deliberate choice of altruism in all our thoughts and actions, so that it becomes inconceivable to knowingly harm others.

Jigme Lingpa

THE CONDITIONS THAT PERPETUATE SUFFERING

The origin of pain, the demon of desire that rears its head
   to strike,
Entwined with poisoned objects of desire,
Contrives a prison whence there's no escape:
The breeding ground of weariness and woe.

We yearn for happiness and strive for it.
But overmastered by the power of ignorance
And caught upon the sharpened point of sorrow and its cause,
We are ourselves the place wherein our pain is all prepared.

Like moths attracted to the bright form of a flame,
Like deer, like bees, like fish, like elephants,
By sound, by smell, by taste, by touch are we betrayed,
Bound up with the five objects of desire.

Commentary by Kangyur Rinpoche

Desire is the source of suffering both in this life and the next. Like moths drawn to the lovely candlelight that destroys them, people are attracted to the pleasing sound of flattery, enticed by the aroma of tobacco, the taste of meat, a lover's soft touch, and the caress of silken robes. Thus people are deceived and destroy the path to their own freedom.

Lured by the sweet sound of a lute, the deer is shot with poisoned arrows; the bee is drawn by the perfume of the flower and is ensnared in its petals; the fish is caught on the hook, unable to resist the taste of the bait; and the elephant, craving contact with its mate, perishes in the quicksand. Beings are enticed by the objects of the senses and are constantly bound up with them.

It is as Vasubandhu says,

> Living beings, each and every one,
> Are lured by these five senses all the time.
> And overwhelmed thereby both night and day,
> What happiness can they attain?

CHAPTER 5

Giving Up the Causes of Suffering

True renunciation is not a constraint but a freedom. It comes from the strong desire to end the frustration inevitably created by the ordinary preoccupations of life. Someone who renounces the world to escape from the prison of illusion is like a bird escaping from its cage to fly in the sky. It does not matter whether the cage is made of gold or base metal: it is still a prison. Whether individuals are rich or poor, famous or unknown, whether they experience success or failure, pleasure or pain, they often end up unhappy and frustrated. Renunciation essentially means simplifying one's mind, one's words, and one's activities, by letting go of what obstructs inner freedom. Constraint creates frustration; renunciation produces a real sense of joy.

Renunciation does not mean depriving oneself of what is truly good and useful in life but rather getting rid of unnecessary burdens. When hermits repeat ten times the magic mantra "I need nothing," they are not making their life insipid but trying to get rid of the endless distractions that take over the mind and leave them with the bitter taste of lost time. They want to unclutter their life to devote themselves completely to what is truly enriching.

The advice that follows is often very direct and blunt. This is probably intentional since for most of us the desire for renunciation is not a natural impulse!

45

The Fourteenth Dalai Lama, Tenzin Gyatso

When the teachings say we need to reduce our fascination with the things of this life, it does not mean that we should abandon them completely. It means avoiding the natural tendency to go from elation to depression in reaction to life's ups and downs, jumping for joy when you have some success, or wanting to jump out the window if you do not get what you want. Being less concerned about the affairs of this life means assuming its ups and downs with a broad and stable mind.

Dilgo Khyentse Rinpoche

Spending all your life trying to achieve ordinary worldly goals is like trying to net fish in a dry riverbed. Clearly understanding this, make a firm decision not to allow your life to pursue such a useless course.

Nyoshul Khen Rinpoche

What makes the Dharma not only useful but necessary? To answer this question, look around and reflect upon your situation in this world. If you do so, without blinding yourself to reality, you will see that what all beings have in common is suffering.

We all suffer in one way or another. A boss has a boss's suffering, and a worker has a worker's suffering. When you see your boss pass by in the street, you might think, "He has a good social position, he lives in a big house and drives a nice car; he must be happy." But this is rarely the case. That man is suffering, too. Maybe he is worried about losing his position; or he has too much work; or he is tormented by the ambition to get ahead in politics, for instance; or he may have big family problems. He probably has a long list of other problems too. Even the president of a big country like the United States has to worry about losing his country's approval or being unable to influence the rest of the world. Even if he succeeds, he is still under constant pressure to keep in control of events. The ordinary worker, meanwhile, is forced to do this and that, following the orders of his superiors, and his work is often tedious and poorly paid.

Is it possible to find a solution to these problems? In the everyday world, the answer is probably no. You might think that by giving a large sum of money to a beggar, you would make that person happy. For some time, maybe. But soon, instead of being satisfied with that sum and enjoying being able to feed and clothe himself, he will want twice as much. Chasing after possessions never brings happiness since the efforts we have to make to get them, protect them, and increase them are already a kind of suffering. No one is ever satisfied with his or her wealth and power. That would be too easy.

Think about the number of people who suffer because they are disabled, sick in hospital, dying of hunger, or war victims. Think about the families torn apart by strife or deprived of a loved one who has just died. Perhaps you don't have this kind of problem right now, but who knows when your turn will come?

Although the modern world has reached an unimaginable level of development in science and technology, there is no machine and no trick to end suffering and produce happiness.

To end suffering—not only by relieving its symptoms but by eradicating its root cause—is precisely the aim of the Buddha's teaching.

So how should we proceed? We must first realize that the true cause of suffering is not outside, but inside. We suffer because of all sorts of negative emotions such as attachment, anger, repulsion, pride, jealousy, confusion. Those emotions are real mental poisons. They are based on a wrong way of understanding and lead only to suffering. This is explained in the Buddha's teaching but can also be understood directly through genuine objective reflection. That is why true spiritual practice consists of working on one's own mind.

The mind is very powerful. It can create happiness or suffering, heaven or hell. If, with the help of the Dharma, you manage to eliminate your inner poisons, nothing from outside will ever affect your happiness, but as long as those poisons remain in your mind, you will not find the happiness you seek anywhere in the world.

To work on the mind is a very vast subject, and the whole Dharma is dedicated to that. Yet, the essence is this: the main reason for which the mind generates a multitude of concepts, negative emotions, and habitual tendencies is the strong clinging to "I," "me," and "mine." Because of that clinging, one suffers when one does not obtain whatever that "I" wants, and one suffers when one encounters what that "I" does not want.

Through meditating over and over again on the nature of mind, one can gradually dissolve ego-clinging. Among all the methods to achieve that result, the most profound is the meditation on bodhichitta, that is, love and compassion. To be full of love for all sentient beings and consider others more important that oneself is the very root of Dharma.

The Fourteenth Dalai Lama, Tenzin Gyatso

THE MEANING OF TRUE RENUNCIATION

If you have a deep and complete understanding of the four noble truths and that understanding is based on the knowledge of emptiness, you will also understand the nature of the cycle of suffering in general and, in particular, your own condition. Through that you will have a sincere and considered aspiration for liberation. That is true renunciation.

But if you have tried every means to make your way in society and have failed, and you then say, out of disgust or desperation: "I give up!" because you can find nothing better to do, that is not real renunciation; it is just defeatism. A true practitioner of the Dharma renounces with courage and full knowledge of the facts.

In the Buddha's mantra *Om muni muni mahamunaye swaha*, the word *muni* means one who is capable and has confidence in his own resources. It is with this attitude that we should abandon the cycle of suffering and not in a spirit of discouragement, groaning and saying, "I'm so fed up."

Genuine renunciation involves determination to overcome ignorance, our real enemy. This determination begins to manifest when we realize that we are slaves of mental confusion and that there is little space for true happiness in our lives. When this feeling becomes unbearable, our only preoccupation is to get free.

Then it is important to share that feeling with all beings, as infinite as space, being fully aware that, just like us, they want to be happy and not suffer. Then selfless love and compassion—which means a deep desire to free others from suffering—will arise, culminating in the wish to attain enlightenment to liberate all beings from ignorance and the suffering it creates.

Shabkar

If you go back to the source of the suffering of samsara, you will only find ignorance. Ignorance of what? Of the fact that beings and things are devoid of true reality, in that they do not exist in themselves and by themselves.

How does ignorance manifest? If one night you pass by a coiled rope on the ground in the dark, you might think it is a snake curled up and be so terrified that your heart races. Similarly, when we are immersed in the darkness of ignorance, we have a mistaken perception of the temporary meeting of our body and consciousness.

Unable to clearly discern its true nature, we take it as an "I." That "I" in fact has no reality.

As a result, we create a distinction between "I" and "other": we are attached to the one and reject the other. Based on this double process of attraction and repulsion, all the other mental poisons arise, and under their influence, we take birth in the various higher and lower worlds of samsara in which we do a mixture of beneficial and harmful deeds with unfortunate consequences.

Milarepa

The sound of thunder, although deafening, is harmless;
The rainbow, despite its brilliant colors, does not last;
This world, though it appears pleasant, is like a dream;
The pleasures of the senses, though agreeable, ultimately
  lead to disillusionment.

Drigung Jigten Gönpo

When we look at death and the impermanence of all things,
Our ordinary projects are just a joke.
How can you believe in the eight worldly preoccupations,*
Which are as transient as the colors of the rainbow?

* Happiness and sadness, gain and loss, fame and obscurity, good or bad reputation.

Jamgön Kongtrul Lodrö Thayé

The following words were uttered as an aspiration prayer in the solitude of the mountains by the aspiring hermit Yönten Gyamtso, as an admonition to himself and to invoke the compassion of the wisdom deities.

Masters of the Oral Tradition, victorious buddhas and
  bodhisattvas,
Powerful Avalokiteshvara and precious Tara,* hold with
  your compassion
One who, forgetting death, thinks only of the business of
  this life,
Squandering his freedoms and favorable conditions!

This human life is as fleeting as a dream:
Whether it is happy or unhappy,
May I, without caring about joys and sorrows,
Sincerely practice the supreme Dharma!

This human life is like a flame exposed to the wind:
Whether it is long or short, may I,
Without letting my ego tighten its grip,
Sincerely practice the supreme Dharma!

The reasonings of the intellect are deceptive illusions:
Whether they are right or wrong, may I, disdaining them
As the trifles of the eight worldly preoccupations,
Sincerely practice the supreme Dharma!

Companions are like a flock of birds perched on a tree:
Whether they be united or dispersed,
May I, taking the reins of my destiny,
Sincerely practice the supreme Dharma!

* Avalokiteshvara is the buddha of selfless love and compassion. Tara, a feminine form of the Buddha who vowed to be reincarnated as a woman constantly until she reaches enlightenment, is the compassionate activity of all buddhas.

This illusory body is like an old ruin:
Whether it is robust or decrepit, may I,
Unhampered by seeking clothes, food, and medicines,
Sincerely practice the supreme Dharma!

As for knowledge that is useless in time of need,
Like a deer's antlers, never mind if I know it or not.
May I, without placing my trust in ordinary knowledge,
Sincerely practice the supreme Dharma!

The trappings of a lama make me look
Like a dog turd wrapped in brocade.
Whether I have them or not, may I,
By seeing the rottenness of my own head,
Sincerely practice the supreme Dharma!

Friends and relatives are like visitors to a market:
Whether they are friendly or hostile, may I,
Cutting the ropes of attachment from the bottom of my
    heart,
Sincerely practice the supreme Dharma!

Material goods are like a treasure found in a dream:
Whether I have them or not, may I,
Without seeking profit by flattering those around me,
Sincerely practice the supreme Dharma!

Social rank is like a baby bird landing on the top of a tree:
Whether it is high or low, may I,
Without yearning for the cause of my own problems,
Sincerely practice the supreme Dharma!

Quickness to analyze is like the snout of a pig:
Whether it is sharp or blunt, may I,
Without vainly spouting the foam of anger or enthusiasm,
Sincerely practice the supreme Dharma!

Meditative experiences come and go like a summer torrent:
Whether they increase or decrease,
May I, without being like a child chasing a rainbow,
Sincerely practice the supreme Dharma!

These freedoms and favorable conditions are like the
    wish-fulfilling gem:
Without them, I would be unable to apply the instructions.
May I, without wasting them while I still have them,
Sincerely practice the supreme Dharma!

The glorious master illuminates the path of liberation:
Without having met him, I would have no means
To comprehend the ultimate nature of things.
Not jumping into the abyss, now I know where I'm going,
May I sincerely practice the supreme Dharma!

This supreme teaching is like a panacea:
Without hearing it, there is no way to know what to do
    or not do.
No longer swallowing deadly poison, now I can distinguish
    the beneficial from the harmful.
May I sincerely practice the supreme Dharma!

This alternation of joys and sufferings is like the cycle of
    the seasons:
Without realizing that, how could I get tired of cyclic
    existence?

With the certainty that suffering will again be my lot,
May I sincerely practice the supreme Dharma!

Like a stone in water, one sinks to the bottom of samsara:
Now if I do not seize the rope of compassion
That the Three Jewels offer me, later it will be impossible.
May I sincerely practice the supreme Dharma!

The qualities of liberation are as precious as an island
    of jewels:
Without knowing them, there is no way to arouse one's
    courage.
Recognizing the unassailable gains of the conquerors,
May I sincerely practice the supreme Dharma!

The life stories of enlightened beings are like ambrosia:
Without reading them, one cannot develop faith.
Knowing where lies victory or defeat,
And no longer buying my own suffering,
May I sincerely practice the supreme Dharma!

Altruistic aspiration to enlightenment is like a fertile field:
If one does not develop it, there is no way to attain
    buddhahood.
Without abandoning through indifference the
    accomplishment of the noble goal,
May I sincerely practice the supreme Dharma!

This mind is like a turbulent monkey:
Without taming it, there is no way to correct the negative
    emotions.
Ceasing to indulge in foolish pantomimes,
May I sincerely practice the supreme Dharma!

This belief in an "I" accompanies me like a shadow:
Without getting rid of it, there is no way to reach the land
 of bliss.
Never fraternizing with the enemy once it is captured,
May I sincerely practice the supreme Dharma!

These five mental poisons are like fire smoldering under the
 ashes:
Without extinguishing them, one cannot rest in the
 unaltered nature of the mind.
Ceasing to harbor venomous snakes in my breast,
May I sincerely practice the supreme Dharma!

This rigid character is like the old leather of a butter bag:
Without softening it, I cannot mix my mind with the
 Dharma.
Not letting my own child do whatever it likes,
May I sincerely practice the supreme Dharma!

These inveterate bad habits are like the flow of a river:
Without interrupting them, I will always do what is opposed
 to the Dharma.
Ceasing to supply arms to my enemies,
May I sincerely practice the supreme Dharma!

These perpetual distractions are like endless ripples on
 water:
Without renouncing them, I cannot stabilize my mind.
Ceasing to give birth to samsara while I am free to choose,
May I sincerely practice the supreme Dharma!

The master's blessings are like the heat that warms the earth
 and water:

Unless they enter me, I cannot recognize my own nature.
While this shortcut is possible, without following a thousand
   detours,
May I sincerely practice the supreme Dharma!

This solitary place is like a summer valley of medicinal herbs:
Without staying here, I cannot develop spiritual qualities.
Now that I'm in the mountains, without wandering in the sad
   villages,
May I sincerely practice the supreme Dharma!

This desire for comfort is like the demon of poverty living in my
   own home:
Without separating from it, I will always find ways to create
   suffering.
By not making offerings to a hungry devil as if he were a god,
May I sincerely practice the supreme Dharma!

Attention and vigilance are like the door-bars of a fortress:
Without them, the comings and goings of illusions will never stop.
Never leaving the latch undone in the presence of thieves,
May I sincerely practice the supreme Dharma!

The natural state of mind is like immutable space:
Unless one discovers it, efforts to apply antidotes will never end.
Instead of putting fetters on my own legs,
May I sincerely practice the supreme Dharma!

The nature of pure awareness is like a stainless crystal:
Without realizing it, one does not acquire the certainty that it has
   no root or foundation.
Not seeking elsewhere what is already within,
May I sincerely practice the supreme Dharma!

The natural simplicity of mind is like an old friend:
If its face is unfamiliar,
Any practice is just deceptive illusion.
Instead of groping my way with my eyes closed,
May I sincerely practice the supreme Dharma!

May the two aspects of the mind of enlightenment arise in
    my mind
Thanks to the Buddha's essential instructions transmitted by
    Atisha
And practiced by holders of the oral lineage.
May all my actions be in harmony with the supreme Dharma!

Our ordinary actions are as useless as wandering in the
    desert,
Our efforts only make the mind more rigid,
Our thoughts just reinforce our delusion,
And everything that ordinary people claim to be Dharma is a
    cause of entanglement.

Multitudes of activities that never succeed,
Crowds of thoughts without any meaning,
Thousands of needs with no time to cater to them:
May I abandon all this agitation and practice the oral
    instructions!

If I want to act, I will take the words of the conqueror as my
    witness.
If I do something, I will mingle my mind with the Dharma.
If I want to practice, I will read the lives of the masters of the
    Oral Lineage.
Indulgent habits, what else can I do with you?

Taking the most humble place, with the wealth of satisfaction,
Freed from the shackles of the eight ordinary concerns,
    courageously engaged in practice,
Receiving the master's blessings and achieving realization as
    vast as space,
May I enter the lineage of the Oral Tradition!

Pema Lingpa

Pema Lingpa had retired to a mountain hermitage at a place called "The Heights of Golden Valley." He lived there alone for a long time in a bamboo hut. Looking down into the valley at the people going about their business from morning to night, a deep sadness came over him. "Well, it seems that I'm as distracted by worldly affairs as those villagers down there!" he said. And he composed the following advice to encourage himself:

> *Namo guru swasti siddham!*
> Homage to the master. May spiritual accomplishment
>   triumph!
>
> O master, Lotus Born, I pray:
> May the teachings of the Buddha
> spread through your blessing!
>
> Pema Lingpa, the tramp of this base era,
> Since your mother gave you birth
> You have forgotten to think about death.
> Distractions have made you lose your head.
> All beings of the six modes of existence
> Wander in samsara, caught by desire and attachment,
> Desiring this and rejecting that.
> See everything as bubbles on water
> Or a mirage in the sky!
> Remember that nothing lasts, Pema Lingpa!

It is certain that the beings who are born
On the four continents will eventually die.
In all the past generations,
You will not find anyone who did not die.
That will be the fate of the people of the present.
And it will be the same for those to come.
Troubled by the uncertainty of the fatal hour,
Think of death, Pema Lingpa!

You were born in that mire of samsara, your homeland.
Until the age of nine your parents took care of you.
Then you wandered in human society
And though no one taught you, you were a pretty good
     craftsman.
Now you're just a common slave,
A peddler of the sacred!
Although you are a holder of the word of Uddiyana,*
You are distracted by the lures of attachment and aversion.
Abandon those illusions, Pema Lingpa!

At the dawn of the Year of the Monkey, the thirty-seventh
     of your life,
You discovered profound treasures as Uddiyana had
     prophesied.
Having become the custodian of many deep instructions,
You left them in idleness and indifference,
Without practicing them entirely.
Like water welling up beneath a cave,

---

* Uddiyana (Tib. Orgyen, o rgyan) refers here to Padmasambhava, who is said to
have been born in a lotus in the lake Danakosha in Uddiyana, a former country
in northwestern India, corresponding probably to the Swat valley in Pakistan,
from which originated many other great Buddhist teachers, including Garab
Dorje, the first human master of the Dzogchen tradition.

Negative emotions multiplied without your noticing them.
Transform your mind, Pema Lingpa!

You haven't given up the desire for food and wealth,
You're caught in the snare of greed and self-attachment.
Obsessed with your ego, consumed with desire, you fool
   yourself.
Spreading your own praises for friends and companions
Who lure you with their goods and delicacies,
You're a fool, unable to accumulate merit and wisdom.
Cut the attachment to the ego, Pema Lingpa!

You pamper your body and dress it with ornaments,
When it's an illusion borrowed from the four elements.
The objects of the six fields of perception
That your five senses apprehend, trick your mind.
You hope that your illusory body, tormented
By unpredictable birth, sickness, old age, and death,
Will be eternal, but it will disappear.
Cease to cherish it, Pema Lingpa!

You are mean to ordinary people,
Although you are linked to them by many karmic ties.
You lack pure vision toward practitioners of the Dharma.
You do not respect your sacred bonds
With those to whom you have a spiritual connection.
You have no respect for the wise,
Nor any gratitude to those who do you good,
And no sadness in the vicious cycle of samsara.
Put a stop to all that, Pema Lingpa!

They are firmly established in the Great Vehicle,
They have mastered their minds by study, reflection,
    and meditation,
They have acquired perfect assurance in the phases of
    creation and completion
And are expert in the three stages of the path,*
But you see only the faults of those sages,
And you despise others:
You're like a fool who walks
Toward a precipice, eyes wide open.
Cultivate pure vision, Pema Lingpa!

Your homeland is the prison of Mara,† the instigator
    of obstacles.
Friends and relatives are Mara's tempters.
Food and riches are Mara's brigands.
Samsara is the stake he will tie you to,
Mara's rope is your laziness.
Mara comes from your attachment to self.
You don't know your own nature and never cease to
    procrastinate.
Abandon the eight worldly concerns, Pema Lingpa!

---

* These stages probably correspond to the three vehicles, Hinayana, Mahayana, and Vajrayana.

† Mara (Tib. *bdud*: demon, devil), in the sutras, refers to an evil spirit or negative force that creates hindrances to progress toward enlightenment. In the context of Buddhist meditation practice, those hindrances are categorized as the "four demons." They are (1) the demon of the aggregates (the physical and mental components of the person), which constitute the support of suffering in samsara, (2) the demon of negative emotions, which are the cause of suffering, (3) the demon of death, which means not only death but also the momentary nature of all things (subtle impermanence is also suffering) and (4) the divine demon, which means the distraction and attachment to pleasant things that are taken as real.

You only appreciate immediate gratification.
Your life runs out, day after day, night after night,
Your body is aging, month by month, year by year,
Your mind is sinking in the mud of ignorance,
And you leave your practice for later!
You never understood what was for your own good,
Stubborn and without Dharma, you are fooling yourself.
Just think about it, Pema Lingpa!

You adopt the appearance of an ascetic,
Without having realized the essence: the unborn state.
You will not be Buddha simply by pretending!
Apply yourself determinedly to the real meaning.
Since understanding alone is not enough to realize it,
Without clarifying the mind in its depth,
You will never exhaust the confusion of concepts.
Resolve the essence, Pema Lingpa!

Abandon the vain activities of the world,
And, far from everything, free from ordinary activities,
In a secluded place far from the crowds,
In the shelter of a cave, spacious and open,
Alone, cast off concern for body and mind.
Adopt the seven-point posture of Vairochana.*
With the intention of helping all beings,

---

* The seven-point posture of Vairochana: (1) the legs are crossed in the vajra posture, commonly known as "lotus posture," (2) the hands are placed on the lap in the gesture of equanimity, the right hand on the left with the tips of the thumbs touching, (3) the shoulders are open and forearms slightly apart from the trunk, (4) the spine is straight, (5) the chin is slightly tucked in against the throat, (6) the tip of the tongue touches the roof of the palate, (7) the gaze is directed straight ahead or slightly downward, following the nose, eyes open or half closed.

Unite your mind with the mind of your master.
Visualize him constantly above your head, Pema Lingpa!

Original mind is not composite.
Fundamental mind is empty by nature.
Manifest mind is omnipresent.
The mind of the six fields of perception apprehends their six
    objects.
The mind of the six classes of beings is driven by karma.
Deluded mind clings to an "I."
The nature of mind is free from impurity.
Be perfectly sure of that, Pema Lingpa!

When you cultivate inner calm,
Whatever thoughts may come to you,
Recognize them with great clarity.
Stare at them and free them in their nakedness,
Then rest in that state.
Alternating formal meditation and postmeditation,
With inner peace will come joy and bliss,
And you will taste the ultimate flavor of insight.
Maintain the constancy of your meditation, Pema Lingpa! . . .

Overcome by lassitude and renunciation,
I, Pema Lingpa, a monk from Bhutan,
Sang this little song of sixteen pieces of advice
That arose in my mind.
May they be useful to beings
And not deserve the censure of the learned!

Patrul Rinpoche

*This story about Patrul Rinpoche was told to the author
by Nyoshul Khen Rinpoche.*

PATRUL RINPOCHE AND THE THIEF

It was near the monastery of Dzamthang. Patrul Rinpoche was
sitting, not on a throne in a temple, but on a grassy knoll. He had
just finished teaching *The Way of the Bodhisattva* in detail to several
thousand people, when a member of his audience wanted to offer
him a horseshoe-shaped silver ingot. As usual, Patrul Rinpoche
refused the offering, but the man nonetheless laid the ingot at his
feet and walked away briskly.

Soon after, Patrul Rinpoche stood up and went on his way,
leaving on the mound all that had been offered to him. A thief,
knowing that the master had received a silver ingot, followed him,
intending to steal it.

Patrul Rinpoche used to travel alone, often without a specific
destination, and would spend his nights under the stars. That
night, while he was asleep, the robber approached him stealth-
ily under cover of darkness. Next to Patrul Rinpoche there was
a small cloth bag and a clay pot to make tea. Not finding what he
sought, the thief started rummaging surreptitiously in the master's clothing, when suddenly, awakened by the thief's hand,
Patrul exclaimed:

"*Ka-ho*! What are you doing rummaging in my clothes?"

Frightened, the man replied brusquely,

"Someone gave you a silver ingot. I must have it. Give it to me!"

"*Ka-ho*!" exclaimed the master again. "Look what a hard life
you lead, running right and left like a fool! Have you come all
this way just for a piece of silver? Poor you! Now listen! Go back
quickly the way you came and at dawn you'll arrive at the bank
where I was sitting. The silver is still there."

The thief was skeptical, but he had searched the master's

belongings enough to know that he was no longer in posses-sion of the ingot. It seemed most unlikely that the coveted offer-ing would be in the place indicated, but he still went back on his tracks. By hunting around the mound, he finally found the piece of silver that Patrul had simply left there.

The robber, who was no longer young, lamented:

"*A-dzi!* This Patrul is surely a true master freed from all attach-ment. By trying to steal from him, I have just created some very bad karma!"

Tormented by remorse, he retraced his steps in search of Patrul Rinpoche. When he finally found him, Patrul exclaimed:

"*Ka-ho!* You're back, always running up hill and down dale! What do you want this time?"

Overcome, the thief broke into tears:

"I haven't come back to steal anything from you. I found the ingot, and I really regret having acted so badly toward a true spiri-tual master like you. To think that I was ready to take away from you what little you have! I beg your pardon. Bless me and accept me as a disciple!"

Patrul Rinpoche reassured him:

"Don't bother to confess or ask me for forgiveness. From now on, practice generosity and invoke the Three Jewels. That will be enough."

Some time later, people got wind of the story and started to beat the thief. When Patrul Rinpoche heard about it, he sharply rebuked them:

"If you hurt this man, it's as if you were hurting me. So leave him alone!"

Milarepa

MILAREPA AND THE HUNTER

One day, the famous hermit-poet Milarepa, after installing his disciples in retreat, withdrew to a cave to practice his own meditation in tranquility. The chosen location seemed to offer an ideal environment. The beautiful scenery, the solitude, the support of the local deities, the singing of the birds and gentle babble of a clear brook combined in perfect harmony.

So it was a shock when a ferocious barking disturbed the quiet of the place. The hermit soon saw from a promontory the interruption that was coming his way. He saw a black stag rushing toward him, breathless and terrified.

Great compassion arose in his heart. He made a wish to teach the Dharma to that animal so that it might be released from its plight and sang it this song:

> I prostrate myself at the feet of Marpa of Lhodrak!*
> Listen, deer whose head is crowned with splendid antlers,
> As long as you seek to run away from anything in the outside world,
> You will never be liberated from the hallucinations of ignorance.
> The time has come for you to renounce all this delusion.
> The maturation of karma is too fast for you:
> How could you escape it in an illusory body?
> If you want to run away, flee into the essence of mind!
> Run to the dwelling place of enlightenment:
> It is sheer delusion to want to escape anywhere else.
> Therefore put an end to your confusion and stay with me!
> Overcome by the fear of death,

*The great translator Marpa (mar pa chos kyi blo gros 1012–97) was the spiritual master of Milarepa. He lived in the province of Lhodrak in southern Tibet. The well-known story of the arduous trials to which Marpa subjected Milarepa before agreeing to give him teaching can be found in Lhalungpa, *The Life of Milarepa*.

You hope to be safe on the other side of the hill
And fear being caught on this side.
But it is hope and fear that make you wander in samsara!
I will teach you the Six Yogas of Naropa*
And show you how to meditate on the Great Symbol.

He sang in a voice as melodious as that of Brahma. Anyone who heard him would have fallen under his charm. The deer, in tears, lay down at his feet.

The hermit was wondering where the barking he had heard came from when a red-coated bitch appeared, barking furiously. Milarepa, saddened, directed his compassion toward her in turn and sang this song:

I prostrate myself at the feet of Marpa of Lhodrak!
May he bless me that I may calm the hatred of beings!
Wolf-faced dog,
Hear the song of Milarepa!
You take everything you see as an enemy.
And your heart is full of hate.
Reborn as a cruel beast,
You live in hunger and suffering.
The poisons that torture you never subside.
If you do not take possession of your own mind,
What will you gain by seizing outside prey?
It's your mind that it is time to conquer!
Give up your hatred and stay with me!
Right now, under the influence of your unbearable
    aggressivity,
You fear losing the deer on the other side of the
    mountain
While hoping to catch it on this side.

* Naropa was the Indian master of Marpa. He transmitted the teachings of the particular practices of the six yogas: inner heat, illusory body, dream, clear light, *bardo* ("intermediate states," particularly between death and rebirth), and transference of consciousness.

But it is hope and fear that make you wander in samsara!
I will teach you the Six Yogas of Naropa
And show you how to meditate on the Great Symbol.

Moved by the immense compassion of the hermit, the dog's hatred was appeased, and she lay down by the deer.

Milarepa said to himself that a sinister figure would surely come after the two animals. And indeed, he appeared, sweaty and rolling his eyes. He was a hunter named Kirawa Gonpo Dorje. Foaming with rage at the sight of the dog and the deer lying quietly near Milarepa, he inveighed brutally against the hermit and shot an arrow at him that missed its target.

Milarepa, thinking that a human being should at least be as capable of understanding as an animal, advised him to listen to his song before shooting any more arrows.

I pray to all the great accomplished beings!
May they bless us that we may be free from mental poisons!
You, the man with the face of an ogre, hear the song of Mila!
It is taught that the human body is a rare jewel,
But looking at you, I see nothing precious!
You, evil man who looks like a demon,
You run after the pleasures of this life,
But in doing so, you're heading for a fall.
Yet if you conquer the desire within,
You will obtain true accomplishments.
You will never control outer phenomena.
Now it's your mind that you need to master!
You will not satisfy your desires by killing the deer;
But if you put an end to the five inner poisons
You will fulfill all your wishes.
The more you try to defeat your outer enemies,
The more they come in greater numbers.
If you simply master your own mind,
You will put an end to all adversity.
Instead of spending your life in harmful acts,

You had better practice the Supreme Dharma!
I will teach you the Six Yogas of Naropa
And show you how to meditate on the Great Symbol.

Still suspicious but struck by the animals' behavior and the unusual power of this lama, the hunter inspected the cave to see if he was not dealing with a charlatan, but, finding nothing in it but a handful of roots and leaves, he felt such intense faith that he offered Milarepa everything he owned, including the life of the deer, and asked to serve him. Milarepa was delighted at the repentance of the hunter and accepted him as his disciple.

The hunter, moved by the rectitude and kindness of the hermit, burst into tears and himself composed a song to Milarepa, in which he prayed for guidance. But when he decided to return to his family to settle his affairs and return as soon as possible, Milarepa dissuaded him by singing the following advice:

You, the hunter, listen to me!
The storm thunders, but it is only empty sound.
The rainbow has beautiful colors,
But it vanishes quickly.
Worldly things, even when enjoyable, are only a dream.
Desirable objects provide great pleasure,
But give rise to harmful actions.
Composite things seem to last forever,
But are soon destroyed.
What we had yesterday we lack today.
He who was alive last year is no longer there this year.
Foods we eat for our well-being change into poison.
The former good companion becomes an enemy
And those we protected with benevolence now cover us
    with insults.
The evil you've done, it's you it will hurt.
Among a hundred heads, your own is the dearest.
Of your ten fingers, cut any, and it's you who suffer.
Of all wives, it's your own that you cherish the most.

Now it is time to do something for yourself!
Life is fleeting, and soon death will knock at your door.
To postpone your spiritual practice is not reasonable.
In fact, your dear ones push you into samsara.
It is time for you to follow a spiritual master:
You will find happiness in this life,
And even more happiness in lives to come.
It's time to practice the Dharma!

Upon hearing this song, Gonpo Dorje was fully converted to the Dharma and abandoned any idea of returning home. When he had received all the necessary teachings from Milarepa, he made them an inner experience through meditation and reached ultimate realization.

Thus he became one of Milarepa's heart disciples, while the dog and the deer were released from their lower rebirth. He became famous under the name of Kira Repa, and you can still see his bow and arrows in the cave of Milarepa.

PART TWO

The Foundations of Practice

CHAPTER 6

Taking Refuge

All our lives we try to protect ourselves when our welfare, our possessions, things that are dear to us, or our very existence are threatened. We are looking for safe places to take refuge, and we seek help from those who are able to defend us.

But we also spend our whole life suffering from our ignorance and the mental poisons it produces, especially hatred and attachment, and those woes are far crueler and more durable than the simple vagaries of our existence. To protect ourselves from such evils, we must go back to their source, namely, ignorance. But how can an ignorant person overcome his or her own ignorance? By relying on beings who have already done so and following the path they have traced. That is the role of the Three Jewels in Buddhism: the Buddha, which means the Awakened One, who shows us how to get free from suffering; the Dharma, the path taught by the Buddha; and the Sangha, the community of those who follow that path.

In other words, the Buddha is the guide, the Dharma is the path, and the Sangha the traveling companions. In Vajrayana, the esoteric vehicle of Tibetan and Indian Buddhism, the spiritual master embodies the essence of the Three Jewels: his mind is enlightenment, or Buddha; his words are the teaching, or Dharma; and his body is the community, or Sangha.

According to Buddhism, taking refuge in the wisdom of enlightenment is the first and indispensable step toward liberation from suffering. It is the starting point of the path.

73

The ultimate, or inner, refuge is none other than our own mind. Through recognizing its essence, the luminous wakefulness of awareness that shines continuously behind the clouds of confusion, one is naturally protected from the very causes of suffering. Preserving the continuum of awareness, we no longer fear the cognitive or emotional obscurations, because they no longer affect our consciousness. The function of the external refuge is to lead progressively to the understanding and eventually the realization of the inner refuge.

The Fourteenth Dalai Lama, Tenzin Gyatso

Through study and reflection, we understand the origin of suffering and how it unfolds and is perpetuated. Then we learn how to reverse this process and acquire the conviction that it is possible to be liberated from it. We also understand how important it is, if we want to break free, to have a correct view of the nature of things, that is to say, emptiness, the absence of independent existence.

When we assimilate the meaning of the four noble truths, and particularly the possibility of the cessation of suffering and the path leading to it, we acquire an unshakable confidence in the teaching, the Dharma, which is the real refuge, then in the Sangha, the community of Dharma practitioners, and particularly the followers of the Mahayana who are inspired by altruistic love and have generated the "mind of enlightenment," or bodhichitta, and finally in the Buddha, or enlightenment itself, which is the ultimate accomplishment of the path of liberation. That confidence is not blind faith. It is based on real understanding.

Padmasambhava

The cause of wanting to take refuge is fear of the miseries of samsara, trusting the Three Jewels as the place of refuge, and, moreover, accepting the Three Jewels to be the objects of refuge and the protectors of refuge. Through these three, you give rise to the intention of taking refuge.

With what particular attitude does one take refuge? You should take refuge with a sense of responsibility for the welfare of others. You should take refuge with this attitude, as you will not attain true and complete enlightenment simply by renouncing samsara and desiring the result of nirvana:

> In order to free all sentient beings from the miseries of samsara,
> I will take refuge until I and all the sentient beings have achieved
> supreme enlightenment!

You may ask, "If one is protected by taking refuge, does that mean that the Buddhas appear and lead all sentient beings?" The reply is that the Buddhas cannot take all sentient beings out of samsara with their hands. If they were able to do that, the Buddhas with their great compassion and skillful means would have already freed all beings without a single exception.

"Well then," you may ask, "by what is one protected?" The answer is that one is protected by the (practice of the) Dharma.

CHAPTER 7

Altruistic Love and Compassion

Altruistic love and compassion are the heart of Buddhist practice. They are considered to be the "essence of the great vehicle," the "path traveled by all the buddhas of past and present, and which will be traveled by all the buddhas of the future," the method "which alone is sufficient, and without which nothing can be accomplished." In the Buddhist sense, altruistic love is defined as "the wish that all beings may find happiness and the causes of happiness," and compassion as "the wish that all beings may be free from suffering and the causes of suffering."

These two can be summed up as unconditional kindness toward all beings in general that is ready to manifest at all times toward any individual in particular. It is a way of being in the world for others that is cultivated until it permeates one's entire being. It does not mean catering to the wishes and whims of others without discrimination, and it certainly does not mean wishing success to those who pursue harmful goals. We should take into account the different elements of each situation and ask, for example, what are the consequences, both short- and long-term, what will really be for the good of this or that person, or if an action will help a small number of individuals or a large number.

Love and compassion must be informed by wisdom. This is based on understanding the immediate and ultimate causes of suffering. By suffering, we mean not just the obvious sufferings of which we are so often the victims or witnesses, such as disease, war, famine, injustice, and poverty, but also their deep causes, namely, the mental poisons. As long as our mind is clouded by confusion, hatred, attachment, jealousy, and arrogance, suffering, in all its forms, will always manifest.

Buddhism teaches that the source of these mental poisons is ignorance of the nature of beings and things, which creates a gulf between our perceptions and reality. We take as permanent what is impermanent. What we take as happiness is often only a cause of suffering, for instance, wealth, power, fame, and fleeting pleasures. Things appear to us as inherently "pleasant" or "unpleasant" and beings as inherently "good" or "bad." The "I" that perceives them seems equally real and concrete. This mistake leads to powerful reflexes of attachment and aversion that inevitably lead to suffering.

Our love and compassion take on a new dimension when we understand that suffering is not inevitable and it is possible to stop the suffering of beings. In his first teaching at the Deer Park near Benares, the Buddha expounded the four noble truths: the truth of suffering, which must be understood; the truth of the causes of suffering, ignorance and the negative mental states that ignorance breeds, which must be eliminated; the truth of the cessation of suffering, which we must attain, and the truth of the path, which must be followed in order to end suffering.

When combined with joy at the qualities and successes of others and impartiality toward all beings, love and compassion are the basis of the mind of enlightenment, or bodhichitta, defined as the wish to attain buddhahood in order to liberate all beings from suffering and its causes. This desire must be accompanied by a determination to do everything in one's power to remedy suffering, not just for a limited time, but for as long as there are beings and those beings continue to suffer.

How can we cultivate love and compassion? The first step is to realize that deep down we want to be happy and want not to suffer, and that it is the same for all beings, including animals. This right not to suffer, so often disregarded, is perhaps the most fundamental of all.

Buddhist compassion ideally aims to put an end to all suffering, whatever it might be and whoever it affects. It is not based on any moral judgment and does not depend on how others behave. It is not limited to our loved ones or those who treat us favorably but embraces all beings without exception, be they friends, enemies, or strangers.

Yongey Mingyur Rinpoche

When I began to practice meditation on compassion, I found that my sense of isolation began to diminish, while at the same time my personal sense of empowerment began to grow. Where once I saw only problems, I started to see solutions. Where once I viewed my own happiness as more important than the happiness of others, I began to see the well-being of others as the foundation of my own peace of mind.

Shantideva

All the joy the world contains
Has come through wishing happiness for others.
All the misery the world contains
Has come from wanting pleasure for oneself.

Is there need for lengthy explanation?
Childish beings look out for themselves,
While Buddhas labor for the good of others.
See the difference that divides them! . . .

By bringing joy to beings, I please the Buddhas also,
By wounding them, I wound the Buddhas too.

The Fourteenth Dalai Lama, Tenzin Gyatso

Compassion and generosity must be accompanied by detachment. Expecting something in return for them is like doing business. If the owner of a restaurant is all smiles with his customers, it is not because he loves them but because he wants to increase his turnover. When we love and help others, it should not be because we find a particular individual likeable but because we see that all beings, whether we think of them as friends or enemies, want to be happy and have the right to happiness.

Nyoshul Khen Rinpoche

Why is bodhichitta, the mind of enlightenment, so important? Because it is the immediate antidote for attachment to that sense of "I" that is the origin of samsara, the cycle of suffering. The unfounded belief in an illusory self pushes us to cherish ourselves and reject others, which finally turns against us and is the main cause of our sufferings in samsara. It is therefore essential to meditate all the time on love and compassion until we love others more than ourselves. That is the lifeblood of our spiritual practice and must always remain so.

Shabkar

Now I have some heart-advice to give you: a sky needs a sun, a mother needs a child, and a bird needs two wings. Likewise, emptiness alone is not enough. You need to have great compassion for all beings who have not realized this emptiness—enemies, friends, and strangers. You need to have compassion that makes no distinctions between good and bad. You must understand that compassion arises through meditation, not simply from waiting, thinking that it may come forth, by itself, from emptiness.

The same number of years you spent meditating on emptiness, you should now spend meditating day and night on compassion, a compassion a hundred times stronger than that of a mother for a child burnt in a fire; an unbearably intense compassion that arises when thinking about the suffering of sentient beings.

Once such compassion is born, you must practice until you come to think, with fierce energy, "Until enlightenment, I shall do whatever is possible to benefit all beings, not omitting a single one, no matter what evil actions they commit, and no matter what difficulties I must endure." . . .

If someone has compassion, he is a Buddha;
Without compassion, he is a Lord of Death.

With compassion, the root of Dharma is planted,
Without compassion, the root of Dharma is rotten.

One with compassion is kind even when angry,
One without compassion will kill even as he smiles.

For one with compassion, even his enemies will turn into friends,
Without compassion, even his friends turn into enemies.

With compassion, one has all Dharmas,
Without compassion, one has no Dharma at all.

With compassion, one is a Buddhist,
Without compassion, one is worse than a heretic.

Even if meditating on voidness, one needs compassion as its essence.
A Dharma practitioner must have a compassionate nature.

Compassion is the distinctive characteristic of Buddhism.
Compassion is the very essence of all Dharma.

Great compassion is like a wish-fulfilling gem.
Great compassion will fulfill the hopes of self and others.

Therefore, all of you, practitioners and laypeople,
Cultivate compassion and you will achieve Buddhahood.

May all men and women who hear this song,
With great compassion, benefit all beings!

Jigme Lingpa

Love means wishing for the happiness of others.
Like a loving mother cherishing her child,
One's body, wealth, and virtue all amassed one gives for
    others' benefit,
While training to endure the harms that they inflict.

Compassion is a powerful state of mind,
An inability to tolerate the fact that others suffer.
Beings in the six realms are entrapped by sorrow and its
    cause,
And seeing this brings tears to one's eyes.
Joy is to delight in other's pleasure and success;
It is to cultivate the wish that all have happiness.
It is a joy one feels when they achieve it for themselves
And is the wish that they should never be deprived of it.

Impartiality is freedom from attachment and hostility,
When sides and factions are all seen as equal,
When enemy and friend and neither—
All are treated with an evenhanded kindness.
We should practice these four attitudes, remembering
That all is without true existence.

Dilgo Khyentse Rinpoche

In each of our countless lives in beginningless samsara, we must have had parents. In fact, we have taken birth so often that, at one time or another, every single sentient being must have been our mother or father. When we think of all these beings who have been our parents wandering helplessly for so long in samsara, like blind people who have lost their way, we cannot but feel tremendous compassion for them.

Compassion by itself, however, is not enough; they need actual help. But as long as our minds are still limited by attachment, just giving them food, clothing, money, or simply affection will only bring them a limited and temporary happiness at best. What we must do is to find a way to liberate them completely from suffering. This can only be done by putting the teachings of Dharma into practice.

True compassion is directed impartially toward all sentient beings, without discriminating between those who are friends and those who are enemies. With this compassion constantly in mind, we should perform every positive act, even offering a single flower or reciting a single mantra, with the wish that it may benefit all living creatures without exception....

The great teachers of the past considered the most precious teaching to be the inseparability of voidness and compassion. Over and over again, they cultivated love, compassion, joy, and equanimity—the four limitless thoughts out of which the ability to help others arises effortlessly. Famous for practicing in uncompromising adherence to the teachings, these masters trained themselves first through careful study of the Dharma and then through direct experience in meditation. That is the right way to make progress on the path that leads to the great bliss of ultimate Buddhahood....

It is said, "To wish happiness for others, even for those who want to do us harm, is the source of consummate happiness."

When we reach this level, compassion for all beings arises by itself in a way that is utterly uncontrived....

It is very important to meditate with your whole being on bodhichitta until it becomes clear just how meaningless and frustrating the activities of this life really are. You will be touched and saddened by the debilitated condition of beings in this dark age, and a strong feeling of determination to be free from samsara will arise. If these attitudes truly take root, the qualities and achievements of the Mahayana, the great vehicle, are sure to grow from them. But if that genuine determination to be free from samsara is not firmly implanted in your mind, your Dharma practice will never be able to fully develop....

All sentient beings are the same in wishing to be happy and not to suffer. The great difference between oneself and others is in numbers—there is only one of me, but countless others. So, my happiness and my suffering are completely insignificant compared to the happiness and suffering of infinite other beings. What truly matters is whether other beings are happy or suffering. This is the basis of bodhichitta. We should wish others to be happy rather than ourselves, and we should especially wish happiness for those whom we perceive as enemies and those who treat us badly. Otherwise, what is the use of compassion?

The Seventh Dalai Lama, Kelsang Gyatso

Even the eagle, king of birds, cannot fly if he is missing a wing.
Many find the wing "perception of emptiness,"
But only those who have also the wing of bodhichitta
Fly to the omniscient state of Buddhahood.

Shantideva

May I be a guard for those who are protectorless,
A guide for those who journey on the road.
For those who wish to cross the water,
May I be a boat, a raft, a bridge.

May I be an isle for those who yearn for land,
A lamp for those who long for light;
For all who need a resting place, a bed;
For those who need a servant, may I be their slave.

May I be the wishing jewel, the vase of plenty,
A word of power, and the supreme healing;
May I be the tree of miracles,
And for every being the abundant cow.

Just like the earth and space itself
And other of the mighty elements,
For boundless multitudes of beings,
May I always be the ground of life, the source of varied
    sustenance.

Thus for everything that lives,
As far as are the limits of the sky,
May I be constantly their source of livelihood
Until they pass beyond all sorrow.

Kangyur Rinpoche

Focusing on all sentient beings, practice the four boundless qualities: love, which is the wish that they be happy; compassion, the
wish that they be free from suffering; sympathetic joy, which is to

feel happy when they are happy; and impartiality, which is to treat them impartially as equals, without attachment or aversion.

Of these four, the meaning of the term "boundless love" is that one focuses on boundless sentient beings (as the object of concentration) and that boundless merit comes to the meditator.

For compassion and the others there are three categories: compassion focusing on sentient beings; focusing on phenomena; and without concepts. The first is that of ordinary beings and takes the form of wishing that all may be free from suffering. The second, focusing on phenomena, is that of sublime beings of the Shravaka and Pratyekabuddha vehicles who, since they have realized the no-self of the individual, designate merely the phenomena of the aggregates as sentient beings; it takes the form of the wish that they may themselves be free from suffering. The third, being without concepts, takes the form of viewing sentient beings as illusion-like through realizing the no-self of phenomena, and wishing they be free from suffering. This is the compassion that the sublime beings of the Great Vehicle have. . . .

How should one meditate on these four boundless qualities? Divide beings into three categories: friends, enemies, and those that are neither. Begin by concentrating on your parents, relatives, and friends, and meditate by wishing that they may meet with happiness and so forth. After that, do the same focusing on beings who are neither your friends nor your enemies. Finally, meditate focusing on all those for whom you feel enmity. The meditation is said to be perfect and complete when your compassion for your enemies and your relatives and friends becomes the same.

Atisha

Son,
Originally pure nature of mind
Is imbued with an overwhelming compassion for all beings.

That compassion is born from emptiness,
And it is to emptiness that it returns.

Son,
All things of samsara and nirvana arise from mind-in-itself,
In which no one has ever seen the least cause or condition.
On examination, the mind is seen to be like a rainbow in the sky.
Know that emptiness and compassion are like the sky and the
rainbow.

Son,
See everything like waves in motion,
That ruffle the surface of the deep ocean:
They arise from the ocean itself,
And sink back into the ocean.

Nobody has ever seen the least demarcation
Between the moving waves and the depths of the ocean.
Likewise compassion for beings immersed in illusion
Arises spontaneously out of emptiness.
It springs forth from emptiness
And to emptiness it returns.

The Fourteenth Dalai Lama, Tenzin Gyatso

CULTIVATING COMPASSION

Before cultivating love and compassion, it is important to understand what these two terms refer to. In the Buddhist tradition,
they are seen as two aspects of the same feeling of benevolence:
love is the desire that all beings may be happy, and compassion is
the wish that they may be free from suffering.

Then we must ask ourselves whether it is possible to cultivate love and compassion and to have less and less anger, hatred, and jealousy. My answer is yes without hesitation. Although, for now, you may not agree with me, I ask you to remain open to that possibility. Let's think about it together, and perhaps we will find some answers.

All kinds of happiness and all sufferings can be included in two categories: those of the mind and those of the body. For most of us, it is the mind that plays the most decisive role in feelings of well-being and ill-being. In comparison, the role of our physical condition is secondary, unless we are seriously ill or in abject poverty. However, the mind can be affected by the most insignificant events. So it is appropriate to make more effort to pacify the mind than to ensure one's physical comfort.

It is possible to transform your mind

Despite my limited experience, I am convinced that with regular training it is quite possible to transform one's mind in a positive way, cultivating thoughts, attitudes, and tendencies that are beneficial to oneself and others, and reducing those that are harmful.

What we call "mind" is a very curious phenomenon. Sometimes it is rigid and resistant to any change, but it can also become very flexible provided we make constant efforts to transform it and become convinced, by reflection, that this change is not only possible but necessary. For that it is not enough to make wishes or prayers. There has to be reasoning based on experience. And we cannot expect this transformation to happen overnight because our old habits resist any kind of quick solution.

How to cultivate compassion

Egocentrism, which affects us all in varying degrees, prevents us from feeling love and compassion toward others. But to be truly happy, one must have a mind at peace, and peace of mind will come only through altruistic love. Of course, to cultivate compassion, it is not enough to believe in its benefits or marvel at the beauty of such feelings. We have to make an effort and use all the circumstances of daily life to change our thoughts and behavior.

One must also know precisely what those words really mean. Usually, love and compassion are mixed with desire and attachment. The love parents have for their children, for example, is biased and limited compared to the unconditional love that the Buddha is talking about.

Similarly, the feeling of being in love is usually more a form of attachment, based on mental projections and fantasies, than true altruistic love. The best evidence for this is that once these projections change, the feeling disappears and sometimes turns into its opposite. Desire can be so strong that the one to whom we are attached appears to us to be free from defects, even if they really have a lot, and at the same time, we exaggerate their qualities. Such distortions of reality are signs that our love is motivated more by our personal needs rather than a real concern for others.

It is possible to experience a love without partiality. It should not come from a simple emotional reaction; it should be based on reflection and lead to a firm commitment. Then it will no longer depend on how others treat us. The goal of the Buddhist practitioner is to cultivate this kind of love, sincerely wishing happiness to all beings in the universe. This is obviously not easy.

Let us reason like this. Whether others are beautiful or ugly, benevolent or cruel, they are all sentient beings like us. And like us, they want to be happy and not suffer, which is their right, just like us. Recognizing that all beings are equal in their aspirations and their right to happiness, we feel a sense of empathy that brings us closer to them. As we get accustomed to this impartial altruism, we finally experience a sense of universal responsibility.

I know that some people will say, "To wish that all sentient beings be happy is unrealistic." They think it is more effective to start with the beings with whom we have a direct link and then gradually expand the circle, and it is pointless to think of all beings as a whole because their number is unlimited.

In other contexts, this objection would have some relevance, but our goal is to extend our kindness to all forms of life that can experience well-being and suffering. This universal love is already very powerful in itself, and it is not necessary to identify with each of the beings in particular to make it effective.

With time and patience, we can come to experience such universal love. Obviously, self-centeredness and, at a deeper level, our belief in an ego existing as an autonomous entity, will do everything possible to dissuade us. Unconditional love is only really possible when the concept of an independent self has faded away. This does not prevent us from starting right away, at our level, and gradually progressing.

Where to start?

We must begin by addressing anger and hatred, which are the biggest obstacles to selfless love. As we all know, these extremely powerful emotions can turn our minds upside down. If we do not control them, they will poison our entire existence and make it impossible to taste the joy of loving all others.

If you are among those who do not see anger as a negative emotion and find that in certain situations that exasperate you, a burst of anger seems to give you renewed confidence and energy, carefully consider in what state your mind is in those moments. The energy that your anger brings is blind energy. You cannot know with certainty what effects, positive or negative, it will produce in the end. When you lose your temper, you close the access to the rational part of the brain. So the energy of anger is rarely reliable and can lead us to act in ways that are sometimes highly destructive.

When it reaches a certain intensity, it makes us lose all reason, and we can hurt not only others but also ourselves.

To manage difficult situations, fortunately we have an energy as powerful as that of anger, but this time it is controllable, as it comes from anger's most effective antidotes: kindness, patience, and reason. The moderation that these qualities engender is often interpreted as a sign of weakness. Personally, I think it is true inner strength. Compassion is certainly benevolent and peaceful by nature, but it gives great power, while those who easily lose patience are unstable and not sure of themselves. I think it is giving vent to anger that is a clear sign of weakness.

When a conflict arises, try to stay humble and sincerely seek an equitable solution. Some people will take advantage of you, or your detachment may provoke an aggressive reaction. Then adopt a firm attitude, but without losing your compassion, and if, to assert your position, you must take strong action, do it without anger or malice.

You should understand that in fact, even if your opponents seem to harm you, ultimately they are mainly harming themselves. To control the instinctive egotistical reflex, which is to fight back, remember you are trying to practice compassion and help others not to suffer the consequences of their actions. If you adopt measures that were chosen with calm, they will be even more effective, powerful, and adapted to the situation.

Friends and enemies

Those who create this kind of difficulty for us are generally not our friends but our enemies. So if we really want to learn something, we should consider our enemies to be the best teachers we could possibly find. The practice of patience is indeed essential for cultivating love and compassion, and we could not perform that practice if we had no enemies. They deserve our gratitude since it is they who ultimately contribute most to our peace of mind. We might add that it often happens, in and around our personal lives, that enemies become friends as circumstances change.

It is of course natural to want to surround ourselves with friends, but I do not think that friendship comes from aggression, anger, jealousy, or fierce competition. The best way to make friends is to be kind toward others. If you really care about others, are concerned for their well-being, help them, and serve them, you will have more friends and elicit more smiles. What do you get from that attitude? Lots of support when you need it. But if you neglect the happiness of others, in the long term it is you who will be the loser.

I love laughter, but there are different kinds of laughter. There is artificial, sarcastic, diplomatic, or hypocritical laughter. Those kinds can cause suspicion and even fear. But genuine laughter creates an impression of freshness, which I believe is a characteristic of human beings.

Defeating the enemy within

Anger and hatred are our real and constant enemies. It is they, not our temporary adversaries, that we need to fight and conquer. As we have not trained our minds to weaken their power to harm, those emotions continue to disrupt and negate all our efforts for inner peace.

To eliminate the destructive potential of anger and hatred, we must understand that they are rooted in the pursuit of our own well-being to the detriment of others. This selfishness is not only the source of anger; it is also the root cause of all our troubles. As it relies on a misleading perception that prevents us from seeing the true nature of things, someone who aspires to cultivate love and compassion must understand the illusory nature of this enemy within and how it inevitably produces its adverse effects.

For this, we must first get to know our own mind. Paying great attention to the study of the way it functions and observing it in an almost scientific way, we discover a multitude of mental states that differ depending on the object that is perceived, the way it is perceived, the intensity of that perception, and so forth. We must then distinguish among all those states, seeing which ones are useful and beneficial and should be encouraged, and which ones cause difficulties and suffering, and need to somehow be eliminated. This analysis should be the essential practice of the Buddhist practitioner.

The Buddhist scriptures speak of eighty-four thousand types of harmful thoughts, to which correspond eighty-four thousand methods, or antidotes, taught by the Buddha. So do not expect to find, as if by magic, the miracle cure that will free your mind from all disturbing forces. In order to obtain significant results, it is necessary to apply many different methods for a long time and have patience and determination. Do not expect to attain enlightenment straight away from your first steps on the path of Dharma!

Buddhist teachings on love and compassion often use aphorisms like: "Do not worry about your own welfare but prefer that of others." These formulas can sometimes frighten us, but they need to be understood in their context, that of a training aimed at teaching us to be genuinely concerned with the suffering of others.

Before wanting to take care of others, one must first be able to love oneself. Loving oneself is not based on a sense of personal debt for which one is accountable to oneself but simply on the fact that by nature we all strive to be happy and not suffer. It is only after accepting this benevolence toward oneself that it is possible to extend it to all others.

Impartiality

Since genuine compassion is necessarily universal and impartial, to achieve it, we must first cultivate impartiality toward all beings. According to Buddhism, those we consider as friends and relatives in this life could have been our worst enemies in a previous life. The same reasoning can be applied to those we currently consider as enemies. Even if they do us great harm, they could have been our best friends or even our mother in past lives. Reflecting on the fluctuating and interchangeable nature of our relations, which means that each individual may manifest in turn as a friend or an enemy, we learn to see things from a more impartial perspective.

This mental training requires a certain detachment, but there again we must understand what is meant by that term. Some people think that Buddhist detachment is synonymous with indifference. But this is wrong. It simply means standing back from the superficial considerations that involve classifying one person as a friend and another as an enemy, with all the emotions that result from that. This type of detachment is the opposite of indifference to others because it is the very basis for the authentic compassion that one feels for all beings impartially.

Dilgo Khyentse Rinpoche

THE ALCHEMY OF SUFFERING

By sincerely training in the meditation practice of exchanging suffering for happiness, you will eventually become capable of actually taking on others' illnesses and curing them and giving them your happiness in reality. Moreover, those with harmful intentions, even evil spirits who try to steal people's life force, will be powerless to harm either you or anyone else if you exchange their suffering and hatred with your happiness and peace.

There are some extraordinary pith instructions that explain in more detail how to make this practice more effective.

First, it is important to start by arousing a deeply felt warmth, sensitivity, and compassion for all beings. To do so, begin by thinking about someone who has been very kind and loving to you; in most cases, this could be your own mother. Remember and reflect on her kindness—how she gave you life, how she suffered the discomforts of pregnancy and the pain of childbirth, how she looked after you as you grew up, sparing no effort. She was ready to make any sacrifice for you and to put your welfare before her own.

When you feel strong love and compassion, imagine that she is undergoing terrible sufferings, that she suffers in agony before your very eyes, being dragged along the ground or tortured. Then imagine that she is starving, just skin and bones. She stretches her hands out to you, imploring you, "My child, do you have anything you can give me to eat?" Imagine her reborn as an animal, a terrified doe being chased by hunters and their dogs. In panic, she leaps off a high cliff to escape them but falls with unbearable pain, shattering all her bones; still alive, but unable to move, she is finished off by the hunters' knives.

Continue to imagine your mother (or another person that you have taken as the object of your meditation) undergoing situation after situation of suffering. An intense feeling of compassion will irresistibly well up in your mind. At that moment, turn that intense compassion to all beings, realizing that each one of them must surely have been your mother many times and deserves the same love and compassion as your mother of this present life. It is important to include all those whom you now consider to be enemies or troublemakers.

Reflect deeply about everything that all these beings are going through as they wander endlessly in samsara's vicious cycle of suffering. Think about old, infirm people unable to care for themselves; about all those who are sick and in pain; people who are desperate and impoverished, lacking even the most basic necessities; about people suffering famine and starvation, the pangs of hunger and thirst; those who are physically blind—and about those who are spiritually destitute, starved of the nourishment of Dharma, and blind to any authentic vision of truth. Think about all those who suffer as slaves to their own minds, constantly maddened by desire and aggression, and about those who harm one another without respite. Visualize all these sentient beings as a crowd in front of you and let all the different forms that their suffering takes arise vividly in your mind.

With an intense feeling of compassion, begin the practice of "exchange." Think of all those who suffer and consider that as your breath goes out, all your happiness—all your vitality, merit, good fortune, health, and enjoyment—is carried out to them on your breath in the form of cool, soothing, luminous white nectar. Make the following prayer: "May this truly go to my enemy and be entirely given to him!" Visualize that they absorb this white nectar, which provides them with everything that they need. If their lives were to be short, imagine that now they are prolonged. If they need money, imagine that now they are wealthy; if they are sick, that now they are cured; and if they are unhappy, now imagine them so full of joy that they feel like singing and dancing.

As you breathe in, consider that you take into yourself, in the form of a dark mass, all the sickness, obscurations, and mental poisons of others, and that they are thereby completely relieved of all their afflictions. Think that their sufferings come to you as easily as mountain mist wafted away by the wind. As you take their suffering into you, you feel great joy and bliss, mingled with the experience of emptiness. Repeat this, again and again, until it becomes second nature to you.

This precious, vital practice can be practiced both in and out of meditation sessions. You can use it at any time and in all circumstances, while engaged in the activities of ordinary life, whether you are sick or well.

Sometimes, visualize that your heart is a brilliant ball of light. As you breathe out, it radiates rays of white light in all directions, carrying your happiness to all beings. As you breathe in, their suffering, negativity, and afflictions come toward you in the form of dense, black light, which is absorbed into your heart and disappears in its brilliant white light without a trace, relieving all beings of their pain and sorrow.

Sometimes, visualize yourself transformed into a wish-fulfilling jewel, radiant and blue like a sapphire, a little larger than your own body, on top of a victory banner. The jewel effortlessly fulfills the needs and aspirations of whoever addresses a prayer to it.

Sometimes, visualize that your body multiplies into infinite forms of yourself, which travel throughout the universe, immediately taking on all the sufferings of each and every being they encounter, and giving away all your happiness to them.

Sometimes, visualize that your body transforms into clothes for all those who are cold and need clothing, into food for all those who are hungry, and into shelter for all who are homeless.

The exchange of self and others can also be used as a way of dealing with the negative emotions that cause us so much suffering. You can practice using any one of them, for instance, desire. Desire is the compulsive attraction and attachment we feel toward a person or an object.

Start by considering that if you tame your own desire, you will be able to reach enlightenment in order to best help beings and to establish them all in Buddhahood. Then think about someone you do not like. Arousing great compassion for that person, add all his desires to your own, and think that as you take them, he becomes free of them. Progressively take all beings' desires, whether manifest or latent, upon yourself, and as you do so, think that all beings become free from desire and achieve enlightenment. This is the way to meditate on taking negative emotions according to relative truth.

To meditate according to absolute truth, arouse in yourself an overwhelming feeling of desire. Fuel it by adding the desires of all beings, to make a great mountain of desire. Then look right into it. You will see that desire is nothing but thoughts; it appears in your mind but does not itself have even the tiniest particle of independent existence. And when you turn the mind inward to look at itself, you become aware that the mind, too, is without any inherent existence in either past, present, or future. The nature of the mind is as insubstantial as the sky.

Using these same methods, you can meditate on anger, pride, jealousy, and ignorance, as well as on anything else that obscures the mind.

Of all the practices of the bodhisattvas, this is the most essential. There is no obstacle that can disrupt it. Not only will it help others, but it will bring you to enlightenment, too. As a beginner you may not be able to help beings outwardly very much, but you should meditate constantly on love and compassion until your whole being is imbued with them.

Gyalse Thogme

This is an excerpt from the biography of Gyalse Thogme by Palden Yeshe.

A LIFE OF COMPASSION

Once, when Gyalse Thogme was sixteen, a benefactor of the monastery asked him to leave for Sakya on an important task and to return the next day. Halfway to Sakya, in a desert plain, the young Thogme came upon a bitch who was starving to death. She was on the verge of eating her own pups. He felt great pity for her, and wondering what he could do to help, decided to carry them all back to E, his monastery. He would then have to travel all night to make up for the time lost. He set off, carrying the dogs on his back. It was very hard. Finally, however, he arrived back at E and finished taking care of them. Before setting off again, he thought he had better have a sip of water. It was then that he came upon the man who had sent him on his errand.

Astonished at seeing him there, the man asked, "Hey, didn't you go?" When Thogme explained what had happened, the man cursed him and said, "There's such important business at stake, and here you are with your great compassion!"

Thogme had been rebuked so sternly that he did not dare take his sip of water. He set off again at once, walked all night, and accomplished his task in Sakya early in the morning. Returning immediately, he arrived back at E just before sunset. Seeing this, the man who had sent him was amazed. He begged Thogme to forgive him for the scolding he had given him. He added, "What you did is wondrous indeed!"

Another time, when he was about twenty, all the monks of E were leaving for Chöbar when Thogme saw a crippled woman weeping by the main door of the monastery. He asked her what was wrong. She explained that she was crying because the monks were leaving. As she would be left behind, there would be no one left to give her alms. Thogme told her not to despair. He would return to fetch her, he promised.

He carried his belongings up to Chöbar and rested for a short while before leaving again with a rope. His friends called him from afar, asking where he was going. Thogme said that he was going back to get the crippled woman, but they did not believe him.

When he got back to E, however, he found that he could not carry both the woman and her things. So first he carried her clothes and mat a certain distance, and then came back to carry the woman. In this way, carrying in turn the woman and her belongings, he eventually reached Chöbar. His friends were astonished. They had thought at first that he had just gone to collect firewood.

When Gyalse Thogme was about thirty, a sick beggar used to stay outside near his door. His body was completely infested with lice. Thogme used to give him whatever food and drink he had, bringing it to him discreetly at night to avoid making a show of his generosity. But one night the beggar was not in his usual place, and Thogme set out in search of him. Finding him at last as dawn broke, Thogme asked him why he'd gone away.

"Some people told me I was so disgusting that when they walked by, they could not even look at me, and they kicked me out," said the beggar.

Hearing this, Thogme was overwhelmed by compassion and wept. That evening he brought the beggar to his room and gave the man his fill of food and drink. Then Thogme gave him his own new robes, taking in exchange the beggar's rags, Thogme put them on and let the lice feed on his body.

It was not long before he looked as though he had been stricken by leprosy, or some other disease. He was so weakened and disabled by sickness that he had to stop teaching. His friends and disciples came to see him, wondering whether he had fallen seriously ill. They soon saw the condition he was in.

"Why don't you be a good practitioner again?" they admonished him.

Some quoted from the scriptures: "If your compassion is not totally pure, do not give your body away."

Others begged him, "For your sake and ours, don't carry on like this. Get rid of those lice!"

But Thogme said, "Since time without beginning, I have had so many human lives, but they have all been in vain. Now, even if I die today, I will at least have done something meaningful. I will not get rid of the lice."

He kept feeding the lice for seventeen days, but they gradually died by themselves, and he was free of them. He recited many mantras over the dead lice, and made *tsa tsas** with them. Every-one now marveled at the purity of his mind and his loving-kind-ness, and everywhere he became known as Gyalse Chenpo, "the Great Bodhisattva."

His compassion was so strong that he was able to help and transform not only human beings but animals, too. Mutual ene-mies, such as wolves and sheep and deer, forgot their cruelty and their fear. They would play peacefully together in his presence and listen with respect to his teachings.

Once, a hermit meditating on the inner channels and energies encountered obstacles to his practice. Losing control of his mind, he began to run about naked. A female wild sheep came upon him; she circled him, threatening to butt him with her horns. When the hermit saw this, he recovered his self-control and realized what had befallen him. Hearing of the incident, Thogme teasingly said that this sheep was an expert in dispelling the obstacles of great meditators. When Thogme became sick, the same sheep showed many signs of distress. Three days after his passing, she suddenly died also below Thogme's hermitage.

He was so serene, self-controlled, and kind that whoever stayed near him naturally became detached from worldly concerns. And then came the last months of his life.

He first showed signs of sickness to encourage his disciples to be diligent—by making them feel sad and to show how sick-ness can be used on the spiritual path. He said that no treatment was likely to help, but to calm everyone, he took some medicine nonetheless, and let prayers and ceremonies be performed on his behalf.

---

* *Tsa tsas*: small sculptures in the form of a stupa symbolizing the Buddha's enlightened mind, usually made of clay. One can incorporate sacred relics or the ashes or bones of a deceased person or animal with the prayer that they may be freed from the lower realms of existence and attain buddhahood.

When someone asked him if there were any way to prolong his life, Thogme said, "If my being sick will benefit beings, may I be blessed with sickness! If my dying will benefit beings, may I be blessed with death! If my being well will benefit beings, may I be blessed with recovery! This is the prayer I make to the Three Jewels. Having complete certainty that whatever happens is the blessing of the Three Jewels, I am happy, and I shall take whatever happens onto the path without trying to change anything."

His close disciples begged him to consider whether medical treatment or anything else they could offer him would be of any benefit.

But Thogme said, "I have reached the limit of my years, and my sickness is severe. Even the attentions of highly skilled physicians with ambrosia-like medicine would be unlikely to help much." And he added:

> If this illusory body, which I cling to as mine, is sick—
>   let it be sick!
> This sickness enables me to exhaust
> The bad karma I have accumulated in the past,
> And the spiritual deeds I can then perform
> Help me purify the two kinds of veils.*
>
> If I am in good health, I am happy,
> Because when my body and mind are well,
> I can enhance my spiritual practice
> And give real meaning to human existence
> By turning my body, speech, and mind to virtue.
>
> If I am poor, I am happy,
> Because I've no wealth to protect,
> And I know that all feuds and animosity
> Sprout from the seeds of greed and attachment.

*The two veils: the obscuration of the negative emotions and the cognitive obscurations.

If I am rich, I am happy,
Because with my wealth I can do more positive actions,
And both temporal and ultimate happiness
Are the result of meritorious deeds.

If I die soon, that's excellent,
Because, assisted by some good potential, I am confident that
I shall enter the unmistaken path
Before any obstacle can intervene.

If I live long, I am happy,
Because without parting from the warm, beneficial rain of
    spiritual instructions
I can, over a long time, fully ripen
The crop of inner experiences.

Therefore, whatever happens, I shall be happy!

And he continued:

"I've been teaching these pith instructions to others, and I must practice them myself. As it is said, 'What is called sickness has no true existence whatsoever, but appears within the display of illusory phenomena as the ineluctable result of wrong actions. Sickness is the teacher that points out the nature of samsara and shows us that phenomena, manifest though they may, have no more true existence than an illusion. Sickness provides us with the grounds for developing patience toward our own suffering and compassion for the suffering of others. It is in such difficult circumstances that our spiritual practice is put to the test'.

"If I die, I'll be relieved of the pains of my sickness. I can't recall any task that I've left undone, and what's more, I realize how rare an opportunity it is to be able to die as the perfect conclusion of my spiritual practice. That's why I'm not hoping for any cure for my illness. Nevertheless, before I die, you may complete all your ceremonies."

CHAPTER 8

The Six Perfections
or Transcendent Virtues

If we compare the altruistic desire to attain enlightenment for
the good of all to the wish to go on a journey, the journey itself
would be the practice of the six transcendent virtues—generosity,
discipline, patience, joyous effort, concentration, and wisdom—
that will perfectly accomplish the double acquisition of merit and
wisdom. Those virtues can only really be called "transcendent" if
they are practiced with the understanding that the three aspects
of whatever one does—the subject, object, and the action itself—
are empty of intrinsic reality. In other words, the first five virtues
become truly transcendent insofar as they are impregnated with
the sixth, wisdom. Transcendent generosity, for example, is not
just the act of giving, but a natural expression of freedom from
the notions of "I" and "mine." It then performs the dual function
of relieving the immediate suffering of those in need and contributing to the enlightenment of those who practice it. That enlightenment is the ultimate remedy for suffering.

Sakya Pandita

Equipped with the powerful body of the perfectly pure view,
  free of elaborations,
With the limbs of perfectly pure meditation, free from distraction,

105

And the turquoise mane of perfectly pure action,
This is the meditator, like a lion of the snows.

Wearing the armor of unlimited accomplishment of the
     benefit of beings,
With the horse of the two accumulations spurred by courage,
Bearing the sword of wisdom that slays the horde of
     mental poisons,
This is the meditator, like a hero on the battlefield.

Rich with the treasure of the three unstained disciplines,
Providing beings with material goods and protection
     against fear
And leading them on the path of liberation through the gift
     of Dharma,
This is the meditator who gathers beings to work for
     their good.

This describes the three kinds of supreme meditators.

Drigung Döndrup Chögyal

Generosity free from expectation is like the confidence of
     a sower:
Whatever needs to grow will grow, and nothing will be lost.
Thus extract the quintessence of your gifts:
That is my advice from the heart.

The triple discipline* is like the sword of a hero.
It cuts the bonds of cyclic existence

---

* The three disciplines are: (1) refraining from doing evil, (2) doing as much good
as possible, and (3) helping beings.

That negative emotions hide.
Be mindful, careful, and full of restraint:
That is my advice from the heart.

Patience is like unbreakable armor
That anger is unable to pierce:
Under its protection, virtues grow.
Through it, obtain the marks of a Buddha:
That is my advice from the heart.

The three kinds of joyous effort* are like spurs
Spurring a superb mount. With them,
The supreme Dharma will quickly free you from cyclic
    existence.
Apply this sovereign method to achieve the ultimate goal:
That is my advice from the heart.

Meditation in equipoise is like a vast palace.
By establishing yourself in it peacefully, you take rest from
    conditioned existence.
Train yourself without distraction in deep concentration:
That is my advice from the heart.

Wisdom is like a flawless eye
Whose vision penetrates all phenomena without
    confusing them.
Maintain this torch of the path of liberation:
That is my advice from the heart.

---

* There are three types of joyous effort, or diligence: (1) armor-like effort, which is resistant to all adverse circumstances, (2) effort in action, which can take the path of awakening to completion, and (3) insatiable effort, which is never satisfied with what we have already done and never lets the commitments that we have taken weaken or decline.

Jigme Lingpa

Virtue that is filled with loving-kindness and compassion
Is generosity when practiced for the sake of beings.
It is discipline when free from self-concern
And patience when untiring for the sake of others.

It is diligence when done with vibrant joy
And concentration when enacted with one-pointed mindfulness.
It is wisdom when there is no clinging to the reality of things.
From virtue such as this the six perfections never separate.

Atisha

"What are the best elements of the path?" Khu, Ngok, and Drom
asked Jowo Atisha.
   Atisha replied:

The best scholar is one who has realized the absence of true existence.
The best monk is one who has subdued his mind.
The best quality is great altruism.
The best instruction is to always watch your mind.
The best medicine is to know that nothing has independent existence.
The best conduct is one that is not in accord with those of the world.
The best achievement is the progressive reduction of negative
   emotions.
The best sign of accomplishment is the steady decline of desires.
The best generosity is nonattachment.
The best discipline is pacifying the mind.
The best patience is humility.
The best effort is abandoning ordinary activities.
The best concentration is the unaltered state of mind.
The best wisdom is to not believe in the real existence of anything.
The best teacher is the one who attacks your hidden faults.
The best instruction is one that hits your secret faults.
The best friends are mindfulness and vigilance.

The best incentives for practice are enemies, obstacles, illness,
    and suffering.
The best method is to not alter the mind.
The best benefit is to have set someone on the path of Dharma.
The best way to help others is to turn their mind to the path of
    liberation.

Geshe Potowa Rinchen Sel

We wander from time immemorial
In this vast ocean of suffering of the three realms of samsara
Through not knowing our own minds.
This misunderstanding is due to our obscurations;
Those obscurations come from not having been able to
    acquire merit and wisdom;
That ignorance comes from lack of faith;
And that lack of faith, from not having death in mind.

Now that you are frightened by the sufferings of samsara,
You want to attain liberation and the omniscience of
    buddhahood;
To do that you must know your own mind.
To know it, you must purify your obscurations,
And for that, acquire merit and wisdom.
To acquire those two things, faith is essential,
And genuine faith will not appear
Without having death in mind.
When you really think about death,
Nothing but the Dharma will seem useful to you,
You will not feel the slightest attraction to the perfections
    of the world.

GENEROSITY

Drigung Döndrup Chögyal

The wealth we have accumulated is like bees' honey;
It takes all our efforts and in the end others get it
  instead of us.
Produce merit and practice generosity.
That's my advice from the heart!

Mipham Rinpoche

Even if I cling to my possessions,
I will have no choice but to leave, abandoning everything.
So I will cultivate generosity and achieve
What is best for this life and the next!

Giving, however small, produces great effects;
Even great wealth does little good.
Even if through being generous in the past, I am rich in
  this life,
If I give nothing in this life, I'll be poor in the next.

They are accumulated, protected, and lost.
Riches have faults without number!
Even if the earth was covered with riches,
The desire of beings would still not be satisfied.

Apart from food, shelter, and a few other things,
Everything is redundant and a cause of torment.
Give and your wealth will grow
Like the waters of a river swelling in summer.

Kangyur Rinpoche

The nature of generosity is to have no attachment to material wealth and to have a giving, openhanded attitude toward others. There are three kinds of generosity: the giving of material possessions, the giving of protection from fear, and the giving of the sacred Dharma.

The gift of material things

Those who are only beginning to train in the general activities of the Bodhisattvas—and this is particularly true for the practice of giving—will find themselves much hampered by feelings of niggardliness and will experience difficulty even in making gifts of food. They must train themselves gradually like the man in the story who started out by transferring small objects from one hand to another, with the thought that he was simply giving. In the end, he was able to perform feats of great generosity.

The gift of protection from fear

This means to protect the lives of those who are imprisoned or are being punished and tortured. It means to protect wild animals that are being chased by hunters, or cattle and sheep destined for the slaughterhouse, and to help people who are endangered by disease and evil forces. It also means to train one's mind in the aspiration actually to liberate all beings from the endless sufferings of samsara—the source of constant fear—and to bring them to the perfect ease of nirvana.

Beginners should practice generosity according to their true capacity. For the danger is that, if they do not have the ability to give what is difficult to give, and overreach themselves imprudently, they will fall into discouragement and regret, and there is a risk that the attitude of the Bodhichitta will be lost.

The gift of Dharma

The true gift of Dharma is to impart instruction to others according to their mental capacity. However, it is difficult for people who are on the level of aspirational practice to give teachings in this way, since they are unable to expound the Dharma clearly either in word or meaning. At this stage, one should consider the altruistic attitude as the main practice and endeavor earnestly, with mindfulness and vigilance, in the task of clearing away defiled emotions according to the instructions of one's spiritual teacher.

For someone whose mind is free, untouched by the eight worldly concerns and uncluttered by distraction and busyness, the main thing is to bring benefit to others. One should then teach the Dharma to others according to their type, capacity, aspiration, and character, from the principles of karma through to the Great Perfection.

DISCIPLINE

The essence of discipline is the firm decision to refrain from harming others and even from having the idea of doing so. It is a repudiation of all that is contrary to the precepts. The teachings on discipline are expounded under three headings: (1) the avoidance of negative actions of thought, word, and deed; (2) the undertaking of positive actions, and (3) benefiting others.

PATIENCE

Gampopa

To practice patience for purely selfish ends, and not in order to help others, is to act like a cat, whose sole purpose is to kill the mouse.

Kangyur Rinpoche

Patience is essentially the ability to bear with suffering. It is the fertile soil in which the flowers of Dharma (in other words, the three disciplines) can grow and spread their perfume of good qualities. Encircling these flowers like a protective fence are the three kinds of patience. The first is the patience to bear the sufferings and difficulties that occur while one is striving for the twofold goal: Buddhahood for one's own sake and the accomplishment of the welfare of others. The second kind of patience is the ability to put up with the injuries that others might inflict, while the third kind is the ability to confront, without fear or apprehension, the doctrine of emptiness and other profound teachings....

The mischiefs that flow from anger are boundless. Just as it is impossible to remove the briars from a forest of thorns (so that the only way to escape harm is not to go there or shoe our feet with leather), it is impossible to halt the onslaught of adversity. Irritated and dismayed by what we do not want, we experience impulses of anger and resentment that are hard to control, and everyone's mind gets infected in the same way. The first thing to occur is the perception that a given object is in some way unwanted, and then feelings of displeasure arise. If, however, we are able to bring the impulse under control before it hardens and becomes established, the arduous practice of patience will prove a good friend. As the proverb says, "Hit the pig on the snout; clean the butter lamp while it is still warm.*"

When we are criticized by someone, our hearing faculty and consciousness all interact so that the statement provokes a strong feeling of displeasure. A sharp sensation of pain is experienced as if an arrow had pierced our heart and torn it open. Nevertheless, if the situation is examined properly, we can see that the words

* An angry pig that charges will flee immediately if it is struck on the snout with a stick, because of the shock. It is much easier to clean a butter lamp while it is still hot before the butter hardens.

themselves are just like an echo. Even if they appear to hit their mark, they are (in themselves) unable to inflict real damage. But what normally happens in this kind of situation? Our habitual way of thinking, which identifies the word with the thing it designates, takes the words as genuinely harmful, and the interplay of assailant and assailed is set in motion. Thus we are disturbed and suffer.

In our present situation, all the causes of physical and mental suffering—beating, fighting, robbing, slander, and the like—seem to come from other people. But the cause of them all is in ourselves. They are like booming echoes returning to their source. Indeed, if we had no ego-clinging, there would be no one for the enemy to attack, so we should reflect how situations of conflict are called forth by our own past actions.

Moreover, if we think about it, we can see that patience can only ever arise in adversity. Thanks to the hostility of enemies, we can embark on the ship of patience and sail upon the ocean of the Mahayana, gaining for ourselves the precious jewel of bodhichitta, the source of immediate and ultimate benefit for self and others. Enemies should therefore be looked upon as the object and source of patience. They are as worthy of offerings as the sacred Dharma itself!

As regards patience in connection with ultimate reality, it is important to reflect on the following point. If one investigates closely to see where the injury lies—in the aggressor, in the action itself, or in the victim of aggression—one will discover that it cannot be found anywhere. As we have explained, when different circumstances coincide, it is the mind, with its tendency to construct existential situations, that fabricates the problem there and then. And if one examines the mind, it will be found not to possess any constant and immutable characteristics.

When one tries to trace a design on water, the pattern dissolves in the very instant of its drawing. In the same way, as soon as the violence of hostile thought is allowed to subside (for it is incapable of remaining on its own, unsupported by other factors), a totally pure and spacious state of mind appears—the primordial great emptiness free from concepts. To preserve this state of openness, this simple presence, in which there is nothing to be lost or gained, accepted or rejected, without being distracted by other things is called, on the profound path of the Madhyamika, the "purification of negative emotions in ultimate reality."

In conclusion, the arduous practice of patience has three phases: the earnest embracing of hardships, the patient toleration of the wrongs done by others, and the patience that is a fearless conviction with regard to ultimate reality. If the last kind of patience is lacking, the other two can never rise above the worldly path. On the other hand, if those two are absent or weak, then however much one may wish to acquire the qualities of the path and fruit, through the practice of generosity and the other five paramitas, it will be difficult to achieve the object of one's aspirations. It is comparable to the difficulties encountered in trying to go somewhere, all alone and without an escort, following a path that is haunted by enemies, robbers, and wild beasts. Therefore, we should summon up our courage and train in patience, cultivating strength of heart.

Chengawa Lodrö Gyaltsen

If it is happiness you seek,
First tolerate suffering.
Without experiencing tears,
You will not appreciate laughter.

Shantideva

Harmful beings are everywhere, like space itself.
Impossible it is that all should be suppressed.

But let this angry mind alone be overthrown,
And it's as though all foes had been subdued.

To cover all the earth with sheets of leather—
Where could such amounts of skin be found?
But with the leather soles of just my shoes
It is as though I cover all the earth! . . .

All the good works gathered in a thousand ages,
Such as deeds of generosity,
And offerings to the Blissful Ones—
A single flash of anger shatters them.

No evil is there similar to anger,
No austerity to be compared with patience.
Steep yourself, therefore, in patience,
In various ways, insistently.

Those tormented by the pain of anger,
Never know tranquility of mind—
Strangers they will be to every pleasure;
They will neither sleep nor feel secure. . . .

If there's a remedy when trouble strikes,
What reason is there for dejection?
And if there is no help for it,
What use is there in being glum? . . .

I am not angry with my bile and other humors—
Fertile source of pain and suffering!
Why then take offense at living beings?
They too are impelled by circumstance. . . .

Although it is their sticks that hurt me,
I am angry at the ones who wield them, striking me.
But they in turn are driven by their hatred;
Therefore with their hatred I should take offense. . . .

So, like a treasure found at home,
That I have gained without fatigue,
My enemies are helpers in my Bodhisattva work
And therefore they should be a joy to me.

Since I have grown in patience
Thanks to them,
To them its first fruits I should give,
For of my patience they have been the cause.

Shechen Gyaltsap

Look at the real nature of the harm that is done to you. It is as elusive as a drawing on water. Let your resentment subside by itself. When the stormy waves of thoughts have vanished, the mind becomes like the cloudless sky that has nothing to win or lose.

Patrul Rinpoche

*This story about Patrul Rinpoche was told to the author
by Nyoshul Khen Rinpoche.*

TESTING THE PATIENCE OF A HERMIT

One of the main concerns of Patrul Rinpoche was to ensure that practitioners remained alert and focused on their training, while preventing them from straying into complacency. One day he heard about a hermit who had been living for a long time in total seclusion and decided to go visit him. He arrived unannounced and sat in a corner of the cave with a doubtful air and a smirk.

"Where do you come from and where are you going?" asked the hermit.

"I came from the place my steps brought me from, and I'm going in the direction in front of me," answered Patrul.

Puzzled, the hermit continued:

"Where were you born?"

"On earth."

The renunciate was not sure what to make of this unexpected visitor. A moment later, Patrul asked him why he lived in a place so far from everything.

"I've been here twenty years. Right now, I am meditating on the perfection of patience," replied the hermit without hesitation, with a hint of pride in his voice.

"That's a good one!" exclaimed Patrul Rinpoche.

He leaned toward the hermit as if to confide a secret to him, and whispered in his ear:

"For two old frauds we're not doing badly, are we?"

The renunciate exploded with anger.

"Who do you think you are coming here shamelessly to disturb my retreat? Who asked you to come this way? Can't you let a humble practitioner like me meditate in peace?"

"And now what happened to your nice patience?" Patrul asked calmly.

Langri Thangpa

*These well-known anecdotes about Langri Thangpa
are to be found in many texts. Here is the version from
the writings of the great yogi Shabkar.*

Once upon a time there was a couple whose children had all died in infancy. When they had another child, they consulted the omens. "He will only survive," they were told, "if his parents say he's the son of a spiritual master." The mother took her newborn son to the cave where the great sage Langri Thangpa was meditating and laid the child before him, saying simply: "This is your son." The hermit said nothing, and raised the child with the help of a devoted woman who lived nearby. Time passed, and the rumor spread that this pure monk had sinned. A few years later, the boy's parents came respectfully to see the hermit and gave him generous offerings. "We beg you to forgive us. When you had done nothing wrong, we spread a false rumor about you. We owe the survival of our child to your kindness." Maintaining his usual serenity, Langri Thangpa gave the child back to his parents without saying a word.

The monk falsely accused

One day a monk of the monastery of Ratreng was accused of stealing a kettle that had simply been misplaced. He went to the abbot: "It was nothing to do with me," he said. "What should I do?" The abbot gave him this advice: "Accept the blame for it, and offer tea to all the monks. In the end, your innocence will be recognized." That is what the monk did. That night, he had dreams of good omens indicating that his whole being was deeply purified. A little later, they found the kettle, and the monk was cleared of all suspicion. When the abbot heard the news, he concluded with these words: "That's the right way to behave!"

JOYOUS EFFORT

Kangyur Rinpoche

THE THREE KINDS OF LAZINESS

(1) People are inextricably entangled in the affairs of this world. They are engrossed in them, overwhelmed by the bustle of mundane activities and society. They cling to their dear ones; they repudiate their adversaries; they immerse themselves in the accumulation, preservation, and increase of wealth. And from all these cares, they cannot free themselves; they are like silkworms imprisoned in the cocoons of their own making.

(2) Moreover, they are overpowered by the laziness of discouragement and tell themselves that they are unable to accomplish even those achievements of Dharma that are only slightly difficult. Destitute of energy in the practice of virtue, they constantly postpone it.

(3) They put themselves down with thoughts like, "Oh, but how could I ever do such things?" To wallow in this kind of depression is to cut oneself off from the Dharma.

People like this have no chance of gaining freedom, foundering as they do in the ocean of the three kinds of laziness. It is as though they were on a leaking ship; they have no prospect of gaining the other shore. . . .

One should overcome those three kinds of laziness with a courageous, armorlike diligence, impervious to any adverse circumstance, and never transgress one's pledge to benefit others nor allow one's diligence to weaken, either in intention or action. This indeed should be irreversible under all circumstances, regardless of the qualities of the path that might arise.

Shakyamuni Buddha

I have shown you the methods
Leading to liberation,
But know that liberation
Only depends on yourself.

Milarepa

Without expecting quick results,
Practice sincerely until your last breath!

Dilgo Khyentse Rinpoche

AN ANECDOTE ILLUSTRATING DETERMINATION

One day at Samye monastery, the great master Ma Rinchen Chok participated in a philosophical contest* with Gyalwa Choyang, a disciple of Padmasambhava. When Ma realized he had lost the debate, he said to himself, "I will go to India to deepen my knowledge of the teachings" and, rising immediately, he ran for the first few miles of his journey to India. Our desire to learn and practice the path should be as ardent as that.

---

* Tibetan Buddhists often engage in lively philosophical jousting during which they debate the most difficult themes of the Buddhist doctrine. In the eighth century, when Padmasambhava and other great masters introduced Buddhism to Tibet, many Tibetans went to India to meet the main holders of Buddhism, learn Sanskrit, and become capable of translating all the available texts into Tibetan. Ma Rinchen Chok was one of the foremost well-trained translators.

Gyalwa Yangönpa

As an old parchment that curls around itself,
Negative tendencies tend to come back.
New habits are easily destroyed by circumstances.
You will not cut through delusion in an instant.
All you who consider yourselves great meditators,
Spend more time in meditation!

Milarepa

At the beginning nothing comes, in the middle nothing stays, in
the end nothing goes.*

CONCENTRATION

Kangyur Rinpoche
Giving up attachment to wealth

The fleeting pleasures of this world are like the canopies of clouds
that appear one moment in the sky and are gone the next. People
immerse themselves in these enjoyments, claiming that they are
necessary for their livelihood and indispensable for their survival. And yet the life of humankind is no more than a flash of
lightning—a swiftly passing interlude, which can in no way be
extended beyond its term and is all the while attended by three sufferings, rampant like a gang of thieves: the suffering of change, the
suffering of suffering, and all-pervading suffering in the making.

In particular, wealth and enjoyments are the occasion of ruin in
this life and those to come. Beings are in a situation that is like a

---

* Milarepa is saying here that at the beginning of spiritual practice, nothing
seems to change in our way of being. Then after some time, changes occur, but
are not stable. Finally, when our practice becomes stable and deep, our inner
peace, wisdom, and other spiritual qualities are no longer subject to fluctuations.

turbulent river rushing irresistibly toward the sea. They are constantly tormented and exhausted by the tasks of accumulating, preserving, and augmenting their possessions. Their minds are pulled this way and that by desires, and they are never satisfied. When they possess a few riches, they become puffed up and look down on others. Fearful of losing what they have, they grow mean and stingy. They are so tight-fisted that they do not even eat their own food or wear their finery. As a result, they wander after death in the limitless ocean of the lower realms.

Wealth and precious possessions gained by evil means, and sinful thoughts and actions issuing from false and deceitful attitudes, are black like summer clouds heavy with rain. They are the source of unbounded suffering both in the present and in future lives. By contrast, those who own little are safe from enemies and robbers. Those who know contentment have reached the summit of riches.

Giving up attachment to bad company

On the whole, ordinary people are foolish and behave like spoiled children. Their mindstreams are clogged with wrong thoughts, and their actions are unvirtuous. They praise themselves and say unpleasant things about others; they are filled with the venom of the defilements. Their attitudes and conduct are as poisonous as a snake's tongue, and they are surrounded by the harsh atmosphere of conflict. For such people, negative states are constantly on the increase. . . .

Giving up attachment to objects of the senses

Until one is able, through the practice of clear insight, to tame the elephant of one's mind, which is intoxicated and driven wild by the deceptive poisons of desire objects, one will never truly perceive the latter's defects, for they always appear as positive qualities. There is nothing more specious and liable to deceive people than the objects of the senses.

Therefore, until the time comes for the compounded aggregate of this physical form to fall apart—in other words, when death occurs and the body is placed on a bier and carried away by four men or loaded on an ox and transported to the cemetery—we should dwell in peaceful woodland glades or other places of solitude, away from the distractions of business and society.

In praise of solitude

Secluded places and places of solitude in the wild* where there are no irritating and harmful circumstances are a delight to the spirit. It is there that weariness with samsara will develop. There one will avoid the society of people whose attitudes are false, who are engaged in the worldly occupations of trade, agriculture, and so on. Likewise, one will not be harassed by the obligation of paying taxes, or commissioned for compulsory service and the payment of duties. One will no longer be fretting about whether one has enough to live on; one will be free from the troubles of wage earning and the need to depend on helpers or attendants or indeed on anyone else. Out in the wilds, there are only the carefree birds and wild animals, the sound of whose voices does not grate upon the ear.

In places such as these, noble beings find a joyful abundance of all that they need: pure water and all kinds of fruit and edible plants. Natural caves are found in the rocks, and shelters of grass and leaves are spacious enough to accommodate the four kinds of

---

* These are traditional names for places at a greater or smaller distance from settlements and that are thus not agitated by the activities of ordinary life.

activity.* How wonderful if we could find such pleasant dwellings, rejoicing in the cool shade of the trees!

The actual practice of concentration

Practitioners should stay in solitude and rest in concentration without allowing themselves to be carried away by distraction even for a moment. This constitutes the higher training of the mind.

Because body and mind are interrelated, if one adopts a correct physical posture, the subtle channels with their energies will be straight, and this will facilitate the birth of realization in the mind. It is therefore important to sit on a comfortable seat and adopt the seven-point posture of Vairochana.

(1) The legs should be crossed. (2) The eyelids should be lowered, and the eyes should be gazing along the line of the nose. (3) The body should be kept straight, not leaning to one side or another. (4) The shoulders should be level. (5) The chin should be slightly tucked in so that the nose is in line with the navel. (6) The tip of the tongue should rest on the palate behind the teeth. (7) The breath should be allowed to rise and fall slowly and naturally. This posture is referred to as the life-tree or vital axis of the mind, for it helps to prevent it from getting lost in distraction, like tying a feeble sapling to a firm support.

One must then persevere in concentration, keeping the mind balanced in equipoise and focusing it exclusively on the specific object of concentration, without letting it stray elsewhere, even to virtuous objects (let alone negative ones), and without letting it lapse into a vague blankness. The object on which the mind should focus one-pointedly may be with or without form, and from time to time, one should through investigation make sure that the mind is focused on its positive target. It is thus that one engages

---

* Eating, sleeping, walking, and sitting.

alternately in the practices of analytic and "resting" meditation. A beginner might concentrate on an image (of the Buddha), for example. The time of meditation should be gradually extended. At length, all that appears to the mind, contrived and fixed upon by thought, will vanish into emptiness, the ultimate reality. This is not a state of nothingness in which nothing can be perceived. All phenomena, forms and so forth, appear unobstructedly, but they have no true existence; they lack all concrete attributes, with the result that there is in fact nothing real to observe.

When the mind remains in a state without torpor or excitement, dwelling one-pointedly on its object, undisturbed by thoughts, this is "calm abiding" (shamatha). The perfect recognition of the mind's nature of primal wisdom or the absence of clinging to the object of concentration is the postmeditation or "insight" (vipashyana). Shamatha and vipashyana partake of the same nature. The Cloud of Jewels gives the following definition:

> Shamatha is the one-pointed concentration of the mind.
> Vipashyana is perfect discernment.

Jigme Lingpa

As soon as you think of meditating, immediately enter the flow of mindfulness of the present moment of awareness. If you maintain that continuously, there is no risk of the slightest mistake, the slightest confusion, or wrong direction. It is unawareness that leads to wandering in the cycle of suffering.

If you recognize this mindfulness, your mental confusion will disappear of itself. Whatever thoughts arise from within that mindfulness, simply remain in the recognition of the observer that notices that a thought is happening without following the thoughts or rejecting the arising of thoughts. In that way not only are thoughts liberated by themselves, but they become a support of the path.

Undercurrents of thoughts that go unnoticed are as if set in stone. They establish repetitive patterns that solidify to perpetuate the endless cycle of existence.

Thoughts recognized by mindfulness are like drawings on the surface of water, which disappear as soon as they are drawn. They vanish without contributing to the creation of proliferating tendencies and do not reinforce the cycle of suffering.

Dzatrul Ngawang Tenzin Norbu

To remedy disturbances to your meditation caused by the arising of different states of mind, there are *five main disturbances* to be recognized: (1) laziness, (2) forgetting the instructions, (3) dullness and wildness, (4) lack of effort, and (5) excessive effort.

Remedy these with the following eight antidotes. Counteract *laziness* with (1) inspiration, (2) endeavor, (3) faith, and (4) the refined flexibility that comes through training body, speech, and mind. Counteract *forgetfulness* with (5) mindfulness, remembering both words and meaning. Counteract *dullness and wildness* with (6) alertness to these states of mind.

When any of these defects occur in meditation, counteract *lack of effort* by (7) making the effort to apply the appropriate antidote. When defects are absent, the antidotes are no longer necessary, and you should counteract *excessive effort* by (8) letting the mind rest in its natural state without antidotes.

As you practice sustained calm, you will experience the gradual pacification of the mind in five steps, which are illustrated by five similes:

(1) Meditation like a waterfall pouring down over a cliff. The thoughts continuously follow one another, and at first seem even

more numerous than usual, because you have become aware of the mind's movements.

(2) Meditation like a river rushing through mountain gorges. The mind alternates between periods of calm and turbulence.

(3) Meditation like a wide river flowing easily. The mind moves when disturbed by circumstances, but otherwise rests calmly.

(4) Meditation like a lake lightly ruffled by surface ripples. The mind is slightly agitated on the surface, but remains calm and present in its depth.

(5) Meditation like a still ocean, an unshakable, effortless concentration in which antidotes to discursive thoughts are redundant.

Sustained calm can momentarily limit negative emotions, but cannot eradicate them. Their full uprooting can be achieved only by the discriminating insight that recognizes the true nature of all phenomena during meditation and that is aware of everything as empty illusion during postmeditation. Sustained calm is thus the concentration aspect of meditation, while profound insight is its wisdom aspect. Shamatha prepares the mind for the insight of vipashyana to show the practitioner that all phenomena are inherently devoid of substantial existence. Both sustained calm and profound insight should be permeated by compassion. Uniting sustained calm and profound insight will eventually lead to a state of sameness in which all concepts of subject and object disappear.

WISDOM

Kangyur Rinpoche

In all, there are three kinds of wisdom: the wisdom of hearing, the wisdom of reflection, and the wisdom of meditation. Gradual training in these will result in the perfect accomplishment of vipashyana, primordial and nonconceptual wisdom. This wisdom destroys the defilements that prevent the attainment of liberation and removes the cognitive obscurations that prevent omniscience. It is the unmistaken knowledge, first, of ultimate reality, the profound nature of things, and second, of all phenomena that arise within the sphere of deluded perception. Equipped with such knowledge, one is able to pass swiftly through the city of existence, which karma and defilements have made so difficult to cross. Thus, one goes beyond suffering and reaches nirvana with ease.

The six transcendent perfections, generosity and so forth, are causally interrelated and are arranged progressively in terms of subtlety and elevation. They are called transcendent because they are all combined with transcendent wisdom.

Drigung Jigten Gönpo

Full of vigor, the son of a barren woman
Climbed a ladder made of rabbit's horn
And swallowed the sun and the moon,
Thus plunging beings in a sea of darkness:
That's what the belief in a self is like.

Ratna Lingpa

Namo guru! Homage to the teacher!
I bow at the feet of Lotus Born Vajra,
Manifest body of the Conqueror Infinite Light
Emanating from the vast space of the absolute
    dimension
Free of concepts, to fulfill the hopes of beings.

I, Rinchen Pal, a lawless vagabond
Only fit to sleep naked,

Giving vent to my crazy thoughts
Sang this song without head or tail.

When I contemplate the outside world,
I only see the deceptive appearances of relative truth,
Ethereal shimmers devoid of ultimate reality.
I, the aimless wanderer, have peace of mind.

When I look at my thinking mind,
I only see movements without trace, like those of the wind.
Ungraspable presence where birth and death are one.
I, the aimless wanderer, have peace of mind.

The painful nature of cyclic existence
Is as illusory as last night's dream:
Ungraspable and devoid of reality.
I, the aimless wanderer, have peace of mind.

Liberation, all bliss,
Only the pure essence of my own mind.
Its nature is emptiness, beyond any reference point.
I, the aimless wanderer, have peace of mind.

The duality of samsara and nirvana
Is only concepts of good and bad.
It is actually a nonduality beyond all reference point.
I, the aimless wanderer, have peace of mind.

CHAPTER 9

Purifying Obscurations and Acquiring Merit

To be sure of reaching our destination when we undertake a long journey, we must get rid of anything that can create obstacles and bring along provisions and other essentials for the trip. On the Buddhist path, that corresponds to the two stages called "purification" and "accumulation." Purification does not mean washing some kind of original impurity out of our human nature. If our nature was inherently bad, it would be useless to try to make it pure, just as we cannot make a piece of coal white by washing it, even for centuries. Rather, we purify, or remove, the obscurations that veil our true nature or what we might call our "original goodness." This purification is like extracting gold from its ore: the impurities are removed to reveal its brilliance and natural perfection. Or it can be compared to the wind driving away the clouds that hide the sun: the sun's light remains unchanged. It was already bright even when hidden.

Buddhism distinguishes two types of obscuration that must be eliminated by this process: the obscuration of disturbing emotions such as desire, hatred, ignorance, pride, and jealousy, and the more subtle conceptual obscuration, which prevents us from seeing the ultimate nature of things.

To make this purification possible, it is necessary to fulfill a number of requirements and conditions. That process is called "the acquisition of merit and wisdom." The acquisition of merit is achieved by the practice of the first five transcendental virtues described in the previous chapter (generosity, discipline, patience, joyous effort, and concentration), while the acquisition of wisdom, the sixth transcendent virtue, comes from recognizing the ultimate nature of reality.

Dilgo Khyentse Rinpoche

In past lives, and in this life until now, we have brought harm to others countless times by lying to them, cheating them, stealing from them, bringing ruin upon them, assaulting them, killing them, and all kinds of other wrongdoing. This accumulated negativity is what has kept us trapped in samsara, and it is now the chief hindrance to our progress on the path. It sustains the two kinds of obscuration that fall between us and the experience of the buddha-nature: obscuration by emotions and obscuration of what can be known.

Our situation is not completely hopeless, however. As the Kadampa masters used to say, "The only good thing about wrongdoing is that it can be purified." Negative actions are compounded phenomena, so they must be impermanent; therefore, as the Buddha said, there can be no fault so serious that it cannot be purified by the four powers.

These four powers are the means through which purification of all wrongdoing can be effected.

The first power is the power of *support*. Support here refers to the person or deity to whom we acknowledge and confess our faults, and who thus becomes the support for our purification.

The support might be Vajrasattva*—for instance, or the Thirty-Five Buddhas of Confession,† or your own spiritual teacher.

The second power is the power of *regret*. Regret arises naturally when we realize that all the suffering we have experienced until now in all our numerous rebirths in samsara has been caused by our own wrongdoing. As long as you remain unaware of the consequences your actions will bring, you will just go on behaving like a fool; but once you see clearly how all your past wrongdoing is what has kept you wandering in the interminable suffering of samsaric existence, you are bound to be stricken with deep remorse about all the negative actions you have committed, completely losing any urge to repeat them.

But regret by itself is not enough; the negative actions of the past still have to be purified. This is done with the third power, the power of the *antidote*. All negative actions committed with body, speech, and mind must be counteracted with their antidotes: positive actions of body, speech, and mind. In answer to your fervent prayer, visualize wisdom nectar flowing from Vajrasattva's body and pouring into you and all sentient beings through the crown of the head. It fills your body and theirs and completely washes away all obscurations, wrongdoing, and negativity, until at the end no trace is left; your body has become completely pure and as transparent as crystal. Vajrasattva smiles. Melting into light, he dissolves into you. Feeling that Vajrasattva's mind and yours have

---

* In the practice of Vajrayana, the "diamond vehicle," the visualization of Vajrasattva and recitation of his mantra is used for practices to purify the obscurations of body, speech, and mind. As with all practices of the Vajrayana, deities are not regarded as external entities, endowed with autonomous existence, but as aspects of the buddha-nature (*tathagatagarbha*) that is naturally present in every being and represents the essence, or potential, of buddhahood, the fundamental nature of all sentient beings.

† Thirty-five buddhas having a particular ability to help those who invoke them to purify their negative actions.

become one, remain for a while in a state of luminous voidness, beyond any concept.

The fourth power is the power of *resolve*, the determination never to repeat those harmful actions again, even at the cost of your life. Until now you might have been blind to the fact that wrongdoing is what causes suffering, but from now on you have no excuse not to change your ways. Nor is it right to think that since negative actions can be purified so easily, they do not matter very much; you have to make a resolute decision, from the very core of your being, that whatever happens you will never do any action that contradicts the Dharma. This will require constant mindfulness and diligence.

Through these four powers, your obscurations will vanish, and all the qualities inherent in the enlightened state will begin to shine, like the sun emerging from behind the clouds.

Dilgo Khyentse Rinpoche

Om.
Great Compassionate Bhagavan Vajrasattva,
Immaculate color of conch, most excellent form,
Pure and brilliant, spreading the light of one hundred
    thousand suns,
Hero, resplendent with a thousand rays of light,
Knower of the triple existence, renowned as the teacher,
Only friend of all the beings of the three realms,
Loving protector, god of compassion, please listen to me.

Since beginningless time
I have taken wrong paths, lost my view, and wandered in
    the rounds of existence.
In former lives, I was mistaken in committing wrong
    actions and misdeeds.

For all these evil deeds, whatever I have done, I feel strong
    remorse and regret.

Increasing and intensifying the power of this proud*
    karma,
I have sunken into the ocean of samsaric misery.
The burning flames of anger have scorched my stream of
    being.
The dense darkness of delusion has blinded intellect.
My consciousness is submerged near the bank of the
    ocean of desire.
The mountain of intense pride has pressed me down into
    the lower realms.
The raging gale of envy has tossed me about in samsara.
The demon of believing in an ego has tied me down
    tightly.
I have fallen into the abyss of craving like into a pit of
    embers.
Intense suffering has burned me like unbearable flames.

These miseries are difficult for me to bear.
And with the intense fire of the power of evil deeds
    burning me,
The sprouts of consciousness and sense organs have
    suffered.
Since this is overwhelming my illusory body of
    aggregates,
Compassionate and loving protector, can you bear it?

---

* "Proud" here refers to the fact that, against all evidence, we believe in a real and
solid "I" and assert it strongly in relation to "others."

I am foolish and deluded, a great sinner with evil karma.
By the power of karma I am reborn as Rudra* in the
  realm of desire.
I feel remorse for this rebirth! This karma is exhausting!
I feel weary and I regret, but the karma cannot be
  changed.
The force of karma is like the flow of a river.
How can the river of karmic power be immediately
  reversed?
All these ripenings result from my own karma.

Although I entered the teachings, I have been unable to
  follow them.
My body, speech, and mind have fallen prey to evil deeds.
Forced about by the fierce storm of karma,
I have for countless former eons
Wandered through the dark dungeons of samsara.
So, protector, through your compassionate blessings,
May you purify my obscurations of karma and negative
  emotions
And establish me right now in your presence, like a loving
  mother.
Brilliant like the sun and radiant like the moon,
Your compassionate face is captivating to behold.

Since beginningless time, blinded by the cataract of
  ignorance,
My eyes have been unable to perceive you.
So where do you stay right now, protector of beings?

* Rudra is the demon who embodies the attachment to ego and phenomena and,
in particular, a mistaken understanding of nonduality.

By karma's most overwhelming and fierce power,
I am completely terrified, afraid, and fearful.
So, as I utter this lamentation of pure yearning,
And make a destitute cry of great loss,
Loving protector, unless you regard me with compassion
    right now,
At some point, when I die and pass away and my mind
    parts from my body,
Separated from my spiritual friend and companions,
    I will be taken away by Yama.*
At that time, without being accompanied by my world
    and relatives,
Alone I will be carried by the power of karma.
Since I will then be without protector and refuge,
Without any postponement or delay of time,
Assiduously, right this moment, perform your liberating
    activity.

Beings like me, tormented by karma,
Have falsely discriminated since beginningless time,
Therefore not escaping from the samsaric places of the
    three realms.
Throughout all my lives in countless eons,
I have taken a countless number of material bodies.
Thus, if the flesh and bones were gathered, they would
    equal the size of the world.
If the pus and blood were gathered, they would fill a great
    ocean.
If the residual karmas were gathered, there would be an
    inconceivable amount beyond description.

* The lord of death.

Though I have journeyed through the three realms and
    continued through births and deaths,
My actions taken have been futile and such a waste!
Compared to all these countless rebirths,
The actions of just one single lifetime,
If engaged in for the sake of unexcelled enlightenment,
This amount of action would have value.
But if I pass away without bringing forth this value,
The force of karma is strong and negative emotions are
    powerful.
Through this I incarnate in the trap of flesh and blood
    and wander in samsara.
I am then imprisoned in existences with unbearable
    sufferings.
Such intense and endless misery
Is due to misdeeds and results from my own karma.
With your great compassion, interrupt this stream of evil
    karma!
Reverse this karmic wind of disturbing emotions.

When through ignorance and powerful karma
I perpetually wander within the darkness of unknowing,
Won't you accompany me with the light of your wisdom
    lamp?
When I cannot bear the ripening of evil deeds,
Won't you carry out your activity with great compassion?
When I fall into the abyss of perversity,
Won't you catch me with your hand of swift compassion?
When I suffer from the overwhelming disease of the
    three poisons,
Won't you cure me with your compassionate medicine of
    skillful means?

When I am scorched in the painful flames of karmic
    ripening,
Won't you shower down a cool stream of compassion?
When I sink down into samsara's swamp of misery,
Won't you pull me up with your compassionate hook of
    skillful means?

Having purified again and again the samsaric abodes of
    the three realms,
When at some time I attain the fruition,
There will be no point in asking for your noble
    compassion.
But while I am left here due to the power of residual
    karma,
Who else can I turn to for compassion?

Daka, you possess the strength of compassion,
And since the karmic residue of previous ties is powerful,
Do not be vague, indifferent, or indolent,
But regard me sincerely, victorious deity of compassion.
Lead me out of the swamp of samsara and guide me
    quickly
To the supreme state of the three dimensions of
    Buddhahood.

Anonymous text

HOW TO MAKE NEGATIVE EMOTIONS
PART OF THE PATH TO ENLIGHTENMENT

Namo ratna guru
Homage to the jewel that is the master!

Here are instructions on how to use powerful thoughts of hatred or attachment to train on the path by using both forms of bodhichitta. The tantras speak of using negative emotions as the path, but that would be impossible if we leave them just as they are. In the collection of the sutras, there are also many teachings on how to apply one's mind to these emotions and use them on the path while radically overcoming them.

Take the example of desire-attachment. When this occurs, either spontaneously or by contact with a particular external object, reflect as follows:

"This is desire. If I do not get rid of it, purify it, or overcome it, it will lead me to unimaginable suffering and to the lower worlds of existence. But if I purify and control it, it will lead me to perfect buddhahood. So that's what I'll do."

Then mentally take your enemy, the emotion of desire-attachment, and let it grow more and more, as you would if you were meditating on altruistic love. Finally, add all the desires of all beings, including those that are only latent, so that they completely fill your mind. Then think that through that all beings become free from desire and attachment and reach buddhahood. This is the way to practice using the relative bodhichitta.

Your own desire, as big as a mountain, only came about through thoughts, and the same goes for others' desire, and desire in itself is only a production of mind. But when your mind observes itself, it can be seen that past thoughts no longer exist, future thoughts have not arisen, and present thoughts are devoid of form or any other perceptible characteristic. Thoughts are like space: they have no independent existence. What we call desire is actually just a name without any reality in itself.

Remain in meditation on that reflection for as long as you can. That is the way to deal with emotions using ultimate bodhichitta. . . .

Practice in the same way focusing on hatred and all the other negative emotions.

I wrote these lines following my master's advice, without adding or deleting anything. May the merit and excellence of these profound instructions for integrating disturbing emotions on the spiritual path extend to the furthest reaches of space.

Jigme Lingpa

Beginners in meditation have not yet acquired the force of habit, and all sorts of phenomena—for instance, suddenly becoming rich—can arouse strong negative emotions in them such as desire, anger, or confusion. But if you stare directly at those emotions as soon as they arise, you will see that they are nothing else but awareness. That is what we call "contemplating the true face of negative emotions." When you see the real nature of those emotions, discursive thoughts, conceptualization, and attachment cease by themselves.

Look into space in front of you, eyes fully open, and whatever thoughts may arise in your mind at that moment, do not look at what has arisen but where it has arisen from. The thoughts will disappear without a trace.

Kangyur Rinpoche

If with mindfulness and meticulous vigilance and care you assess your actions correctly, adopting what is to be adopted and repudiating what is to be repudiated, down to the slightest gesture of your hands, the mouthing of a single syllable, or the conception of a single thought, you will not be brought low by any adversity threatening your practice. Everything you do will be transformed into the perfectly pure practice of the path, the all-important accumulation of merit.

CHAPTER 10

The Spiritual Master

Uniting with the Mind of the Teacher

"Guru yoga," or union with the nature of the teacher, is an essential practice of Tibetan Buddhism, which is based on deep devotion to the spiritual master. We should understand that the depth and dimension of this devotion transcends any notion of "blind faith." The devotion discussed here arises from the recognition of the immeasurable qualities of enlightenment of which an authentic spiritual teacher is the living example. The practice consists of mixing our mind with the teacher's mind through meditation, which enables us to break the limits of our confused and limited vision. Our narrow inner sphere mingles with the immense space of the teacher's enlightenment.

From the ultimate point of view, it is simply rediscovering the true nature of our mind, its luminous emptiness and original freedom. But this process can rarely occur without the catalyst which is the practice of guru yoga.

Through the outer teacher we can recognize the inner teacher. We read in many tantras and commentaries that, of all the practices of Buddhism, guru yoga is the most essential and the most effective for removing obstacles and progressing swiftly and surely on the path. For this reason it is crucial to rely on an authentic spiritual master who has all the qualities of wisdom and compassion described in the teachings.

Kangyur Rinpoche
The importance and the qualifications of a spiritual teacher

It is said that when a log of ordinary wood lies in the forests of the Malaya mountains, that great garden of medicinal plants, it will be impregnated with the moisture dripping from the leaves of the sandalwood trees and will gradually imbibe the sweet perfume of sandal. In just the same way, if you are able to frequent a spiritual master, you will quickly acquire the latter's qualities.

Fully qualified teachers

In the present age of decadence, it is extremely difficult to come upon accomplished spiritual masters who exhibit all the signs of authenticity as described in the sutras and the tantras. Nevertheless, it is essential to rely on spiritual friends whose minds are like excellent earth, well tilled both by the knowledge of the precepts of the three vows, as explained in the texts, and by faultless conduct, unstained by negative emotion. The earth of their minds should be moist with the knowledge of both the words and meanings of the sacred texts and their commentaries, themselves the source of their own freedom; and it should be saturated with great compassion and a loving concern for all that lives.

It is thus that brilliant flowers will blossom: the four ways in which masters attract disciples who are fortunate in treading the path of liberation. The latter are like bees that come and savor the quintessential nectar of instruction. These four ways are: (1) a generosity that is completely free from attachment, (2) a way of teaching that is attuned to the disciples' minds, (3) the ability to introduce them to the practice that leads to freedom, and (4) the fact that the teacher practices what he or she preaches.

False teachers

Some teachers, however, are like "wooden millstones." They practice the Dharma dishonestly and out of pride, like Brahmin priests, merely in order to preserve a line of incarnate lamas or a family lineage or out of concern for the reputation of their monastery, fearing that their ecclesiastical residence or tradition might otherwise decline. Trying to secure wealth or religious patrimony with such an evil motivation is like bathing in a filthy pond; such people are made even dirtier by the experience. Thus to receive, study, and explain the teachings and to build stupas, make statues, and so forth, with such motives as these is not true Dharma. Indeed, it will be the person's ruin. This is why the root text speaks of bathing in a filthy pond. Empty and noisy boasting about qualities contributes nothing to the mind's discipline, just as a wooden millstone is incapable of grinding barley and cannot produce flour. Such teachers bring their disciples to ruin.

Again, there are some people who, though their minds are filled with defilements and are no different from ordinary beings, have, as the karmic result of some trivial generosity in the past, obtained the position of a teacher in this life. They put on airs and persuade themselves that they are somebody after all, preening themselves and becoming puffed up with pride because they receive offerings, honors, and service from their devotees who go bowing and scraping in front of them—fools who know nothing about the true characteristics of a genuine spiritual master!

Then there are other imposters—those who have only a smattering of the teachings. They have taken the vows and embraced the tantric commitments. But they are ignorant of the precepts, and their discipline is quite distorted. They have no idea of the three trainings, and their minds, awash with defects, are base and degenerate. They pretend to teach and give instructions. It is sheer guesswork, yet they behave as though they were soaring in the skies of realization. Moreover, they do not actually care for their disciples, and the drawstrings of love and compassion have broken. Attendance on such "insane guides" inevitably leads to the precipice of negativity, to the abyss of the lower realms, and to ever-increasing evil.

The teacher's knowledge should be greater than that of the disciple. If this is not the case, and if people who are supposed to be teachers are lacking in bodhichitta, it is a great mistake to follow them, attracted perhaps by their fame and personal charisma. It is evident that the blind cannot be led by those who are themselves "blind guides." Therefore, to place one's trust in someone whose eye of wisdom is closed is a serious error in both the immediate and the ultimate term. Teachers like this are unconcerned that their disciples are acting contrary to the Dharma. They make a pretense of caring for them because they enjoy being served and respected. And their disciples help them, believing that they are serving their teachers, despite the fact that such "masters" are immersed in the eight worldly concerns and their actions are quite destitute of any underlying wisdom or valid purpose. Associating with such people and in such a way deprives disciples of any chance of understanding what behavior is to be adopted and what is to be rejected. They will consequently wander in the darkness of the lower realms.

For the above reasons, aspirants may well be devoted and sincerely interested in practicing the Dharma, but if they fail to check whether their teachers are truly qualified and commit themselves regardless, they will be throwing away their present qualities as well as those to come in relation to the path. Their very human existence, endowed with eight freedoms, which they have only just obtained after waiting so long, will be rendered meaningless. Their situation is like someone going toward a dark mass of poisonous snakes thinking that it is the cool shadow of a tree. Expecting shade and coolness, they hope to refresh themselves but will be punished for their mistake with a poisonous bite. As it is said in the *Vidyadhara Pitaka*:

> They, disciples, fail to judge him truly.
> He is ignorant and has no answers to their questions:
> This teacher is a demon for his students.

Authentic spiritual teachers

But masters who are steeped in the sacred scriptures and their commentaries, whose eyes of wisdom are open wide, and who, through their extraordinary realization of the three trainings, are skilled in liberating their disciples' minds—teachers such as these are supreme, their minds replete with every quality of doctrine and realization.

They are the peerless source of all qualities on the path and of all supreme and ordinary accomplishments. Authentic spiritual masters act with the intention of leading beings of every kind along the path of freedom.

Seeing all appearances as dreams and illusions, their minds are like space. Even if their actions and words seem at variance with mundane conventions, it is a mistake to judge them wrongly, for there are many purposes behind such actions, as they train beings according to their wisdom.

True spiritual masters are greater than anyone in the world. They are expert in cutting through the doubts of their disciples related to the words and meaning of the teachings or to the practice and the dispelling of obstacles. Spiritual masters are not downcast when others abuse and criticize them. However exhausted they may become, physically, verbally, and mentally, in the service of others, they bear everything with patience. . . . And it is through the practice of their essential instructions that beings cross over the sorrowful ocean of existence and reach the land of freedom. Spiritual masters are thus like great ships. They are true guides, able to teach the common path without mistake, who can explain the sense of the sublime sutras of definitive meaning as well as the tantras....

Those who rely properly on such teachers with faith and unfeigned devotion will automatically acquire all the advantages of favorable samsaric birth (health, longevity, beauty, good fortune, family, wealth, and intelligence), together with all the qualities of enlightenment (loving-kindness, compassion, and so forth). Such qualities will shower upon them like falling rain.

Dilgo Khyentse Rinpoche

The teacher is like a great ship for beings to cross the perilous ocean of existence, an unerring captain who guides them to the dry land of liberation, a rain that extinguishes the fire of the passions, a bright sun and moon to dispel the darkness of ignorance, a firm ground that can bear the weight of both good and bad, a wish-fulfilling tree that bestows temporal happiness and ultimate bliss, a treasury of vast and deep instructions, a wish-fulfilling jewel granting all the qualities of realization, a father and a mother giving their love equally to all sentient beings, a great river of compassion, a mountain rising above worldly concerns unshaken by the winds of emotions, and a great cloud filled with rain to soothe the torments of the passions.

In brief, he is the equal of all the Buddhas. To make any connection with him, whether through seeing him, hearing his voice, remembering him, or being touched by his hand, will lead us toward liberation. To have full confidence in him is the sure way to progress toward enlightenment. The warmth of his wisdom and compassion will melt the ore of our being and release the gold of the buddha-nature within.

Jamgön Kongtrul Lodrö Thayé

Externally, the teacher appears in human form and teaches the path to liberation. Then comes a time when, through his instructions and his blessings, one comes to a realization identical to his. Then one sees that the inner, or absolute, teacher has always been present. It is simply the nature of one's own mind.

Drigung Jigten Gönpo

If the sun of devotion does not shine
On the snowy mountain of the lama's four kayas,
The stream of his blessings will never flow.
Arouse devotion in your mind with determination!

Shabkar

Just as silvery mist rises
Into the vast, empty firmament,
Will not the form of the lord guru
Appear in the immensity of all-pervading space?

Just as gentle rain slowly descends
Within the beautiful arc of a rainbow,
Will not the guru shower down profound teachings
Within a dome of five-colored light?

Just as rainwater remains
Upon the even ground of a broad meadow,
Will not these teachings remain in the mind
Of your faithful and devoted son?

Just as brilliantly colored flowers
Spring up across the lush, soft moorland,

Will not spiritual experiences and realization
Arise in your son's mindstream?

Shabkar

In the beginning I took the teacher as teacher,
In the middle I took the scriptures as teacher,
In the end I took my own mind as teacher.

From the teacher who showed the path of deliverance,
I received the sacred teachings of individual liberation.
My practice was to shun wrongdoing and cultivate virtue.

From the Bodhisattva teacher,
I received the sacred Mahayana teachings on generating
    Bodhichitta:
My practice was to cherish others more than myself.

From the Vajradhara teacher,
I received the sacred teachings, initiations and
    instructions of the Secret Mantrayana:
My practice was to meditate upon the development and
    completion stages, and the Great Perfection.

From many other teachers,
I received many sublime teachings,
Thus establishing spiritual connections:
My practice was to cultivate faith, respect, and pure
    perception.

Kangyur Rinpoche

GOOD AND BAD DISCIPLES

It is said that disciples should consider themselves as invalids, afflicted from beginningless time by the disease of defilements; they should look upon the Dharma teachings as medicine; and the teacher should be regarded as a skillful physician, while the practice diligently pursued should be considered as the healing process.

With four attitudes analogous to these, disciples should think of the teacher as travelers might consider an escort protecting them from enemies. They should depend upon their teachers as on courageous friends guarding them from danger. Again, they should rely on them like merchants who are dependent on their captain, or travelers dependent on a ferryman (to cross a great river).

Some people who lack confidence in the profound Dharma may have a superficial devotion because they are pleased by circumstantial trifles: gifts, smiles, and other marks of favor. Such shallow, artificial devotion serves no purpose. It is as changing as the weather—there in the morning, gone by the afternoon. Abandon it, for it is fragile and easily altered.

Even with the help of many different methods, some people are very difficult to coax into the Dharma. At first, they are like wild yaks—difficult to herd into the cattle pen. Then they are fractious and unruly when they are instructed and made to study, and anyone who is diligent in the Dharma they detest. The present life is their only interest. In the end, they neglect their vows and samayas and take up with unsuitable friends. They go from bad to worse and stray from the teacher and their Dharma friends, eventually becoming like the wild men of the forests and the outlands, who shun the company of human kind.

Then there are people who, even when they are in the teacher's presence, are constantly preoccupied with all manner of plans. They think that, better than staying with the lama, they ought to be away, practicing in solitude. They rush away, but no matter where they go, they take up with bad friends; their practice and actions degenerate, and they get caught in evil ways.

On the other hand, if they are actually told to go into solitary retreat and apply themselves steadily to spiritual practice, they may well stay there, but they disregard their teacher's instructions and their practice falls apart. They give themselves up to idleness and distractions, failing to do even one session a day. They are no different from the tips of kusha grass, bending here and there as the wind blows.

Then there is a bad sort of person, skilled in trickery and unsatisfied by mere wealth and reputation. People like this covet the prestige of receiving empowerments, transmissions, and instructions as if these were items of merchandise, and they approach the spiritual master with deceitful intentions, laying a trap as though for a musk deer. Without any thought of the master's kindness, their one intention is to get the musk, in other words, the sacred Dharma, and when they have it, the samayas and vows are tossed away. Just like hunters who, having killed the deer, are excited at the prospect of selling the musk, these disciples are thrilled at their new standing, proud of having received such a teaching. People like this, who throw away the sacred links with their teachers, will be wretched in this and future lives.

There are, in general, many individual types of disciple, but they can all be classified in the following three categories, which it is important to understand. To begin with, there are those who have genuine faith, who sincerely receive, reflect, and meditate upon the perfect teachings. They have great interest and devotion and are determined to free themselves from samsara. Then there are those who have the appearance of practitioners, but they are lacking in genuine determination and settle only for success and honor in their present life. Finally, there are those who belong neither to the first nor second category. They are lukewarm, neither hot nor cold. They are foolish and false in their Dharma practice, embracing it simply because other people do so. Without prior consideration, they engage in it rashly and without faith or sincere intention. Their practice of the Dharma is like the meditation of a monkey or the recitations of a parrot. They end up like stray dogs wandering the streets; they are neither practitioners of Dharma nor straightforward worldly people.

By contrast, good disciples don the armor of devotion like Nagabodhi,* who realized the Truth. They have steadfast minds and like Shrijñana† serve the teacher and the doctrine without a care for life and limb. Like Jetsün Mila, they do whatever their teacher tells them, without regard for their own comfort. Disciples like this are liberated merely by their devotion.

Disciples should have faith, the source of all spiritual qualities, and a clear, lucid intelligence unafflicted by doubt. They should have acquired the knowledge that enables them to distinguish virtue from nonvirtue. They should have the great compassion of the Mahayana and a deep respect for vows and samayas. They should be serene and disciplined in thought, word, and deed. They should be broad-minded and on friendly terms with their neighborhood as well as with their Dharma kindred. They should act with generosity toward the pure recipients‡

---

* One of the four closest disciples of Siddha Nagarjuna, Nagabodhi, a Brahmin thief, realized the natural state, emptiness, as his master was explaining to him the pure essence of mind.

† Atisha Dipamkara Shrijñana came to Tibet in 1042. In a vision, Tara, who was his tutelary deity, said to him before he left the University of Vikramashila: "Go to Tibet at all costs! It will help the Dharma in general, and the benefit will be especially great if you associate with the upasaka [Drom Tönpa]. All this, however, will shorten your life by twenty years." Atisha thought that it did not matter as long as the doctrine and beings could be benefited, and he set off at the expense of his life.

‡ Those who are worthy of our generosity are all beings in need, those who are suffering, and the buddhas and bodhisattvas.

and should have pure perception with a sense of propriety toward others.

Good disciples should be (1) like well-behaved children, knowing how to please their teacher and how to avoid displeasing him or her. (2) Even if their teacher scolds them severely and often, as need arises, the students should behave like intelligent horses and restrain their anger. (3) In order to accomplish their teacher's purpose, disciples should be like boats, sailing back and forth without weariness. (4) Like a bridge, they should be able to withstand any circumstance—good or bad, happiness or suffering, praise or blame. (5) Disciples should be like an anvil, unmoved by the summer's heat and the winter's cold. (6) Like servants, they should be obedient and meticulous in carrying out their teachers' instructions. (7) They should be respectful toward their teachers and the spiritual community, with the humility of a street sweeper. (8) They should reflect upon their own shortcomings and avoid all arrogance, like the old bull whose horns are broken and who takes the last place in the herd. In the *Bodhisattva Pitaka* it is said that if disciples act in this way, they will be relying on their teacher correctly.

Do not make distinctions among the teacher's attendants and disciples, liking some and disliking others. And do not make a nuisance of yourself. Try rather to be like a belt,* fitting easily with any company, and like salt,† easily adaptable to anyone, high or low, influential or obscure. Be a pillar of strength against weariness, irritation, and any kind of assault. This is how to serve the teacher and to respect the teacher's attendants and benefactors as well as the vajra kindred.‡ . . .

* Belts readily adjust to different waists.

† Salt melts into food providing its taste while remaining invisible.

‡ In Vajrayana, the disciples of the same master from whom one has received teachings and initiations must be considered with the utmost respect. They become vajra ("diamond") brothers and sisters, meaning that their spiritual connection must be pure and unalterable.

You should aspire to dwell constantly in the company of spiritual masters, custodians of the treasury of Dharma—like swans living in beautiful creeks and flower-filled pools that gently taste the weeds and plants, and like bees that sip the nectar of the blossoms without damaging their color or perfume. It is marvelous indeed to be able to observe the proper conduct as just described, leaving aside all incorrect behavior and cultivating every wholesome attitude. Attend the spiritual master steadfastly without weariness, trying not to be a cause of displeasure. Taste, by the power of faith alone, the qualities of the master's realization!

Patrul Rinpoche

*This story about Patrul Rinpoche was narrated to the author
by Dilgo Khyentse Rinpoche.*

PATRUL RINPOCHE'S DECISIVE MEETING
WITH DO KHYENTSE YESHE DORJE (1800–1866)

Patrul Rinpoche felt unlimited devotion for Do Khyentse, whom he perceived as the Buddha himself.

One day the great yogi Do Khyentse decided to go to the province of Dzachuka, in the guise of a nomad yogi with carefree and unpredictable ways. As Patrul approached him, Do Khyentse addressed him with these words: "Hey! Patrul! If you are brave, come over here!" When Patrul Rinpoche came within reach, Do Khyentse caught him by the hair, pinned him to the ground, and started to drag him along.

Patrul noticed right away that Do Khyentse had been drinking because his breath smelled of beer. He said to himself, "Even a great teacher like him can get drunk and behave in such an inappropriate way!" He thought of the harmful effects of drinking alcohol, as described by the Buddha.

At that moment, Do Khyentse loosened his grip, and releasing

Patrul, stared at him intensely: "Ugh!" he cried. "You mad dog, with a head full of foul thoughts and rationalizations!" Then he spat in his face, showed him his little finger as a sign of contempt and went on his way.

Patrul suddenly realized the significance of this behavior: "I completely misunderstood! This is a profound teaching on the nature of mind he has just given me." He sat in meditation and remained in the spontaneous experience of awareness, as clear as the immaculate sky. It was as if the bright sun was rising, after the dawn that had been the introduction to primordial awareness that he had received from his first master, Gyalwe Nyugu.

Later, Patrul Rinpoche said jokingly about this episode: "'Mad Dog' is the initiatory name that Do Khyentse gave me." And he used that nickname to sign some of his writings.

PART THREE

The Main Path

CHAPTER II

Understanding the Nature of the Mind

When the mind looks at itself, what can it learn about its own nature? The first thing that becomes apparent is that countless thoughts prompted by our feelings, our memories, and our imagination constantly rush through our mind, almost without our knowledge. But is there not also a basic consciousness, always present behind this movement, even in the absence of thoughts, a presence that could be called the fundamental ability of the mind to know or to be conscious?

As thoughts arise, if we look at them closely, can we pin down any characteristic, or attribute, any real existence to them? Where are they located? Do they have a color or a shape? However hard you look, you will not find anything else in the end but the bare faculty of knowing that we have just mentioned. You will find nothing intrinsically real. It is in this sense that Buddhism says that the mind is "empty of independent existence."

How can we make use of this notion of the "emptiness" of thoughts? When a thought or an emotion such as anger arises in our mind, what usually happens? We let ourselves be overwhelmed by it. The thoughts grow and give rise to many other thoughts that disturb us, blind us, and encourage us to say and do certain things, which may be violent, which may hurt others, and which we will probably come to regret. Now it is possible to examine the thoughts before they proliferate, instead of letting this chain reaction occur. Then we will realize that those thoughts and emotions do not have the solid reality that we had imagined, and it will be possible to break free from their grip.

If we can see that thoughts arise from pure awareness, the nature of mind, then dissolve back into it, like waves rising from and falling back into the ocean, it will be a big step toward inner peace because thoughts will have lost much of their power to harm.

Dilgo Khyentse Rinpoche

What we normally call the mind is the deluded mind, a turbulent vortex of thoughts whipped up by attachment, anger, and ignorance. This mind, unlike enlightened awareness, is always being carried away by one delusion after another. Thoughts of hatred or attachment suddenly arise without warning, triggered by such circumstances as an unexpected meeting with an enemy or a friend, and unless they are immediately overpowered with the proper antidote, they quickly take root and proliferate, reinforcing the habitual predominance of hatred or attachment in the mind and adding more and more karmic patterns.

Yet, however strong these thoughts may seem, they are just thoughts and will eventually dissolve back into emptiness. Once you recognize the intrinsic nature of the mind, these thoughts that seem to appear and disappear all the time can no longer fool you. Just as clouds form, last for a while, and then dissolve back into the empty sky, so deluded thoughts arise, remain for a while, and then vanish in the voidness of mind; in reality nothing at all has happened.

When sunlight falls on a crystal, lights of all colors of the rainbow appear; yet they have no substance that you can grasp. Likewise, all thoughts in their infinite variety—devotion, compassion, harmfulness, desire—are utterly without substance. There is no thought that is something other than voidness; if you recognize the void nature of thoughts at the very moment they arise, they will dissolve. Attachment and hatred will never be able to disturb the mind. Deluded emotions will collapse by themselves. No negative actions will be accumulated, so no suffering will follow.

Dilgo Khyentse Rinpoche

The mind has, in general, two aspects, stillness and movement. Sometimes the mind is quiet and free from thoughts, like a calm pool; this is stillness. Eventually, thoughts are bound to arise in it; this is movement. In truth, however, although in a sense there is a movement of thoughts within the stillness, there is actually no difference between these two states—just as the nature of stillness is voidness, the nature of movement is also voidness. Stillness and movement are merely two names for the one mind.

Most of the time we are unaware of our state of mind and pay no attention to whether the mind is still or moving. While you are meditating, a thought might arise in your mind—the idea of going shopping, for instance. If you are aware of the thought and just let it dissolve by itself, then that is the end of it. But if you remain unaware of what is happening and let that thought grow and develop, it will lead on to a second thought, the thought of having a break from your practice, and in no time at all you will find yourself actually getting up and going out to the market. Soon many more thoughts and ideas will arise—how you are going to buy this, sell that, and so forth. By this point you will be a very long way away from your meditation.

It is completely natural that thoughts keep on arising. The point is not to try to stop them, which would be impossible anyway, but to liberate them. This is done by remaining in a state of simplicity, which lets thoughts arise and vanish again without stringing onto them any further thoughts. When you no longer perpetuate the movement of thoughts, they dissolve by themselves without leaving any trace. When you no longer spoil the state of stillness with mental fabrications, you can maintain the natural serenity of mind without any effort. Sometimes, let your thoughts flow, and watch the unchanging nature behind them. Sometimes, abruptly cutting the flow of thoughts, look at naked awareness.

Innumerable thoughts and memories, stirred up by the tendencies to which we have become habituated, arise in the mind. One after the other, each thought seems to vanish into the past, only to be replaced as the next, in its turn, becomes fleetingly present to the mind before itself giving way to future thoughts. Each thought tends to pick up the momentum of the one before it, so that the influence of a string of thoughts grows as time passes; this is called "the chain of delusion." Just as what we call a rosary is in fact a string of single beads, so also what we usually call the mind is really a succession of momentary thoughts; a trickle of thoughts makes the stream of consciousness, the mind-stream, and the mind-stream leads on to the ocean of existence. Our belief that the mind is a real entity is a conclusion based on insufficient investigation. We believe a river we see today to be the same river we saw yesterday, but in reality a river never stays the same even for a second—the water that made up yesterday's river will surely be part of the ocean by now. The same is true for the countless thoughts that run through our "mind" from morning to evening. Our mind-stream is just a succession of instantaneous thoughts; there is no separate entity that you can point out as being a mind.

Now, if we analyze the thought process carefully, it becomes evident that past thoughts are already dead, like a corpse. Future thoughts have not yet been born. As for present thoughts, they cannot be said to have any properties such as location, color, or shape. They leave no traces, and indeed they are nowhere to be found. In fact, there could be no possible point of contact between past, present, and future thoughts. If there were any real continuity between, for instance, a past thought and a present thought, that would necessarily mean either that the past thought is present or that the present thought is past. If the past really could extend to the present in this way, it would also follow that the future must already be present. But nevertheless, ignorant of the true nature of thoughts, we maintain the habit of seeing them as being continuously linked, one after another. This is the root of delusion, and this is what allows us to be more and more dominated by our thoughts and emotions, until total confusion reigns.

It is of vital importance to be aware of the arising of thoughts and to still the waves of thoughts that assail you. Anger, for instance, is an extremely destructive tendency which spoils all the good qualities you may otherwise have. No one enjoys the company of an angry person. There is nothing inherently very frightening about the appearance of snakes, but because they are generally very aggressive, the mere sight of them inspires fear and loathing. Whether in a human or a snake, such a preponderance of anger is nothing more than the outcome of an unchecked accumulation of negative thoughts. If at the very moment an angry thought arises, you recognize it for what it is and understand how negative it is, your anger will calm down of its own accord, and you will always be able to stay on good terms with everyone. On the other hand, if you let that first angry thought give rise to a second angry thought, in no time at all, your anger will be completely out of control, and you will be ready even to risk your life to destroy your adversary.

Mipham Rinpoche

Homage to the precious master Manjushri!
Happiness and suffering depend upon the mind.
We may suffer at the death of one we call "son."
We may rejoice at the death of one we call "enemy."
Yet, suffering and joy do not belong to external objects.

Those who cherish their body protect it.
Those who are not attached are willing to offer it.
Those who have no patience with themselves and others
Are irritated by a simple thorn.
The sage, who holds on to nothing
Has no fear even of hell fire.

Everything depends on the mind, which, in turn,
Obeys the thoughts that come from its own habits;
Thus it is buffeted by endless myriads
Of concepts, pleasures and sufferings. . . .

Alas! If we observe how this lost mind works,
When it is happy, it becomes arrogant and its desires multiply;
When it suffers, it loses courage and wants to be happy;
Whatever happens to it, it never takes the path of lasting
    happiness.
Alas! It wanders endlessly in suffering!

Who can count the number of thoughts,
In just one day, one after another, like ripples on the water?
Exhausted with vain concepts of rejection and appropriation,
By hopes and fears, it buys its own suffering!

This inner conversation that we are powerless to stop
Goes round and round like a wheel.
Its root is the belief in duality:
Without it, there would be no mental constructs.

These constructs spawn mistaken thoughts.
The arrogance of the ego arises, and an endless web
Of thoughts, pursuing pleasure and refusing suffering,
Is woven continuously even into our dreams.

Would I not be better to set down
The useless burden of these troubles
That no one imposes on me
But I inflict on myself?

Nyendrak Lungrig Nyima

Although subject and object are not two,
They appear to us as fundamentally distinct entities.
And through attachment to them, we further strengthen
    this tendency.
Samsara is nothing else but that.

While good and bad actions are devoid of true reality,
By the power of our intention they produce joys and
    sorrows,
Just as seeds of sweet or bitter plants
Give fruits of corresponding taste.

Thus, the world appears similarly
To those with common karma,
And differently to those whose karma is different.

In fact, even if one "goes" to hell or elsewhere,
It is only a change in one's perception of the world.
As in dreams, where the things that appear do not exist,
The root of all our illusory perceptions is the mind.

The nature of mind transcends the notions of existence
And nonexistence, eternity and nothingness:
To this nature is given the simple name "absolute space."

That space, in itself perfectly pure,
That immaculate sky, empty and luminous, with no center or
    periphery,
Has always been in the heart of every being,
Its face obscured by the temporary veil of mental constructs.

It is hard to put an end by force
To the continuous chain of thoughts,
But if, when they occur, their nature is recognized,
Thoughts have no choice
But to be liberated in their own sphere.

Without pursuing past thoughts
Or inviting future thoughts,
Remain in the present moment, and simply recognize
The nature of whatever arises in your mind.
Relax in simplicity, free of intentions and attachments.

Although there is nothing to meditate on
Remain fully present without getting distracted.
By getting used to the way things occur of themselves, without
    altering anything,
Primordial wisdom, self-luminous, will arise from within.

"How is this so?" you might ask.
If you leave cloudy water undisturbed,
It will naturally become clear.
Most other meditations
Are only temporary ways to calm the mind.

The space of great unchanging emptiness
And the simple luminosity of uninterrupted wakeful presence
Have always been inseparable.

You must yourself experience that essential thing
Which is within you: no one can do it for you.

Dilgo Khyentse Rinpoche

When you feel hatred toward someone, your hatred and anger are not in any way something inherent either to that person as a whole or to any aspect of him. Your anger only exists in your own mind. As soon as you glimpse him, your thoughts dwell on all the times he brought harm to you in the past, how he might harm you in the future, or what he is doing to harm you now; even hearing his name upsets you. As you become fixated on these thoughts, full-blown hatred develops, and at that point you feel an irresistible urge to pick up a stone to throw at him, or grab something with which to strike him.

Anger might seem extremely strong, but where does it get the power to overwhelm you so easily? Is it some external force, something with arms and legs, weapons and armor? If not, then is it somewhere inside you? If so, where is it? Can you find it in your brain, in your heart, in your bones, or in any other part of you? Impossible though it is to locate, anger does seem to be present in a very concrete way, as a strong clinging that freezes your mind into a state of solidity and brings a great deal of suffering both to yourself and to others. Just as clouds, which are insubstantial and cannot support weight or be worn as clothing, can nevertheless darken the whole sky and cover the sun, in the same way thoughts can obscure the pristine radiance of awareness. By recognizing the void, transparent nature of mind, let it return to its natural state of freedom. If you recognize the nature of anger as void, it loses all its power to harm.

Mipham Rinpoche

THE NATURE OF MIND:
ESSENTIAL INSTRUCTIONS IN THREE POINTS

The natural simplicity of mind is inexpressible,
Free and vast: it must be recognized by itself.
When all mental fabrication, all conceptualization,
And all attachments disappear naturally,
We call that "recognizing the essence of mind."

Once freed from the net of thoughts,
Not losing the continuity of the presence of the primordial nature,
Without acting or making effort, without seeking anything:
We call that "preserving meditation."

When, like clouds in the sky,
The waves of many thoughts
Neither harm nor benefit the mind, which remains serene,
We call that "liberating the mind in its own nature."

These three essential instructions will be understood
By meditators who cultivate inner experience,
But will be incomprehensible to garrulous intellectuals.

Written by Mipham Namgyal, on the tenth day of the Fire Monkey month.

Shabkar

Spontaneously luminous simplicity: it's just that!
How can you say you don't see
your mind as being the Buddha?
There is nothing to cultivate, so how can you say:
"I haven't practiced much"?

This awakened mind, clearly manifest: it's just that!
How can you claim that you can't find your mind?
This uninterrupted limpid clarity: it's just that!
How can you claim that you don't see the essence of your mind?

Once established in that nature, there's nothing at all to do.
How can you claim you can't do it?
If there's no more duality between rest and movement,
How can you claim you can't remain in it?

In the awakened state, born of itself,
The three aspects of buddhahood* are spontaneously
    accomplished, without effort.
How can you claim you can't accomplish them by practice?

You should just remain in nonaction.
How can you claim you can't do it?

Thoughts arise and are liberated simultaneously.
How can you claim that this remedy escapes you?

This awareness of the present moment: it's just that!
How can you claim you can't recognize it?

Dilgo Khyentse Rinpoche

If you overcome the belief in a truly existing self today, you will be enlightened today. If you overcome it tomorrow, you will be enlightened tomorrow. But if you never overcome it, you will never gain enlightenment.

---

* Literally "the three bodies" (Tib. *sku gsum*, Skt. *trikaya*): *nirmanakaya*, the Body of Manifestation; *sambhogakaya*, the Body of Perfect Enjoyment; and *nirmanakaya*, the Absolute Body.

This "I" is just a thought, a feeling. A thought does not intrinsically possess any solidity, form, shape, or color. For example, when a strong feeling of anger arises in the mind, with such force that you want to fight and destroy someone, is the angry thought holding a weapon in its hand? Could it lead an army? Might it burn anyone like a fire, crush them like a stone, or carry them away like a raging river? No. Anger, like any other thought or feeling, has no true existence. It cannot even be definitely localized anywhere in your body, speech, or mind. It is like wind in empty space. Instead of allowing such wild thoughts to determine what you do, look at their essential emptiness. . . .

Once you overcome the hatred within your own mind, you will discover that in the world outside, there is no longer any such thing as even a single enemy. But if you keep giving free rein to your feelings of hatred and try to overcome your outer adversaries, you will find that however many of them you manage to defeat, there will always be more to take their place. Even if you could subjugate all the beings in the universe, your anger would only grow stronger. You will never be able to deal with it properly by indulging it. . . .

Examine anger itself and you will find that it is nothing but a thought. If that angry thought disappears, it will not lead to an action done in anger, with its negative karmic results. Trample on anger with realization, and it dissolves like a cloud in the sky; and as it dissolves, the notion of "enemy" will vanish with it.

In essence, the mind is what is aware of everything—it is a clarity that perceives all external objects and events. But try to find it, and it turns out to be as impossible to grasp and as elusive as a rainbow—the more you run after it, the farther away it appears to recede; the more you look at it, the less you can find. This is the empty aspect of the mind. Clarity and emptiness are inseparably united in the true nature of mind, which is beyond all concepts of existence and nonexistence.

Dilgo Khyentse Rinpoche

At the moment, the natural clarity of your mind is obscured by delusions. But as this obscuration clears, you will begin to uncover the radiance of awareness, until you reach the point where, just as a drawing on water disappears the moment it is made, your thoughts are liberated the moment they arise. To experience mind in this way is to encounter the very source of Buddhahood, the practice of the fourth empowerment. When the nature of mind is recognized, it is called nirvana; when it is obscured by delusion, it is called samsara. Yet neither samsara nor nirvana has ever departed from the continuum of the absolute. When realization of awareness reaches its full extent, the ramparts of delusion will have been breached, and the citadel of Dharmakaya* beyond meditation can be seized once and for all. Here there is no longer any distinction between meditation and postmeditation, and experience is effortlessly stabilized; this is nonmeditation. In the limitless expanse of Dharmakaya, recite the six-syllable mantra.

Shabkar

All the phenomena of samsara and nirvana,
What appears and what exists,
Are no more than rainbows in an empty sky,
Which appear through a conjunction of causes and conditions.

No matter how they may appear, they are nothing in themselves;
They arise as embellishing ornaments
For the skylike nature of mind—wondrous!

* The absolute dimension of the state of buddhahood beyond all concepts.

Mind—it has no color, it has no shape.
Look for it: it cannot be found at all—
Emptiness!

Leave mind just as it is—
Vivid clarity!

Immaculate, empty, like the infinite sky—
Let mind remain in that very state,
And let it be—raw, brilliant, awake,
Never obscured, utterly transparent.
Leave mind at ease, open, without aim.

When mind merges with that state
Which, like space, is all-encompassing,
All phenomena are understood with utter clarity,
And all the enlightened qualities
Of the various paths and stages arise.

Boundless compassion is born
Toward beings who lack such realization.

Through such training in emptiness and compassion,
Benefit for other beings naturally occurs.

May void, primordial wakefulness
Immaculate as the sky, actually arise,
Vivid, free of obscuration,
In the mind-streams of those who hear this song.

Dilgo Khyentse Rinpoche

To take the uncreated stronghold of the nature of mind, you have to go to the source and recognize the very origin of your thoughts. Otherwise, one thought will give rise to a second, then a third, and so on. In no time, you will be assailed by memories of the past and anticipation of the future, and the pure awareness of the present moment will be completely obscured. If you recognize the emptiness of your thoughts instead of solidifying them, the arising and subsiding of each thought will clarify and strengthen your realization of emptiness. . . .

It is our own mind that leads us astray into the cycle of existence. Blind to the mind's true nature, we fixate on our thoughts, which in truth are simply the manifestations of that nature. But through fixation, pure awareness is frozen into solid concepts such as "self" and "other," "desirable" and "repulsive," and many more. That is how we create samsara. . . .

Lakes and rivers can freeze in winter, and the water can become so solid that people, animals, and carts travel back and forth on its surface. At the approach of spring, the earth warms up, and the waters thaw. What remains then of all that solid ice? Water is soft and fluid, ice hard and sharp. We cannot say that they are identical, but neither are they different—ice is only frozen water, and water is only melted ice. It is the same with our perceptions of the external world. To be attached to the reality of phenomena, tormented by attraction and repulsion and obsessed by the eight worldly preoccupations, is what causes the mind to freeze. Melt the ice of your concepts so that the fluid water of free perception can flow. . . .

Everything we experience—all the phenomena of samsara and nirvana—appears with the vivid clarity of a rainbow and yet, like a rainbow, is devoid of any tangible reality. Once you recognize the nature of phenomena—manifest and at the same time empty—your mind will be freed from the tyranny of delusion.

To recognize the ultimate nature of the mind is to realize the state of Buddhahood, and to fail to recognize it is to sink into ignorance. In either case, it is your mind, and your mind alone, that liberates or binds you....

If you allow your thoughts and feelings to arise and dissolve by themselves, they will pass through your mind in the same way that a bird flies through the sky, without leaving any trace. This applies not only to attachment and anger, but also to the experiences of meditation—bliss, clarity, and absence of thought. Those experiences result from perseverance in practice and are the expression of the inherent creativity of the mind. They appear like a rainbow, formed as the rays of the sun strike a curtain of rain; and to become attached to them is as futile as it would be to run after a rainbow in the hopes of wearing it as a coat. Simply allow your thoughts and experiences to come and go, without ever grasping at them....

Maintain that state of simplicity. Should you encounter happiness, success and other favorable conditions, take them like a dream or an illusion. Do not get attached to them. And should you be struck by illness, calumny, or other trials, physical or mental, do not let yourself be discouraged. Rekindle your compassion by wishing that through your own suffering, the sufferings of all beings might be exhausted. Whatever the circumstances, do not get either elated or depressed, but remain free and at ease in imperturbable serenity.

Minling Terchen Gyurme Dorje

*At the request of his spiritual son Ösel Tenzin,
Gyurme Dorje wove this garland of words as they came to his mind.*

Namo guru ratnaya!
Homage to the precious master!

Awareness, born of itself,
Is primordially pure.
It does not come or go. There is nothing
To be added to it or taken away.
Leave alone whatever may arise in it,
Like the reflections of the moon in water!

Examine the essence of whatever thoughts
And adverse circumstances may arise,
And see them continuously as waves
Constantly falling back into the ocean.

Watch out with the greatest vigilance
For harmful or unvirtuous actions,
Choosing without error
What to do or not to do,
And thus create your own happiness!

Since the Three Jewels know
Whatever you do, say or think,
Cut without hypocrisy the attachments
That you yourself have woven
And in doing so, do something worthwhile!

The joys and sorrows of the illusory world
Are like dreams and mirages.
Letting them evaporate by themselves,
Cut the web of belief in a solid reality!

Phenomena of any kind
Are the play of the ultimate nature.
When you have abolished discrimination
    between good and bad,

Dualistic attachment, the source of hopes and fears,
Is like a thief in an empty house.

In short, meditate without distraction to realize
The natural state free of mental constructs,
And accord all your actions with the Dharma,
Taking your inspiration from the lives of the sages of the past!

Gyalwa Gotsangpa, Gönpo Dorje

HIS LAST WORDS

My mind is like space, without birth and death.
Like space, mind has no center or periphery.
Like space, mind is not bound or liberated.*
Like space, mind has neither high nor low.

Having said this, Gotsangpa remained in equanimity in the natural luminosity of mind itself, the spacelike absolute dimension, and left this world.

Patrul Rinpoche

*This story about Patrul Rinpoche was told to the translator
by Nyoshul Khen Rinpoche.*

INTRODUCTION TO THE NATURE OF MIND

In a mountain meadow, Patrul Rinpoche was sleeping under the stars in the company of his disciple Nyoshul Lungtok, when suddenly he said to him:

---

*From the absolute point of view, the mind has never really been chained by ignorance because its fundamental nature, which is pure enlightenment, is unalterable. Thus, when the veils that mask this nature disappear, the mind is not really "freed," since it was never really enslaved.

"Didn't you tell me that you still haven't recognized the true nature of mind?"

"That's right."

"It's not difficult."

He asked him to come and lie down beside him. Lungtok lay on his back and stared at the sky.

Patrul Rinpoche spoke:

"Do you hear the monastery dogs barking?"

"Yes."

"Do you see the stars shining?"

"Yes."

"Well, the nature of mind is that!"

Instantly, Nyoshul Lungtok saw the nature of his mind. The coming together of his years of meditation, the master's presence, and that particular moment had led to this culmination of his inner realization.

CHAPTER 12

The Hermit

The vocation of the hermit is often misunderstood. Hermits do not withdraw from the world because they feel rejected, because they can find nothing better to do than wander in the mountains, or because they are unable to assume their responsibilities. They make their decision, which may seem extreme, because they have realized that they cannot control their mind and solve the problem of happiness and suffering amidst the endless, futile, and distracting activities of ordinary life. They are not running away from the world. They distance themselves from it to put it in perspective and better understand how it functions. They do not flee their fellow men and women, but need time to cultivate an authentic love and compassion that will not be affected by ordinary concerns such as pleasure and displeasure, gain and loss, praise and blame. Like a musician who practices scales or an athlete who trains the body, they need time, concentration, and constant practice to master the chaos of their mind and penetrate the meaning of life. Then they can put their wisdom to work to help others. Their motto might be: "Transform yourself to better transform the world."

The chaotic situations of ordinary life make it very difficult to progress in practice and develop inner strength. It is best to concentrate solely on training the mind for as long as is necessary. The wounded animal hides in the forest to heal its wounds until it is fit to roam again as it pleases. Our wounds are those of selfishness, malice, attachment, and other mental poisons.

The hermit does not "rot in his cell," as some have imagined. Those who have experienced what it is really like will tell you that one matures in one's hermitage. For someone who remains in the freshness of mindfulness of the present moment, time does not have the heaviness of days spent in distraction, but the lightness of a life fully savored. If hermits lose interest in certain ordinary concerns, it is not because their existence has become insipid, but because they choose, among all the possible human activities, those that will truly contribute to the happiness of self and others.

Sangye Wön Re Dharma Senge

From the perfect Buddha to our present teachers, all the great spiritual masters and scholars have renounced the ordinary affairs of this life and dedicated themselves to the Dharma for the benefit of the teachings and infinite beings.

Without being contaminated by the eight worldly concerns, they have made the duration of their practice the duration of their lives and accepted all difficulties. Without a care for their body and their life, they did nothing but practice the Dharma in wild and lonely places or hermitages. They were not fools or people who did not know what to do with their lives, nor yet sons who did not want to manage the affairs of their families. But if we look at the practitioners of today like us, those who live like these sages are as rare as stars in the daytime. And even if there are a handful of them, they fall under the influence of the circumstances of life, and very few reach the end of the path.

If we really want to attain the ultimate goal of the Dharma, we must fulfill the six conditions that will lead us to appreciate solitude.

The omniscient Longchenpa* describes them thus:

* Gyalwa Longchen Rabjam, perhaps the most eminent scholar and spiritual master of the Nyingma tradition. For more information, see the entry in the biographical notes at the back of this volume.

Being able to rely on one's own strength when the spiritual
    master is not there,
Having no doubts to clear up or obstacles to remove,
Being free of the problems of disease and harmful influences,
Withdrawing from the company of worldly beings,
Having received all the instructions to achieve one's own good
    and that of others,
And having a clear understanding of the final and ultimate view.

Gyalse Thogme

In solitary places,
One has no enemy to defeat,
No family to protect,
No superior to respect,
Or servant to command.
What else is there to do, *mani*-reciters,
Than subdue one's own mind?

Godragpa Sonam Gyaltsen

Mind watching mind,
That's this beggar's experience of practice.

Cherishing others more than myself,
That's this beggar's application of practice.

Gyalwa Yangönpa

In the lonely place The-Thought of-Death-Fixed-in-the-Heart,
The hermit Deeply-Disgusted-with-Attachments
Draws the boundaries of his retreat by renouncing the thoughts
  of this life,
And does not meet those known as the Eight Worldly
  Preoccupations.

Jigme Lingpa

Among the crowds, hatred and attachment grow,
While in the wilderness, good qualities flourish.
So live in the lonely mountains
And watch the spectacle of your mind!

From now on, blown by the wind of renunciation,
Light the fire of emptiness and compassion,
Fan the flames with the fan of attention,
And burn the brushwood of the ordinary mind and its thoughts!

Drigung Döndrup Chögyal

Catering to the eight worldly concerns,
Is to be like a deer caught in a trap: it exhausts its life
In efforts as vain as they are interminable.
Cultivate the spirit of renunciation as best you can:
That's my advice from the heart.

The activities of samsara are like ripples on water:
As your life runs out, they never end.
From now on, only have short-term projects:
That's my advice from the heart.

Jetsün Trakpa Gyaltsen

CUTTING THE FOUR ATTACHMENTS

If you cling to this life, you are not practicing the way.
If you cling to the cycle of existences, you know nothing of
   renunciation.
If you cling to your own good, you're ignoring the bodhichitta.
If you let your mind be attached to anything at all, you do not
   have the view.

Shabkar

Let the length of your practice
Equal the length of your life;
Wander from place to place,
In solitary mountain retreats.

Shabkar

In accordance with the words of my guru, I shall not leave this
place until definite and genuine meditation experiences and realization arise in my being. At night, I won't sleep in the corpselike
posture of ordinary people but will stay cross-legged and upright.
At all times, rather than indulging in idle chatter, I will refrain
from speaking. I will eat once a day, at noon. I will live alone. I will
think of nothing but my guru's instructions. I will not seek com-
forts but persevere in the hermit's life and accept its hardships.
I will avoid all worldly distractions until I achieve stability in my
realization. In short, not letting my body, speech, or mind stray
into the ordinary, I shall practice day and night.

Shabkar

Snow lions don't freeze in snow mountains;
Vultures do not fall out of the sky;
Fish do not drown in water;
Practitioners do not die of hunger.

So, cast away this life's concerns!
Give up plans for the future!

Shabkar

Wondrous—remaining in lucid serenity,
The state of skylike evenness!

Joyous—when day or night, indoors or outdoors,
Eyes open or closed, makes no difference to your
    awareness.

Wondrous—when the world of form appears
Like a rainbow in the unchanging sky of the absolute
    dimension!

Joyous—to dredge the depths of samsara
Bringing all beings to enlightenment!

All you whose wisdom is vast as the sky
Brilliant as the unobscured sun,
Limpid as crystal, firm as an unshakable mountain,
To you I pay homage and go for refuge;
Grant me the waves of your grace.

Rigdzin Chökyi Trakpa

Since attention is the source of all qualities,
Abandon distractions and, like a wounded animal
   who hides itself away,
Remain alone in a secluded place:
That's my advice from the heart.

If you fail to be attentive, you will do no better
Than wild animals that live in the wilderness.
Stimulate your courage by thinking hard how little
   time you have left,
And abandon all distractions:
That's my advice from the heart!

Lhatsün Namkhai Jigme

*Phet!**
If you want to really practice the teaching,
You must not depend on anything or anyone.

If you want to have real diligence,
Eradicate the last trace of attachment to yourself.

If you want to have real pure vision,
See the teacher in all things.

If you want to have real inner calm,
Maintain it day and night.

If you want to have real insight,
Let whatever you perceive dissolve in awareness.

---

* An interjection used to cut the train of thought and awaken the naked clarity
of the mind.

If you want to stabilize your calm and insight,
Stop discriminating between mind in movement and mind
    at rest.

Dudjom Rinpoche

ADVICE FOR RETREAT (FIRST PART)

Understanding that all objects of desire, combined with our habitual tendencies, are obstacles, cultivate an attitude of not wanting them. Concerning wealth and possessions, if you don't know how to be contented with just a little, once you've got one, you'll want two, and it won't be difficult for the deceiving devil of the desirable objects to enter.

Whatever good or bad things people might say, don't take them as true; have no hope or doubt, acceptance or rejection. Let them say whatever they will, as though they were talking about someone already dead and buried. No one but a qualified guru—not even your father or mother—can give correct advice. Therefore, keeping control over your own actions, do not hand your nose-rope to others. Outwardly good-natured, you should know how to get along harmoniously with all without "burning their noses." But in fact, if anyone—superior or inferior—comes to hinder your practice, you should be unshakable, like an iron boulder pulled by a silk scarf. It won't do to be a weak character whose head bends in whichever direction the wind blows, like grass on a mountain pass.

For any practice, from the moment you begin it until you reach its ultimate end—whether lightning strikes from above, a lake springs up from below, or rocks fall from all sides—having sworn not to break your promise even at the cost of your life, you should persevere until the end. From the very beginning, you should come progressively to an established schedule of periods for practice, sleep, meals, and breaks, allowing no bad habits. Whether your practice is elaborate or simple, you should make it even and regular, never sporadic, and not even for an instant should you leave any room for the ordinary.

During retreat, whether your doorway is sealed or not, you must not speak, not spy, or come face to face with others. Having completely discarded the wanderings of the restless mind, expel the stale breath and correctly assume the essential elements of bodily posture. The mind should rest upon clear awareness without wavering even for the time of a finger snap, like a peg driven into solid ground.

A strict outer, inner, and secret retreat will quickly give rise to all the signs and qualities. But if for some important reason you meet someone and talk with them, thinking "after this I shall be very strict," after this transgression the prosperity of your practice will fade and everything will become slacker and slacker. If at the very start you make a resolute, clear-cut decision to remain seated, making your retreat progressively stricter, your practice won't be swept away by obstacles.

There are many ways of checking the particular qualifications and topography of places, but in general a place blessed by Guru Rinpoche and the great accomplished masters of the past, which is not in the hands of people who have broken their sacred links is suitable, or, according to your preference, any utterly solitary place where favorable conditions—food and other necessities—are easily available. . . . Always forsaking outer and inner entertainments, to dwell in nonaction is to dwell in the true solitary place.

As for the actual purification of your nature: the ordinary aspects are the four mind changes; the extraordinary ones are refuge, generation of bodhichitta, purification of obscurations, and the two accumulations. Having practiced each of these assiduously according to the commentaries until you have truly experienced them, you should then consider the most extraordinary guru yoga as the vital essence of practice and persevere in it.* If you do not, growth of meditation will be tardy; and even if it grows a little, it will be vulnerable to obstacles, and genuine realization will not be able to take birth in your being.

So, if you pray with simple and very fervent devotion, after some time, through the transfer of the heart-mind realization of the guru, an extraordinary realization, inexpressible in words, will certainly take birth from within. As Lama Shang Rinpoche says, "To nurture stillness, experiences, and deep concentration—these are common things. But very rare is the realization born from within through the guru's blessings, which arise by the power of devotion."

---

* The four changes of mind arise from the contemplation of the preciousness and rarity of the human body, the impermanence of all things, the ineluctable law of cause and effect, and the imperfections and sufferings of samsara. Guru yoga (*bla ma'i rnal byor*), literally union with the master's nature, is not only the essence of the preliminaries but also of all practices.

CHAPTER 13

Deepening Spiritual Practice

The notion of practice may seem to imply a sense of obligation. It certainly involves a commitment to work on oneself with effort and regularity. That is an indispensable condition for a student to progress toward enlightenment. If a beginner does not practice regularly and does not adopt a certain discipline, it will be quite impossible to stabilize the mind and cultivate altruistic love and other essential qualities.

The practice involves both turning inward and openness to others. It begins with an introspection that makes one aware of the positive and negative aspects of the mind and allows one to encourage the former and correct the latter. Then, while continuing to purify one's own mind, one broadens the scope of one's attention, developing heartfelt concern for all beings who suffer under the influence of those negative aspects of the mind.

Regular practice is also necessary to be able to progressively assimilate the profound teachings of an authentic master. It is essentially a process of inner growth and freeing oneself from the ingrained habits that keep one in the circle of suffering.

The duration of the meditation sessions of a practitioner's day may vary from a few minutes to many hours, or even day and night, in the case of a retreat. Then comes a time, after many years, where the division between meditation and postmeditation dissolves and the mind, finally free, no longer makes a distinction between practice and everyday life.

The instructions that follow are designed to help practitioners to develop and deepen their practice while avoiding the obstacles that will inevitably hamper its development, and to establish a continuity and balance in the spiritual training, until it permeates every moment of one's existence. These instructions given by the sages of the past or present are a direct expression of their own experience. They offer them as if, as the traditional expression has it, they had opened their bosoms "to show us the redness of their heart," without hiding anything. When we meditate on them, we have to connect them to our own inner experience because only then can they take on their full meaning so that their truth, depth, and beauty can become a constant source of inspiration.

Drigung Döndrup Chögyal

Teachings to which one does not apply oneself
Become as meaningless as an echo.
So integrate them in your mind:
That's my advice from the heart.

Phagmo Drupa, Dorje Gyalpo

If you apply yourself continually to the practice
Appearances will become your teacher,
And you will die having realized
That the entire phenomenal world
Is supreme bliss.

Khyentse Chökyi Lodrö

CRUCIAL POINTS OF SPIRITUAL PRACTICE

I bow down to Lord Orgyen, the peerless refuge!

Now that you obtained this human life,
This eminent support, free and well favored,
Don't waste it. By every means,
Extract its quintessence.

Mind is the root of all phenomena.
If, complacent and careless, you neglect to examine it,
It becomes an expert liar.
But when you examine it, it has no root or basis.

All phenomena of samsara and nirvana
Are nothing but the play of pure and impure.
In the fundamental nature, primordially pure and empty,
Neither samsara nor nirvana have the slightest existence.

Emptiness is not a mere nothingness.
It manifests spontaneously as radiant wisdom,
And from it, awareness and compassion shine forth.

Awareness has no name, no characteristics;
From its creativity, the multiplicity of samsara and nirvana
    arises,
Yet, what arises and what makes it arise are not two.
Simply rest in this nonduality.

Motionless, rest in the tranquility of body;
Breathing naturally, rest in the tranquility of speech;

Not chasing after attachments, rest in the tranquility of mind;
Rest in a state of immensity, ease, and freedom.

This awareness of unborn dharmakaya
Is not a product of causes and conditions, but is present of itself,
Vivid, simple, naked,
Unaltered by notions of subject and object,
Unaltered by conceptual efforts.
Rest in this effortless contemplation.
But "rest" is just a word;
In truth there is no one who rests and nothing to rest in.
At all times, without distraction, maintain the recognition
Of the face of dharmakaya, awareness-emptiness.

Deluded samsaric activities have no end;
The more you strive in them, the more they multiply,
And the more thoughts of enmity or attraction invade your
    mind,
Thus creating the cause for being reborn in the lower realms.

Put your trust in the Dharma,
Blend your body, speech, and mind with it;
And thus entering the path of liberation and enlightenment,
At the time of death, you will have no regret.
In this life as well as future lives,
You will go from bliss to bliss.

Contemplate above your head, or in your heart,
The Teacher who shows you the greatest kindness,
As inseparable with the Great Orgyen,
And arouse ardent devotion.

When good or bad events, happiness or suffering arise,
Pray to your spiritual father,
And, merging your mind with his mind
Remain in that state of union.

When the hour of death comes, give up all attachment and
    aversion,
Meditate on Lord Orgyen above your head.
Visualizing your consciousness as a syllable *hri* upon a disk
    of light,
Make it dissolve in the Lord Orgyen's heart.
If you practice this meditation regularly now,
You will remember it easily at the moment of death.
Also pray to be reborn in the Glorious Copper-Colored
    Mountain.*

In brief, the practice of Dharma
Is to sever all that ties to samsara,
To cultivate gentle love and compassion for all beings of the
    six realms,
And at all times, without distraction,
To thoroughly master your own mind.

Although I have no inner realization,
I, a dharmaless fellow who lives on religious wealth
Called Chökyi Lodrö,
Wrote these few pieces of advice,
Simply not to refuse the request
Of the noble and virtuous lady Pelu.

Sarwa mangalam, may all be auspicious!

* The pure realm of Padmasambhava.

CHAPTER 14

View, Meditation, and Action

View, meditation, and action are three themes that define the practice of Buddhism and recur in all the teachings. "View" refers to the way one perceives reality. Based on analysis and contemplation, it enables one to understand with certainty that phenomena do not have the solid reality usually attributed to them. Everything is interdependent, impermanent, and devoid of independent existence. The view particularly means seeing the nature of mind. "Meditation" is the method of gradually assimilating the view by a process of familiarization, until it becomes one with one's being. "Action" is the process of connecting to the world by implementing the experience gained in the view and meditation through one's conduct.

Gyalwa Longchen Rabjam

SIX ESSENTIAL INSTRUCTIONS TO FREE THE MIND

The view focuses on mind itself: recognize its true nature.
The meditation focuses on luminosity: let it reach its full
    brilliance.
The action focuses on illusory phenomena: make
    everything that appears part of the path.
The contemplative experience is the manifestation of
    reality itself: cut the root of attachment.

The fruit is naturally present: give up hopes and fears!
The activity of enlightenment is to benefit beings:
    guide them with compassion!

Atisha

One day Dromtönpa* asked Atisha, "Is it possible to attain buddhahood only by meditating on the view of emptiness?"

Atisha replied, "In whatever you see and hear, there is nothing that doesn't come from your mind. To recognize that mind
is empty awareness, devoid of any substance, is the view. To continuously maintain that recognition without distraction is the
meditation. To maintain that recognition while acquiring merit
and wisdom in the manner of an illusion is the action.

"If you make that a true inner experience, it will manifest in
your dreams. If it manifests in your dreams, it will manifest at
the moment of death. If it manifests at the moment of death, it
will manifest in the intermediate state after death (*bardo*). In that
case, you will be sure to attain the supreme accomplishment."

Jetsün Taranatha

It is essential to put into practice the *view, action,* and *meditation*
together because they are interdependent, like a stack of spears
leaning against each other. Without the view, however good your
actions may be, they will involve a belief in reality and perpetuate
samsara. The view without the action will not complete the acquisition of merit and can also lead one into the abyss of nihilism.
View and action without meditation are as useless as treasure buried underground. Just as an inexhaustible treasure hidden under
the hut of a poor man will not prevent him from being hungry,

---

* The main Tibetan disciple of Atisha and a founder of the Kadampa lineage.

although the view and action may have been explained at great length, without the practice of meditation, they will not enable the mind to mix with the Dharma. In the hour of need, they will hardly be useful.

VIEW

The Fifth Dalai Lama, Ngawang Lobsang Gyatso

All phenomena are primordially pure; they cannot be
    located, and are empty;
Empty though they are, like a magic show, they clearly
    appear to our perception;
What appears to our perception, when we look into its
    nature for something identifiable, is nonexistent.
Nonexistent though it is, it gives rise to the experience
    of all happiness and suffering.

Dilgo Khyentse Rinpoche

All phenomena arise from emptiness through the illusory play of causes and conditions, and it is precisely their empty nature that allows all things to manifest. Just as space enables the totality of the universe to unfold without itself being altered or affected in any way, or just as the sky makes possible the appearance of a rainbow, phenomena are the "adornment" of emptiness but emptiness is never tainted by them.

Geshe Chayulwa

Subject and object are like sandalwood and its
    perfume,
Samsara and nirvana, like ice and water,

Appearances and emptiness, like clouds and the sky,
Thoughts and the absolute nature, like waves and the
   ocean.

Gyalwa Longchen Rabjam

Like reflections on a limpid lake,
The multitude of phenomena manifest
While being empty of independent existence.
Today, understand with certainty
That everything is only empty forms.

Like a clear cloudless sky,
The nature of mind, the king, is the absolute dimension.
Today, understand with certainty
That it has always been unborn,
Empty and luminous, without changing.

Like the clouds that evaporate into space, the multitude
   of thoughts
Are spontaneously liberated in the absolute dimension.
Today, understand with certainty
That, in reality, whatever arises is ungraspable and
   dissolves of itself.

Like beautiful birds soaring in space,
Recognize this mind as space itself.
By spreading the wings of meditative experience and
   realization,
Understand that its nature is the nondwelling absolute
   dimension.

Like the rainbow's colors in an immaculate sky
Is the shimmer of thoughts in the nature of mind.
Today, understand with certainty
That whatever arises is the sovereign mind,
    empty and luminous,
Which transcends any attachment.

As in the example of a melody,
All things result from a number of causes,
Themselves devoid of reality.
Today, understand with certainty
That everything is the primordial nature,
Empty, without root or foundation.

Like clouds in the unchanging sky,
Negative actions and emotions,
And all things good or bad,
Spring from the mind and depend on the mind,
But the nature of mind has neither root nor
    basis.

Just as turbid water becomes clear at rest,
Today, understand with certainty
That by leaving thoughts alone just as they are,
They naturally become limpid by themselves
And are spontaneously liberated in the absolute
    dimension.

Shechen Gyaltsap

Homage to the gurus, buddhas, and bodhisattvas!

I bow to all the masters
Who have attained supreme primordial liberation
And out of compassion remain here,
Dredging the depths of samsara.

I will speak a little about how to destroy one's clinging to
    the notion of reality
With the great medicine, bodhichitta,
The essence of the Mahayana path,
    The road traveled by all the buddhas and bodhisattvas.

Just as there is perfectly clear water
Within the earth,
Within the obscuring emotions,
There is great primordial wisdom.

It is profound, serene, unfabricated suchness,
An uncompounded expanse of luminosity;
Nonarising, unceasing, primordial peace,
Spontaneously present nirvana.

Just as sesame oil pervades sesame seeds,
The essence of the tathagatas
Is primordially present and inseparable from
The basic state of all beings.

Obscured by the deluded notions of subject and object,
Shrouded in the cocoon of the three habitual tendencies,
Like a treasure lying hidden in a poor man's house
This nature remains unrecognized.

Since beginningless time, you have roamed
On the immense plain of existence, which is apparent yet
    unreal.
Alas! Such is the power of ignorance and karma.

Having fully prostrated
At the lotus feet of an authentic master,
You should cleanse the stains of ego-clinging
With the nectar of his instructions.

Although I have not done it the slightest harm,
My enemy, ego-clinging,
Has entrenched itself in my heart since beginningless time
And confined me to the appalling prison of existence.

It has inflicted hundreds of tortures upon me.
Yet, instead of resenting it,
I have put my trust in it and fallen under its power.
Is there any catastrophe, any delusion
Worse than this?

Misplaced patience is contemptible.
Taking the Three Jewels as my support,
Mounting the horse of irrevocable renunciation,
Donning the armor of the four boundless ones*
And rallying the armies of the six paramitas,
Today, with the sharp weapons of emptiness and
    compassion,
I shall slay my foe!

* Love, compassion, sympathetic joy, and impartiality.

One sees, as when mistaking a rope for a snake,
That the self is nothing but a misperception:
It is nonexistent, devoid of intrinsic reality.

By continuously turning the wheel of investigation,
You will gain confidence
In the nonexistence of both beings and phenomena,
And a time will come when you achieve certainty
That the two truths,
The illusory arising of interdependent events
And the emptiness that is devoid of all assumptions,
Are not contradictory, but, in essence, one.

Dudjom Rinpoche

In brief, from the beginning, awareness has never existed as a substantial entity with elaborated characteristics: its nature is primally pure, void, vast, and all-pervasive. As the radiance of voidness is unobstructed, the ocean of phenomena of samsara and nirvana appears spontaneously, like the sun and its rays; thus awareness is not a blank nothingness, totally void, for its natural expression is the great spontaneous presence of the qualities of primordial wisdom.

MEDITATION

Rigdzin Chökyi Trakpa

If you have not acquired inner experience
Nor fully clarified the view through meditation,
You will not manage to do so through philosophical
    debates or just by reading.
Meditate continually: That is my advice from the heart.

The Seventh Dalai Lama, Kelsang Gyatso

During meditation, keep the mind unobstructed as space;
After meditation, regard the flow of events as a rainbow;
Thus the things which so allure the world
Are seen to be insubstantial hallucinations.

Joy and misery are dances within a dream;
Forms and sights are a town projected by a magician;
Sounds are like one's own voice echoed in a cave;
Those who grasp at them are mindless children.

Just as a reflected image distinctly appears
When a man holds his face to a mirror,
All things are both radiantly manifest and empty.
For that very reason is cause and effect unfailing.

Rigdzin Chökyi Trakpa

Mind itself has always been free from mental fabrication:
No need to ruminate about the past or anxiously anticipate
    the future.
Remaining beyond thought, without attachment or
    distraction, whatever happens,
Release thoughts the instant they appear:
That's my advice from the heart.

Without blocking sense perceptions one by one,
Without seeing them as real or following them,
Whatever you perceive, free it in your mind's natural state:
That's my advice from the heart.

Drigung Döndrup Chögyal

The all-powerful mind is like a magician
That makes everything appear, the woes of samsara
    and the happiness of nirvana.
Carefully maintain the recognition of the nature of
    mind:
That's my advice from the heart.

Dudjom Rinpoche

ADVICE FOR RETREAT (CONTINUED)

Having thus cut from within all doubts and misconceptions about the view, to experience that view continuously is called meditation. Apart from this, all meditations with targets are intellectual meditations devised by thought; we do nothing like that.

Without straying from stability in that view, remain free, letting be all perceptions of the five senses in their natural state. Do not meditate on particulars, thinking, "This is this, this is that." If you "meditate," that is the intellect. There is nothing to be meditated upon. Do not let yourself be distracted even for an instant. If you wander from dwelling in awareness itself, that is the real delusion, so do not be distracted.

Whatever thoughts arise, let them arise. Do not follow them, do not obstruct them. You may ask, "Then what should be done?" Whatever manifestations of the phenomenal world may arise, remain in a state of natural freshness, without grasping at them, like a small child looking inside a temple. If you do so, all phenomena remain as they are, their aspect is not modified, their color does not change, their luster does not vanish. Although the phenomenal world is present, if you do not contaminate it with concepts and clinging, all appearances and thoughts will arise as naked primal wisdom, empty and radiant. People of narrow intellect are puzzled by the great number of teachings that are said to be very profound and very vast. So if we were to point a finger at the essential meaning that emerges out of them all, one would say: when past thoughts have ceased, and future thoughts have not yet arisen, in the interval is there not a perception of nowness, a virgin, pristine, clear, awake, and bare freshness that has never changed even by a hair? Ho! That is the natural way of abiding of awareness.

However it does not always remain in that state: doesn't a thought suddenly arise? That is the natural expression of awareness itself. But if you do not recognize it as such at the very moment it arises, that thought will spread out into ordinary thoughts. This is called "the chain of delusion." It is the root of samsara. If you simply recognize the nature of the thoughts immediately as they arise, without extending them, leaving them freely to themselves, then whatever thoughts arise are all simply liberated in the expanse of awareness-dharmakaya. This itself is the main practice uniting the view and meditation of "cutting through solidity."* As Garab Dorje† says, "When awareness arises abruptly from the natural state of the primally pure expanse, that instant of recollection is like finding a gem in the depths of the ocean: this is the dharmakaya, which has not been contrived or made by anyone."

You should meditate like this with great energy day and night, without distraction. Not allowing emptiness to remain in the domain of theory, bring everything back to awareness itself.

* Trekchö (khregs-chod) is a practice of the Great Perfection that cuts through the solidity of the mind's concepts of subject and object.

† Garab Dorje was the first teacher of the lineage of the Great Perfection.

Gampopa

Meditation without knowledge,
May produce temporary benefits,
But it will not reach its true goal.
However much you melt gold or silver,
Once the fire is out, they harden again.

Mokchokpa Rinchen Tsöndru

On the mountain of this illusory body,
The lion cub of consciousness plays.
Those who know training in nonattachment to the
    six senses
Will surely overpower existence and transcendence.

In the nest of ignorance,
The young garuda* of consciousness dwells.
Those who can use the wings of means and knowledge
Will surely soar in the six realms' skies.

Look, look with the mind at the outer world.
Having looked at the outer world,
You'll see that, like a mirror's reflections,
Appearances have no intrinsic nature.

Look, look with the mind at the inner mind.
Having looked at the inner mind,
You'll see that, like a candle untroubled by the breeze,
Mind is clarity without discursive thoughts.

---

* A spectacular bird of Indian mythology with extraordinary powers.

Look, look with the mind between outside and in.
Having looked between outside and in,
You'll see that, like the sun rising in the sky,
Marks [of dualistic experience] unravel in their own ground.

Meditate, meditate with the mind on the profound path of
    means:
Having meditated on the profound path of means,
You'll see that, as if led by an excellent guide,
Mind reaches the place it desires.

Meditate, meditate with the mind on the Great Seal:*
Having meditated on the Great Seal,
You see that, like a spreading forest fire,
Whatever appears helps you.

Turn, turn the mind to begging aimlessly:
Having begged aimlessly,
You'll see that, like snow falling on a lake,
Your thoughts dissolve straightaway.

Mipham Rinpoche

In this world, the myriad transient phenomena
Are the magic of the mind.
Other than the currents of ordinary thoughts,
There is no suffering of samsara.

Happiness comes from the mind, suffering also.
The higher and lower worlds, gods and demons,

---

* The Great Seal or Great Symbol (Skt. *Mahamudra*) is a teaching about the
nature of mind, comparable to that of the Great Perfection.

All that is good and everything bad
Are nothing but the magic of the mind.

Abandoning any desire to do this, or practice that,
Recognize with certainty the nature of mind, the source of
    everything.
When you recognize the unchanging natural state of mind
    in itself,
Remain in the continuum of that presence:
    There you have the essential point of all instructions. . . .

If the armies of the four Maras assail you, it is still the mind;
If gods and demons suddenly arise, it is still the mind;
Even the imbalance of the elements in the body has the same
    origin. . . .
It is the force of habits, from time immemorial,
Which makes the continuous flow of agitated thoughts so
    real, so solid.
Yet their illusory army whose assaults are hard to repel
Have ultimately no more power than mirages. . . .

When at ease, in vast awareness,
As if curing himself from a disease,
The yogi recognizes reality, the nature of the mind,
He remembers the bad habits of his thoughts,
Like servants holding their heads higher than their master's.
He sees the sun of bliss rising in his heart.

When you have subdued the enemy that is your thoughts,
There is no other enemy in the three spheres of samsara,
No devil and no great fear.
Yogi, you have won the ultimate victory.

When you have unlocked mind's secret, when you know the
  experience of reality,
Many cogitations and practices only lead to exhaustion.
Whatever you practice, its fruit can be resumed in
  one essential point:
Mind rediscovering its own nature.

ACTION

Rahulabhadra

On every occasion, pray tirelessly for the benefit of beings. When
you are going to sleep, think: "May all beings attain the absolute
nature!" When you wake up in the morning: "May they awaken as
buddhas!" When you get up: "May they have the body of a buddha!" When you dress: "May they be clad with the ability to be
ashamed to do wrong and show restraint before others!" When
you start a fire: "May they burn the firewood of negative emotions!" When you eat: "May they eat the food of concentration!"
When you open a door: "May they have access to the city of deliverance!" When you close a door: "May they close the way to lower
rebirths!" When you go out: "May I take the path of deliverance
for all beings!" When you go somewhere: "May I lead all beings in
the higher worlds!" When you arrive: "May I liberate the beings
of the lower worlds!" When you see someone happy: "May all
beings find the happiness of buddhahood!" When you witness
the suffering of others: "May all beings be free from suffering!"

Gampopa

Do not argue with the vain,
Do not compare yourself to the wealthy,
Do not denigrate those who want revenge,
Do not resent the powerful.

Abandon a bad custom, even if it comes from your
    father or your ancestors.
Adopt a good custom, even if it is practiced by your
    adversaries.
Do not take poison, even from the hand of your mother.
Gold, even given by an enemy, still has all its qualities....
Some are not impressed when others carry mountains
But consider a bit of wool a heavy burden for
    themselves!

Dilgo Khyentse Rinpoche

THE CESSATION OF NEGATIVE EMOTIONS

As it is said, "The sign of being wise is self-control; and the sign of a mature spiritual experience is the absence of conflicting emotions." This means that to the same degree that one becomes wise and learned, one also becomes serene, peaceful, and subdued— not a reckless person bursting with pride and arrogance. However much your practice progresses year after year, you will have no concern with comfort and discomfort; you'll have no pride at all. You will be always at peace, untroubled by outer events, with a humble mind, beyond hopes and doubts and indifferent to the eight worldly concerns: gain and loss, pleasure and pain, praise and blame, fame and obscurity. There is a saying that goes: "In spiritual practice, the difficulties come at the beginning; in worldly affairs, they come at the end." This means that when you renounce worldly affairs and devote yourself entirely to practice, you may encounter some outer and inner obstacles; but the more you persevere, the more happiness you will find. Conversely, worldly activities can give you ephemeral and superficial satisfactions at the start, but soon you will meet with bitter disappointment....

Discarding all other thoughts, you should be concerned only with the Dharma. You do not need to think about wealth, fame, and power, but should cultivate humility. Do this not only for a few months of retreat but for the entire duration of your life, until the very moment of your death. When death comes, it is of no use to be among many worldly people; it is better to die in an empty cave, one-pointedly absorbed in your spiritual practice. With this frame of mind, the obstacles of Mara will have no place to grasp hold of you....

You must constantly check whether or not you succeed in using the teaching to tame your conflicting emotions. If any practice has the opposite result, increasing your conflicting emotions and your selfishness, it is not suited for you, and you should give it up. Once you have started to practice, don't follow just anyone's advice. Be like a wild animal jumping out of a trap and running as far away as it can. You must be completely free from samsara, not half in and half out....

When you find yourself in the midst of a large gathering, never lose your mindfulness. Preserve the state of uncontrived simplicity and remember the guru's instructions.

You should be like a mother who has been separated from her newborn baby. A woman who has just had a child is extremely loving and attentive to him; and if someone takes the child away from her even for a very short time, she can't stop thinking about him. In the same way, you should never part from mindfulness and vigilance....

Even if death were to strike you today like lightning, you must be ready to die without sadness or regret, without any residue of clinging to what is left behind. Remaining in the recognition of the view, you should leave this life like an eagle soaring up into the blue sky.

When the eagle takes flight into the vast sky, it never thinks, "My wings won't be able to carry me; I won't be able to fly that far." Likewise, when dying, remember your guru and his instructions, and adhere to them with complete confidence.

Dudjom Rinpoche

ADVICE FOR RETREAT (CONTINUED)

Now, how to progress further in the meditation by means of action and how to evaluate it in the light of one's inner experience. As was said before, the most important thing is fervent devotion, to pray to the teacher with ardor from the heart, without ceasing even for an instant to consider him as the real Buddha. We call this "perfect devotion, the universal panacea." It is superior to all other ways of dispelling obstacles and making progress. Levels and paths will be traversed with great momentum.

Regarding meditation's defects: if your meditation sinks and becomes dull, revive alert awareness; if it scatters and becomes wild, relax perception deep inside. Yet this should not be an intentional and forcible retrieval made by the usual meditating mind keeping watch. Be simply mindful not to forget the recognition of your own nature. Preserve this in all circumstances—eating, sleeping, walking or sitting, in or out of meditation periods. Whatever thoughts arise, happy, painful, or defiled, remain without a trace of hope or doubt, rejection or acceptance, and do not try in any way to destroy them with antidotes. Whatever feelings of happiness or suffering there may be, leave them as they are in their true nature, naked, fresh, clear, vast, and limpid. Thus, since for all this there is nothing but a single vital point, do not confuse yourself with all sorts of cogitations. There is no need to meditate upon emptiness as an antidote distinct from undesirable thoughts and negative emotions.* If you recognize the nature of those undesirable thoughts with awareness, at that very moment they will be liberated by themselves, like a snake untying its knot.

Almost everyone knows how to talk about the ultimate hidden meaning of the Luminous Vajra Essence,† without knowing how to put it into practice. It has become just like a parrot's litanies. We who practice it are so greatly fortunate!

Now, there is more to be understood that we must consider carefully. The two deadly enemies that have bound us to samsara since beginningless time until now are the grasper and the grasped. Now that by the grace of the master we have been introduced to the dharmakaya nature residing in ourselves, these two are burnt up like feathers, leaving neither trace nor residue. Isn't that delectable!

Having received the profound instructions upon such a swift path, if you do not put them into practice, they will be just like a wish-fulfilling gem put in the mouth of a corpse—such a pity! Don't let your heart rot; take up the practice.

Beginners will find that the mind, completely invaded by black thoughts, will stray into distraction. Even more tiny thoughts will proliferate unnoticed, until a lucid mindfulness comes back, and you will think sadly, "I have wandered." At that moment, do not do anything like interrupting the course of the thoughts, feeling

---

* The very nature of those thoughts and negative emotions is emptiness. There is therefore no need to superimpose on them, as an antidote, a conceptual emptiness fabricated by the intellect.

† Tib. *od gsal rdo rje snying po*, synonym of the Great Perfection (*rdzogs pa chen po*). It refers to the "essence" of mind, which is "luminous" in its spontaneous capacity of limitless cognition, unobscured by the veils of ignorance. "Vajra," sometimes translated as "adamantine" or "diamond," indicates that this essential nature is indestructible.

regret about your wandering and so on; simply remain in this clear mindfulness and keep on experiencing the natural state. This by itself is enough.

"Do not reject the thoughts; see them as dharmakaya." So goes a well-known saying. However, until your experience of wider vision has been perfected, merely to think "this is dharmakaya" and remain in a blank tranquility involves the risk of being caught in an amorphous equanimity devoid of any characteristic whatsoever. So, to begin with, whatever thoughts arise, just stare at them without analyzing or pondering and rest upon the "recognizer" of the thoughts, without caring about them or giving them any importance, like an old man watching children at play.

Remaining like this you will settle into a kind of stagnation in the natural state devoid of thoughts. When this experience is broken all of a sudden,* instantly a wisdom transcending the mind will arise, naked, fresh, and vivid.

On the path there cannot but be some mixing with experiences of bliss, clarity, and nonthought; but if you remain without even a hair of self-satisfaction, conceited attachment, hope or doubt, that will prevent you from going astray.

It is very important that, always discarding distraction, you practice with one-pointed vigilant mindfulness. If you stray into sporadic practice and theoretical knowledge, you will be satisfied with a vague tranquility; without having reached a decisive experience, you will be only verbally clever, and this will not be at all profitable. As the Great Perfection says, "Theoretical understanding is like a patch; it will fall off," and, "Experiences are like mist; they will vanish." This is how many great meditators are led astray by good or bad minor circumstances and get lost in them. Even when meditation has penetrated your mind, you need to

* This refers to techniques, transmitted from master to student, to break the stagnation of a calm yet dull state of meditation without thoughts, thus awakening the clear recognition of awareness.

cultivate it continuously, otherwise the deep instructions will be left on the pages of the books, and your mind, your Dharma, and your practice will become impervious, so that the birth of genuine meditation will never come. Take care, you old meditators, still novices in practice: there's a danger that you may die with "just the taste of salt in your mouth!"*

After you have practiced continuously over a long period, a time will come when, through fervent devotion or some other circumstance, experiences will metamorphose into realization, and awareness will be seen naked and vividly clear. It is like casting off a veil from your head: there is a vast sense of freedom. It is "the supreme seeing of the unseen." From then on thoughts will arise as meditation. The states of stillness and movement† will be liberated simultaneously.

At first, thoughts are liberated through recognizing them: it is like meeting someone you already know. In the middle, thoughts are liberated by themselves, like the undoing of a knot in a snake. Finally, thoughts are liberated without creating benefit or harm; it is like a thief in an empty house. These three will happen progressively. A strong and total conviction that all phenomena are simply the display of your own awareness will take birth from within. Waves of emptiness-compassion will surge forth. Preferences between samsara and nirvana will cease. You will realize that buddhas and beings are not good or bad. Whatever you do, you will never move from the total satisfaction of the absolute nature, day and night in an uninterrupted vast continuity. As it is said in the Great Perfection "Realization is unchanging like the sky."

---

* This expression seems to mean that one has whatever one needs to practice the Dharma, and one has the intention to use it, but finally, through lack of persistence, one achieves nothing.

† This refers to the two possible states of the mind, still, when there are no thoughts, and moving, when thoughts occur.

Patrul Rinpoche

This story about Patrul Rinpoche was told to the author
by Nyoshul Khen Rinpoche.

One day Patrul Rinpoche asked his faithful disciple Nyoshul Lungtok:

"What lama do you invoke in your prayers?"

"Unfortunately, I'm not able to pray for long."

"Well, maybe sometimes you can't manage, but who do you invoke when you can concentrate?"

"You."

"Why me? This country has no shortage of lamas!"

"If I have positive thoughts, even if it is only for a brief moment, I know that I owe it to you and your teachings. So, I think of the inexhaustible kindness you have shown toward me."

"If that's how you see it, that's okay. You can continue to pray like that."

Dudjom Rinpoche

ADVICE FOR RETREAT (CONTINUED)

Until the expression of the qualities of your inner understanding has reached perfection, it is inappropriate to recount your experiences to anyone who is prepared to listen to them, so keep your mouth shut. Furthermore, don't boast about years or months of retreat but practice earnestly for the duration of your entire human life. Do not belittle the gaining of merit through the cause and effect relationships of relative truth, deceiving yourself with mere words about emptiness.

Village ceremonies, exorcisms, and so on, are just performed to get food, so don't stay long in populated places. Meaningless activities, unnecessary talk, and unprofitable thoughts should be reduced to a minimum. Don't fool others by pretense and deceit, which contradict the Dharma. Don't practice wrong livelihood by making indirect requests and uttering flatteries out of longing for desirable things. Don't associate with sinful people or with those whose views and actions are not in harmony with yours. Disclose your own defects, and don't speak of the hidden faults of others....

You should take along the path all connections, good or bad, both with people who hold you in high esteem and treat you well and with people who dislike you and treat you badly, without making any distinction, caring for them with pure prayers. At all times inwardly keep your spirits high, without losing courage, and outwardly, on the path of action, remain humble. Wear worn-out clothes. Consider everyone, good, bad, or in between, as superior to yourself. Live simply and remain determinedly in mountain hermitages. Set your mind on the condition of a beggar.

Follow the example of the lives and perfect liberation of the accomplished beings of the past. Not blaming your past karma, practice Dharma flawlessly. Not blaming circumstances, whatever they may be, remain steadfast. In brief, taking your own mind as witness, dedicate your life to the Dharma. Thus, at the time of death, free of thoughts about things left undone, you will not be ashamed of yourself. That is the vital point of all practices.

When the hour of your death is approaching, give away whatever possessions you have without being attached to even a needle. At the moment of death, the best practitioners will be joyful, middling practitioners will be without apprehension, and ordinary practitioners will feel no regret.

THE FRUIT

Shabkar

When one looks at one's own mind,
The root of all phenomena,
There is nothing but vivid emptiness,
Nothing concrete there to be taken as real.

It is present as transparent, utter openness,
Without outside, without inside:
An all-pervasiveness
Without boundary and without direction.

The wide-open expanse of the view,
The true condition of mind,
Is like the sky, like space:
Without center, without edge, without aim.

By leaving whatever I experience
Relaxed in ease, just as it is,
I have arrived at the vast plain
That is the absolute expanse.

Dissolving into the expanse of emptiness
That has no limits and no boundary,
All vision, all sound,
My own mind, and the sky all merge.

Not once did the notion arise
Of these being separate and distinct.

In the absolute expanse of awareness,
All things are blended into that single taste—

But, relatively, each and every phenomenon is distinctly,
    clearly seen.
Wondrous!

Deeply intoxicated with the bliss
Of radiant clarity, vivid, brilliant, immaculate,
From my heart, I wished to dance with joy.

Toward all the beings under the skies
Who have failed to realize this,
All-pervading compassion spontaneously dawned;
The urge to sing this song arose of itself.

Without entering into the narrow rock gorge,
Which is mind watching for stillness and movement,
Without being caught in the snare of "view" and
    "meditation" created by the intellect,
Without flying into the dark clouds of dull states of mind,
Without plunging into the storm of agitated thinking,
The great garuda, my own mind,
Flew freely into the wide-open sky of the absolute expanse.

Eyes completely open, encompassing a hundred horizons,
Utterly at ease, the garuda of mind wings its way.
What delight!

In the expanse of skylike evenness,
All phenomena, all the appearances and sounds
Of samsara and nirvana are apparent yet empty:
They are empty, and yet they appear.

Although they appear, phenomena are empty,
Free of the limiting concept "truly existent."

Although they are empty by nature, phenomena do appear,
Free of the limiting concept "nonexistent."
In the vast space of the view
That is itself spontaneously free
From the two limiting concepts, belief in permanence or in
   nothingness,
This joyous song burst forth by itself.

Even more vast than the sky is the view, emptiness.
There, the sun of love and the moon of compassion arose,
And again and again I made boundless prayers
To benefit the teachings and beings.

May all disease and epidemics,
All famine, and all wars be ended,
And may all have happiness and joy.

Rangrig Repa, Kunga Lodrö

When I arrived at the sacred place of the King of Snowy
Mountains,* I had a decisive experience of awareness, clear as a
cloudless sky, profoundly luminous, vast and serene, transcending any notion of enslavement and liberation, transparent, with
no outside or inside. Phenomena did not cease to manifest in
any way, but in that experience of direct awareness, whatever
appeared, whatever manifested, and all movements of thoughts
were clear and limpid, transcending all limits. The more phenomena appeared thus without obstruction, the more the experience
became clear. I understood that whatever appeared was nothing
but spontaneous luminosity. As for the incessant movement of

* Mount Kailash (6,714 m) in western Tibet, one of the most important sacred
mountains of Asia. Many meditators lived there as hermits in caves, including
Milarepa (1040–1123), Gyalwa Gotsangpa (1189–1258) and Lingje Repa (?–1188).

underlying thoughts, I perceived it as the uninterrupted presence of awareness. A conviction arose in me from deep within, unlike anything I had known previously. The very notion of gross or subtle thoughts, or good and bad, no longer applied. All that appeared, everything I perceived, could no longer affect me for better or worse, and no longer provoked any hope or fear.

There was no difference between manifestation and nonmanifestation, and my mind remained perfectly clear, even amidst the multiplicity of events and thoughts. Even when jumping or running, even if my mouth and my eyes were distracted, my mind remained open and relaxed. All discourse about what is or is not, or of being or not being in meditation, had collapsed. There was an uninterrupted continuity of awareness beyond description, in which all mental activity came to exhaustion.

Without it being necessary to distinguish between periods of meditation and nonmeditation, I experienced certainty arising from the depth of my mind.

Gampopa

A drop of water is not much,
But pour it into a lake, and when will it dry up?

PART FOUR

Removing Obstacles and Making Progress in the Practice

CHAPTER 15

Exposing Faults

The Kadampa masters* used to say that the kindest teacher is one who reveals our hidden faults, and thus enables us to see what is holding us back on the path. Reassuring flattery will only serve to sustain our ignorance, our vanity, and our suffering. The rebukes of a true master, one whose sole purpose is to awaken his students, have nothing to do with contempt or a tendency to see defects in others' behavior. Just as the needle of a compass stubbornly and unambiguously points north, they provide their students with precious indications that will save them from wasting time taking wrong directions or getting trapped in their own weaknesses.

After reading some of the following texts, one might think that the authors are castigating themselves. But this expression of humility is a traditional way of presenting the teaching. The disciple knows how to take it: he understands that the teacher is showing him a mirror.

Until we are able to integrate what we have understood through meditation into our everyday life, the smallest obstacle will trip us up, and we will be unable to cope with the vagaries of existence while continuing to grow spiritually. Periods of meditation and

---

* Kadampa: a Tibetan Buddhist school founded by followers of the Indian master Atisha (982–1054) that focuses on monastic discipline, compassion, and study. His teachings are preserved and practiced in all Tibetan lineages. It was under the inspiration of this school that the Gelugpa tradition was founded in the fifteenth century.

postmeditation must reinforce each other, or the fruit of the spiritual path will remain out of reach.

To correct one's faults and achieve stability, it is essential to be vigilant at all times. In the words of a Kadampa master:

> The sword of attention guards the door of my mind!
> If passions threaten, I'll threaten them back!
> I'll release my grip when they release theirs!

Practice requires a sustained effort. If we were naturally free from attachment and anger, and our only concern was for infinite beings, we would already be accomplished, and we would not need to practice. As that is generally not the case, we must keep in mind the meaning of the teachings and carefully observe what we do, say, and think. It is only by assiduous discipline that as practitioners of the Dharma we can deeply and definitively transform our way of being.

Dilgo Khyentse Rinpoche

When you are criticized, accept it as an opportunity to acknowledge your hidden faults and increase your humility. Criticisms are your teacher, destroying attachment and craving. If brought to the path, harsh words and blame will inspire your practice and strengthen your discipline. How can you ever repay such kindness?

The happiness and suffering created by praise and criticism are ephemeral. When you are complimented, instead of feeling proud just regard the praise as if it were something you were hearing in a dream or a fantasy. Tell yourself that it is not you that is being praised but the good qualities you may have developed through spiritual practice. In fact, the truth is that the only people really worthy of praise are those who have attained liberation.

If you point out someone's faults, they will become quite

upset—even if it is your own child or student. If you flatter people, however, attributing to them qualities they do not possess, they will be delighted. If people always agree with us and flatter us, it may make us feel good, but it will not help us to develop the qualities of a Dharma practitioner. What will truly help us most is if someone points out our faults and shows us the right way to deal with them. Gold, through repeated beating and melting, becomes more and more refined. In the same way, by continually recognizing our own faults and applying the teacher's instructions, we will be able to transform our negative qualities into the path of liberation.

When a troublemaker is identified and apprehended, peace returns to the village. Similarly, when our faults are unearthed by a truly kind teacher, enabling us to recognize and eradicate them, peace returns to our being. The true spiritual teacher speaks frankly, striking at the core of our defects in order to lead us to the right path.

Shabkar

THE SHARP NEEDLE

Master, from the invisible realm
Look down upon this miserable person!

I'll point out my own defects
As I'd remove lice with my finger,
I'll toss my defects out the door
As I'd pull a thorn out of my foot and toss it away.

You, Shabkar—
You obtained a free, well-favored human birth,
You met a lama, the embodiment of all the Buddhas,
You received his profound and vast instructions.

As the result of having listened to the Dharma and
    contemplated its meaning,
Your body, speech, and mind should have become tame and
    serene,
But they didn't. They got worse!

Your obscuring emotions should have diminished;
But they didn't. They got worse!

Your mind should have evolved,
But it didn't. It got worse!

This is what you are:
A sack stuffed with the wealth and food given by the faithful,
A bull sleeping like a corpse,
A snake filled with hatred,
A bird filled with desire,
A pig filled with stupidity,
A lion filled with pride,
A dog filled with jealousy,
A hungry ghost filled with greed,
A butcher thirsting to inflict torment,
A cannibal reveling in flesh and blood.

Toward the lama, who is all Buddhas in one,
You lack the devotion that brings tears to the eyes.

Toward your Dharma brothers and sisters,
You lack the pure perception to see them as deities.

Toward all beings, each of whom was once your mother,
You lack the compassion that makes one's hair stand on end.

Toward the vast and profound instructions,
You lack the diligence that spurs one to practice.

Lacking faith and respect,
You are a longtime samaya-breaker,*

Lacking pure perception,
You are shameless.

Lacking compassion,
Your heart is rotten.

Lacking meditation practice,
You are utterly lazy.

Not seeing your faults,
You are blind.

Proclaiming others' faults,
You have a big mouth.

You are a stone anchor dragging to the depths of hell:
You have collected such bad karma,
O Dharmaless accumulator of evil.

You are such a traitor,
Betraying the lama who is all the Buddhas of the three times.

You are such a traitor,
Betraying your vajra brothers and sisters who keep pure samaya.

* Samaya (Tib. *dam tshig*): the engagements of the Vajrayana, involving pure perception of one's teacher, harmonious relations with one's fellow students, and commitment to the practice.

You are such a perverter of the teachings,
Tarnishing the image of the Dharma.

You are such a charlatan,
Outwardly appearing as a practitioner,
Yet acting against the Dharma,
And complaining about the faults of fellow practitioners.

You are the living dead—a zombie, a walking corpse.
Even if you are not possessed by Maras, you are quite mad.

You stuffed dummy, where did you come from?
Man of ill omen, where did you come from?

Look at your "diligence":
Nothing but eating, drinking, and sleeping like a corpse!

Look how you stubbornly refuse to walk toward virtue,
Balking like an exhausted donkey!

Look at how, faster than anyone,
You plunge toward evil like a waterfall!

You can't tolerate a single bad word;
Look how your face convulses with rage!

You are a sack of faults and downfalls—
To whom have you given back your vows?

You carry a great weight of evil deeds;
Where are your virtues?

You are a huge bladder of defects;
Who stole all your good qualities?

You have a full load of the eight worldly concerns;
What have you done with holy Dharma?

You are nothing like a Dharma practitioner—
Aren't you ashamed of yourself?

Old dog without a tail,
Go out and join the other dogs!

Bull with upper teeth*
Go and look for a herd of cattle!

In case you insist on staying,
Will you dare to behave as before?

Man,
If you have any self-respect,
A heart in your chest,
Brains in your head,
Some sympathy for yourself,
Regret your past actions!
Improve your whole behavior!
Now's the time! It's already getting late!

See how
All that is born dies,
All that is hoarded runs out,
All that is gathered gets separated,
And all, absolutely everything, is without essence:
Meaningless activities should be abandoned.

---

* Meaning a bovine in human form. (Cattle only have an upper dental pad.
Humans have upper teeth.)

To practice the essential, divine Dharma,
You must exert yourself in accordance
With the words of your lama and
The Victorious Ones.
O Lama and Three Jewels, look upon me compassionately!

My past actions were wrong,
I regret them from the core of my heart,
I confess them, and promise never to commit them again.

Grant your blessings
So that I may act in accord with the Dharma.
Grant your blessings
So that I may observe the Vinaya.
Grant your blessings
So that I may follow the Sutras.
Grant your blessings
So that I may practice according to the Abhidharma.
Grant your blessings
So that I may accomplish the Secret Mantrayana!*

Patrul Rinpoche

ONE TASTE

If you make the mistake of feeling
Attachment to the illusory things you perceive,
Those illusions will deceive you.

---

* Vinaya: the precepts for monastics and laypeople. Sutras: the discourses of the Buddha. Abhidharma: the systematic presentation of phenomena, including mental states. These three constitute the three sections of the Buddhist canon, known as the "three baskets" (*Tripitaka*), to which is added the "pitaka of the Secret Mantras," the tantras of the Vajrayana.

But if you know that mind and appearances
Are like water and the reflection of the moon,
Both have only one taste.

If an old man's eye is drawn
To the bloom of youth,
The poisonous taste of attachment may arise.
When attachment to the body is liberated in the space
    of the absolute,
Youth and age have one taste.

If you believe too much in the three stages of life
As if they were permanent,
The pangs of death may be cruel.
In the one essence of awareness,
Birth and death have one taste.

If you are too tightly bound
By affection for your friends and relatives,
Separating from them will surely break your heart.
When you know the illusory nature of samsara,
Union and separation have one taste.

If you invest the deity with great hopes,
The fear of demons will only increase.
When you know that the world and beings are the deity,
Gods and demons have one taste.

If you run after your thoughts
A thousand activities will occur to you.
If you watch the mind without thought,
You can relax in nonaction.

If you listen to whatever people say,
There is no limit to what you must do.
When you decide for yourself,
You can resolutely avoid having projects.

Even if others perceive you in a good light,
When you yourself see your own faults,
It is meaningless to pretend to be good.

It is time for this bad fellow to hide his corpse,*
The kingship has fallen into the hands of the fox.†
He has tasted its fruit for a time,
But when the fox is bitten by the icy wind,
The time has come for him to go back to his lair.

If we do everything the people of Marwa say,
It will be hard to see the land of Do,‡
But for one who decides it's time to leave,
Do and Marwa are just two sides of the same pass.

Ha-ha! What miserable talk!
Heh-heh! Just nonsense!
Oh! Oh! It just came out spontaneously!

---

* Patrul Rinpoche is referring to himself.

† This verse alludes to a legend. One day a fox fell into the cauldron of a dyer and came out a beautiful blue color. When he returned to the country, the other animals, not recognizing him, took him for a divine being and showed him the greatest marks of respect, to the point that he was soon made king of beasts. One full moon while the fox sat proudly in his court, other foxes began to yelp in the distance. Unfortunately, the blue king could not help but yelp too. Unmasked, the impostor had barely time to flee to save his life.

‡ Two valleys in eastern Tibet.

Patrul Rinpoche

"DRIVE THEM AWAY WITH STONES . . .!"

I prostrate at the feet of my master!
When I, the old dog that lives in solitude,
Remember the words of my supreme refuge,
I feel like talking in this way:

The first time I met my master,
I felt that all my wishes had been fulfilled,
Like a navigator who comes upon an island of pure gold.
That is called taking the meaning of the teachings to heart.

Later, when I arrived in the presence of my master,
I had a feeling of guilt,
Like a thief who meets a judge.
That is called being brought to order.

Now when I visit my master,
I am hardly more impressed than a pigeon nesting in a temple,
I feel like I'm meeting an equal.
That is called turning your back.

The first time I received spiritual instructions,
I was eager to implement them,
Like a starving man seeking food.
That is called appearing to practice.

Later, when I listened to the teachings,
I was prey to great uncertainty,
Like when you hear someone talking a long way off.
That is what's called not having clarified one's doubts.

Now, when I listen to the instructions,
I have a feeling of repulsion,
As if I was forced to eat my own vomit.
That is called losing the urge to ask for teaching.

The first time I found myself in a lonely place,
I felt perfectly at ease,
Like a traveler returning home.
That is called delighting in being in the right place.

Later, like a young girl living alone,
I could no longer bear
Staying in a lonely place.
That is called not being able to keep still.

Now when I am in a secluded place,
I find that I'm in a pleasant spot,
Like an old dying dog under a cornice.
That is called hiding away to die.

At first when I thought about the view,
The higher it was, the better I liked it,
Like a vulture looking for a place to nest.
That view was confined to mere words.

Later, when I was considering the view,
I was afraid of taking the wrong direction,
Like someone who comes to a crossroads.
That is called remaining perplexed.

Now, when I think of the view,
I feel I've been cheated,

Like a child to whom an old man talks nonsense.
That is called not knowing where you stand.

At first when I thought of meditating,
I was full of enthusiasm,
Like a boy and a girl under the spell of their meeting.
That is called being thirsty for meditation.

Later, at the thought of meditation,
I felt exhausted,
Like a frail person carrying a heavy burden.
That is called having a short meditation.

Now, when I think of meditating,
I cannot stay quiet for a moment,
Like a needle that is trying to stand upright on a stone.
That is called no longer wanting to meditate.

At first when I thought about the action,
I felt constrained by my vows,
Like a wild horse that has just been tethered.
That is called a pretense of discipline.

Later, when I thought about the action,
I felt free to do as I please,
Like an old dog that has ripped out the stake that held it.
That is called abandoning one's vows.

Now, when I think about the action,
I have no restraint,
Like a woman who no longer takes care of her appearance.
That is called not caring about one's condition.

At first when I thought about the goal of the path,
I thought it seemed like a good business prospect,
Like a charlatan who vaunts his wares.
That is called having high hopes.

Later, when I thought about the goal of the path,
I thought it was far away,
Like the other side of the ocean.
That is called not having much enthusiasm.

Now when I think about the goal of the path,
I feel I have no chance of achieving it,
Like a burglar who comes too late, and sees the dawn
    rising.
That is called losing all hope.

At first when I was about to start an explanation,
I was very pleased with my talent,
Like a beautiful woman who arrives at the market square.
That is called loving to talk.

Later, when I started an explanation,
I thought I knew everything,
Like an old man telling stories of the past.
That is called having a nimble tongue.

Today, when I start an explanation,
I feel like exposing my faults,
Like an evil spirit struck by an exorcist.
That is called feeling shame.

In my early philosophical debates,
I really wanted to win,

Like when you go to court for some dubious case.
That is called often yielding to anger.

Later, when I debated,
I felt I was seeking the ultimate meaning,
Like a mediator who strives to have a balanced view
    of things.
That is called mobilizing all one's intelligence.

Now when I debate,
I feel I can say anything,
Like a charlatan touring the boondocks.
That is called having lost all restraint.

When I started to compose texts,
I felt that they came spontaneously
In the manner of great adepts who improvise songs
    of enlightenment.
That is called not modifying anything.

Later, when I composed a text,
I felt I was working on the style,
Like an experienced poet shaping his verses.
This is what is called producing good literature.

Today, when I compose a text,
I feel that it is pointless,
As if I'm writing the guide of a place that I do not
    know.
That is called not wanting to waste ink and paper.

At first when I met my fellow students,
I was animated by an intense spirit of competition,

Like young people gathered for a contest of archery.
That is called being the plaything of desire and
  aversion.

Later, when I was with my companions,
I felt intimate with them all,
Like a prostitute going to a party.
That is called having many friends.

Today, when I am with my peers,
I do not feel like I belong,
Like a leper in a crowd.
That is called feeling lonely.

At first when I saw wealth,
I just felt a moment of pleasure,
Like a child picking flowers.
That is called not trying to acquire assets.

Later, when I saw wealth,
I felt it was impossible to have enough,
Like when you pour water in a leaky vase.
That is called not being very motivated.

Now, when I see wealth,
I think of it as a heavy burden,
Like an old beggar with numerous offspring.
That is called preferring to have nothing.

The first time I had disciples,
I aspired to greatness,
Like a valet who takes the place of his master.
That is called congratulating oneself.

Later, when I had disciples
I felt I was indispensable for them,
Like pilgrims who have reached a sacred place.
That is called doing one's best for others.

Now, when disciples approach me,
I want to scold them!
It's like meeting demons in a lonely place.
That is called wanting to chase them away with stones.

This is the end of the admonition entitled "Chasing them away with stones."
May merit ensue!

Kalden Gyatso

The absurdities of ignorance are growing;
You, wisdom, do you have the heart to sleep?

Desire is becoming increasingly coarse;
You, feelings of repulsion, what swamp have you fallen into?

The splendor of hatred is greater than ever;
You, altruistic love, where did you run to?

Pride is shouting ever louder;
You, humility, did you become deaf?

The pangs of jealousy are more and more tangible;
You, pure vision, I have sought you everywhere in vain.

False views are more and more treacherous;
You, faith and respect, have you totally vanished?

The funeral meal is more and more tasty;
You, virtuous practices, are you about to disappear?

Faults and transgressions fall like rain;
You, vows and precepts, I wonder if you're still there.

The knot of greed tightens more and more;
You, generosity, is your hand broken or paralyzed?

I, Kalden Gyatso, a native of Rongpo, wrote these words of remonstrance to help distinguish faults from their remedies.

Guru Chökyi Wangchuk

Om mani padme hung hri*

*Here is "The mani† that exposes the hidden faults and failings,"
some advice given by Chökyi Wangchuk to Pajo Thogden Chapchöl
and all his spiritual children.*

Hri! Remember us, O Great Compassionate One!
It is inconceivable to have crossed the threshold of the Dharma,
But without wearying of samsara, it is useless.
That's why it's better to recite the *mani.*

You may spend years in solitude,
But without freeing yourself from desire, it is useless.
That's why it's better to recite the *mani!*

You may engage in ascetic practices
And live off the essence of the elements.‡

---

* The mantra of Chenrezi (Avalokiteshvara), buddha of compassion. This is the mantra most frequently recited by Tibetans.

† The *mani* is the usual term by which the Tibetans refer to this mantra.

‡ The practice of extracting, by physical or meditative means, the essence of the elements (space, water, earth, fire, and wind) to regenerate and enhance vitality. This also enabled some ascetics living in deserted areas to survive for years without having access to ordinary food.

Without pacifying your longing for food, it is useless.
That's why it's better to recite the *mani*!

You may strive to listen, reflect, and meditate.
If your mind does not derive any benefit, it is useless.
That's why it's better to recite the *mani*!

You may have good understanding of the meaning of the
nine progressive vehicles.
If you have no compassion, it is useless.
That's why it's better to recite the *mani*!

You may be expert in the view, meditation, and action.
If you have not renounced the ordinary world, it is useless.
That's why it's better to recite the *mani*!

You may have strength, power, and inconceivable qualities.
If you have not mastered your mind, it is useless.
That's why it's better to recite the *mani*!

You may be able to embellish the philosophical doctrines
with words.
If it's the words that interest you, it is useless.
That's why it's better to recite the *mani*!

You may live constantly in remote places.
If you do not renounce activities, it is useless.
That's why it's better to recite the *mani*!

You may renounce companionship and be celibate.
If you do not abandon distractions, it is useless.
That's why it's better to recite the *mani*!

You may understand the meaning of the Great Perfection.
If your thoughts are not liberated, it is useless.
That's why it's better to recite the *mani*!

You may well understand the meaning
Of the equality of self and others.
If it's only pretense, it is useless.
That's why it's better to recite the *mani*!

You may have always stayed with your master.
If you did not acquire his qualities, it is useless.
That's why it's better to recite the *mani*!

You may have received many initiations.
If your mind does not mature, it is useless.
That's why it's better to recite the *mani*!

You may have had thousands of pith instructions.
Without inner experience, it is useless.
That's why it's better to recite the *mani*!

You may have thousands of great teachers.
Without serving them, it is useless.
That's why it's better to recite the *mani*!

You may have spent eons listening to the Dharma.
Without faith, it is useless.
That's why it's better to recite the *mani*!

You may have practiced in many caves.
If you have no accomplishment, it is useless.
That's why it's better to recite the *mani*!

You may claim that you have realized the Great Perfection.
If you still have ordinary dreams,* it is useless.
That's why it's better to recite the *mani*!

You may know how to comment nicely on texts, arguments,
    and instructions.
If you don't recognize your own nature, it is useless.
That's why it's better to recite the *mani*!

Rinchen Phuntsok

ADVICE TO MYSELF

Though you see that the things of samsara have no meaning,
You are feverishly involved in endless activities
Without finding satisfaction.
You, lazy one, don't care about fitting in with others!

When you're up, you get drunk with pride;
When you're down, everyone despises you;
And in between, you arouse jealousy.
Wake up and reflect on the merit of all these activities!

If you are frank, you only make enemies,
If you are hypocritical, your consciousness is weighed with
    karmic debts,
If you combine the two, they call it vacillation.
Undecided one, consider the results of your actions!

---

* As practitioners progress on the spiritual path, they gradually become able to
know when they are dreaming (sometimes called "lucid dreaming"), then they
can change the nature of their dreaming to the point of no longer having ordinary dreams and remaining in a continuous state of luminosity.

If you talk a lot, you're a blabbermouth,
If you say nothing, you are taken for a fool.
If you are sometimes silent and sometimes talk,
  people call it instability.
You, Rinchen, think about the vanity of words!

Patrul Rinpoche

ADVICE TO HIMSELF

On the immaculate pollen bed of an open lotus
Seated on the disc of a full moon, the throne of white light,
The unshakable manifestation of bliss-emptiness in
  divine form:
Master Vajrasattva, sole deity, I trust in you!

Listen, Abu Shri,* so distracted, with such bad karma!
Think how you've been fooled again and again by mistake
  after mistake.
Do you get it?
You're still making mistake after mistake, so watch out!

Stop living a false and empty life.
Drop those deceptions of your own mind
And endless projects that you don't need!

Don't make your head spin with the burden
Of strings of ideas that never come true

* One of the nicknames of Patrul Rinpoche. "Abu" could be translated as "comrade," and "Shri" is the Sanskrit equivalent of the Tibetan *pal* (Glorious), the first syllable of "Palge," the lama of whom he was recognized as the *trulku* (incarnation), hence "Patrul."

And endless distracting activities.
They're just waves on the water: leave them alone!

You listened to hundreds of teachings
Without understanding any.
What's the point?
You reflect then forget when you need it.
There's no point!
You meditate, but it doesn't cure your emotions.
Just drop it!

You've recited many mantras,
But you haven't mastered the creation phase.
You visualize solidity as deities but haven't dropped duality.
You seem to tame demons,
But you haven't tamed your mind.
So your nicely arranged four sessions of recitation . . .
Just drop them!

On the surface you seem so clear,
But you can't relax your mind.
Underneath, you seem so focused,
But there's no freshness.
Your awareness seems to be unshakable,
But what's really stable? Your concepts!
So you can drop that point of concentration
And drop that steady gaze.

Your words may seem sweet,
But they do not help your mind.
Your logic may seem sharp,
But it just foments illusion.
Your advice may seem deep,

But you don't put it into practice.
So drop reading books
That distract your mind and tire your eyes!

You sound your little drum: tom! tom!
It's just making a noise to show off.
You may intone: "Take my flesh! Take my blood!"*
But you haven't stopped cherishing them.
You may sound your cymbals: ching! ching!
But you don't have any concentration.
So drop that fancy kit
Which just looks nice!

Today they want to learn,
But in the end they give up.
Today, they seem to have understood,
But after a while there's nothing.
They may learn a hundred things,
But they do not apply them to their minds.
So drop those disciples
That seem so important! . . .

Endless chatter
Causes attachment and hatred.
You may express surprise or approval,
But in fact, it's a way of speaking ill of others.
What you say may sound good,
But others get irritated.
So drop that gossip.
It only makes your mouth dry!

* This verse refers to the practice of Chö (*gcod*), "cutting (through the ego)" in which one makes an imaginary offering of one's own flesh.

Teaching without personal experience,
Is like having learned to dance from a book.
Even if they seem to listen to you with devotion,
From your side, it's pure deceit.
If you betray the teachings,
Sooner or later you'll be ashamed of yourself.
So drop those sermons
That have the appearance of rhetoric!

Euphoric today,
Angry tomorrow,
People are prey to changes of mood.
They are never satisfied;
Even if they are, they are useless when you need them,
And bring you to despair.
So drop the politeness,
Flattery, and obsequiousness!

There are people who can handle
Religious and secular affairs;
Don't long for such companions, old Abu!
Don't you see that the old buffalo in his stable
Deep down just longs to sleep?

You can't do without eating, sleeping, and shitting;
Don't bother with the rest. It's not your business.
Do what is within your capabilities. Stay quiet in your corner!

Just drop everything! That is the essence!

*Advice written by the yogi Trimé Lodrö (Patrul Rinpoche) for his close friend
Abu Shri (which is none other than himself) to give him some suitable recom-
mendations that he needs to put into practice. And even if there is nothing to
put into practice, the essential point is to let go of everything. And not to be
annoyed even if you don't attain the fruit of the teaching!*

Dodrup Tenpai Nyima

Giving advice in a technical manner sometimes makes it more difficult to understand. So I will speak in everyday language. Anyway, I'm not capable of long and beautiful speeches.

Well, let's get straight to the point. Suppose that the Lord of Death appears before you today. He cuts the fine thread of your existence, interrupts the continuous movement of your life force, and your last breath escapes like a spark. There's your beloved body, which you have so pampered, abandoned on your bed. Your friends and relatives cannot accompany you, and you are forced to leave behind all the goods that you have spent your life accumulating.

In the intermediate state, the bardo, a multitude of fantasies appear to you, as numerous as the stars of the night, and you enter a frightful darkness. Now you are on a terrifying and painful path where the proof of your bad karma will manifest clearly to you. Can you still remain comfortable and relaxed?

It is easy to say, "I will die tomorrow." We may say that life is ephemeral, but in fact, when we hear or teach the Dharma in the morning, and in the afternoon we are busy making long-term plans, are we really thinking of death? The answer is clear.

The past is over. Now, every moment, from dawn to dusk, keep this question in mind: "What must I do to have no regrets when I die?" Don't forget it! This is important, so think about it now!

Talking, walking, urinating, defecating, eating . . . aren't you bored sick with the activities of this life? What do you have better to do than to apply yourself to spiritual practice? A flash of faith in the Three Jewels, or a little compassion that arises in you, and it is already the Dharma!

Tell yourself that if you do not do your best now to practice the noble path, getting another human life once your skull and bones are in the ground will not be as easy as droppings falling from the backside of a horse!

In summer look in your larder and see how many flies cluster on a piece of rotten meat, and you will easily understand that there are many more beings in the lower worlds than in the human realm.

If you mumble prayers without taking the path of liberation, as if you had a tongue of crumpled paper in a wooden mouth, and the old plague of ordinary worries still lurks in you, tell me what can come of this sham of practice? Think hard and make up your mind, once and for all, to devote your time to the Dharma.

Do not trust misleading fake buddhas. Do not seek the protection of the ghosts that inhabit the air. Do not ask advice from harmful friends and other childish people. Give your whole being to the Three Jewels, the only infallible refuge. Never forget to have such devotion that you see your master as the Buddha in person. Do not criticize the great sages. If friends hurt you, do not let resentment invade your mind. If an enemy hurts you, do not let yourself be overwhelmed by lamentation.

When someone speaks harshly to you, if you wonder, "Why has this person spoken to me so nastily?" and that nagging thought fills your heart, it is as if a virulent demon had arisen in you. Tell yourself that such a thought is a demon who wants to harm you and understand that you really need the remedy of wisdom.

Behavior such as amassing and hoarding wealth, or flattering close friends while nourishing malicious thoughts against others, only strengthens attachment and aversion, and condemns you to become the slave of negative emotions. And once you start to serve your negative emotions, all possible afflictions, each one worse than the other, will plague you.

Do you not see that it is through serving those emotions in samsara from time immemorial, that now you are in such a pitiable condition, where your body composed of impure aggregates attracts all sorts of suffering! From now on consider the negative emotions as your enemies and those who hurt you as friends.

When an insect bites your back, you cannot stand it. You cry "*Atsa*! Wretched beast!" So how will you deal with great suffering? Well, it's the same for other beings, who all just want to be happy and not suffer. In children's tales, one speaks of "perfect happiness" and "pitiful suffering." Be aware that everyone feels unhappy as soon as he or she experiences a bit of suffering and see if you can have a good heart. Don't forget it! Don't forget it! Long life to you!

Thus spoke the beggar Jigme to fulfill the wish of Gegen Palge.

Gyalwa Longchen Rabjam

Here's a song to exhort myself and others to bear in mind that the ordinary business of this life and the illusions of this world provide neither benefit nor refuge.

On the mountain of habitual tendencies accumulated since
    time immemorial,
The net of ignorant duality veils the clear light of mind.
Because you do not have the slightest weariness of this world
    of samsara,
Unconscious one, I have some advice for you.

If you do understand, see the misleading nature of this
    ephemeral life,
Reflection and analysis is useless.

If, once more, you fail to take the path of liberation,
Having obtained a human life is useless.

If you do not purify negative actions and develop
    positive ones,
To have entered the door of the Dharma is useless.

If you do not keep in mind the suffering of the lower worlds,
Seeming to practice Dharma is useless.

If you are not thoroughly convinced of the vanity of this life,
Seeming to accumulate merit is useless.

If inwardly you are unsatisfied and unable to have no needs,
Seeming to have few desires is useless.

If, through not having mastered your mind, you are incapable
    of humility,
Seeming to practice patience is useless.

If you have not conquered your anger and pride from within
Seeming to be disciplined is useless

If you have not assimilated the Dharma deep within you,
Seeming to know the sutras and tantras is useless.

If you have not aroused limitless bodhichitta in your heart,
Seeming to practice the Great Vehicle is useless.

If you do not keep your vows and spiritual commitments
    perfectly pure,
Seeming to practice the secret mantra vehicle is useless.

If you have not persuaded yourself to be profoundly weary
    of samsara,
Seeming to be practicing in solitary places is useless.

If you have not truly abandoned your attachment to the reality
    of things,
Seeming to be a good Dharma practitioner is useless.

If you do not take your own mind as the true witness,
Seeming to be a good person in the eyes of others is useless.

If you are not disgusted with the eight worldly concerns,
Seeming to be an excellent practitioner is useless.

If you have not abandoned the dispersions of desire for
    prestige and fame,
Seeming to have many disciples is useless.

If you have not given up vanity, partiality, and thirst for glory,
Seeming to be altruistic is useless.

If you only think of yourself,
Seeming to be generous is useless.

If your altruism is not entirely free of selfish desires,
Seeming to help others is useless.

If you are not moved by your teacher and his teachings,
Seeming to have faith is useless.

If you yourself do not have deep certainty,
Seeming to be a counsel for others is useless.

If you do not see your inner negative emotions as enemies,
Employing external remedies is useless.

Without sadness in samsara, renunciation, and the thought
    of death,
Hoping to attain enlightenment is useless.

If you do not commit yourself to practice in solitude,
Having listened to and reflected on the teachings is useless.

If you are disgusted with the things of the world but still make
    long-term plans,
Meditating in solitude is useless.

If you have not met an authentic spiritual master,
Seeming to follow a spiritual friend is useless.

If you do not sincerely feel infinite devotion,
Seeming to rely on your spiritual master is useless.

If the blessings of the master do not penetrate your heart,
Embarking on the path to liberation is useless.

If you are not able to practice, renouncing worldly things,
Knowing the ultimate nature is useless.

If you have not acquired unfeigned pure vision,
Seeming to have great fervor is useless.

If you do not have fervent and sincere respect,
Seeming to honor your spiritual companions is useless.

If you have not become familiar with your own awareness,
To have received the profound instructions is useless.

If you have not acquired inner confidence, free from duality,
A view that is only general understanding is useless.

If you cannot meditate while remaining free from adopting
    and rejecting,
Meditating using conceptual references is useless.

If you do not understand that your own perceptions are empty,
   without reality,
Seeming to practice nonduality is useless.

If you do not recognize that unobstructed awareness-
   emptiness is the absolute dimension,
Trying to attain the fruit of the path is useless.

If you do apply the antidotes adapted to your mind,
Intellectual talk is useless.

If you do not purify thoughts without rejecting them,
Letting them dissolve in the space of awareness,
Positive thoughts that are doubly illusory are useless.

If you do not purify the five poisons,
Eliminating harmful thoughts as soon as they arise,
The emptiness of nonaction is useless.

If you do not have inner certainty in the view, meditation,
   and action,
Wandering from one sacred place to another is useless.

If you have not exhausted the intellect
And seen the nature of phenomena in its nakedness,
Seeming to be an accomplished yogi is useless.

If you do not know how to rest continually in
   awareness-emptiness,
Seeming to be a great meditator is useless.

If you do not realize the transparency of phenomena,
Recognizing that they have no independent existence,
The introduction to the nature of mind is useless.

If you are not so weary of samsara that you want to renounce
    everything,
Meditating in solitude is useless.

If you do not abandon hopes and fears,
And continue to fear suffering and worry about the future,
Seeming to have high realization is useless.

If you do not discipline your mind by scrupulous behavior,
Seeming to behave like a liberated yogi is useless.

If you do not wander in wild uninhabited places,
Retreats and vows are useless.

If you do not throw to the winds your ambitions for this life,
Seeming to be a good practitioner is useless.

If you remain obsessed with your reputation and infatuated
    with your outward appearance,
Seeming to be a "good lama" is useless.

If you do not forsake the distractions caused by life in society,
Simply to receive everyone's praises is useless.

Now it is time for you to follow the example
Of masters of the past by pursuing the path of liberation.

I have given you this advice from the heart:
Turn your mind inward and you will see that what I say is true.

The first step in the right direction is to turn your back on
    samsara;
The second is to destroy the mistake of taking things for real,

And the final one, to conquer the unchanging land of
awareness.
Like this, you will naturally accomplish your own benefit and
that of others.

*This concludes the third chapter of advice to myself in the form of adaman-
tine songs, the chapter on overcoming attachment to the things of this life.*

CHAPTER 16

Overcoming Inner Demons

When, in the early fourth century BCE, Shakyamuni Buddha meditated under the spreading branches of the Bodhi Tree* at the site of the present town of Bodh Gaya, he suffered in the months before his enlightenment the violent assaults of four maras or demons. The demons that Buddhist practitioners are warned about are not ghosts or external evil spirits, but inner forces caused by our erroneous perception of the world that are powerful enough to cause serious obstacles to our practice.

The texts mention four demons: the demon of the aggregates (the physical and mental legacy of karma that temporarily constitutes our person and forms the support of suffering), the demon of the self, the demon of death, and the demon of afflictive emotions.

When these four demons launched their final assault on the Buddha and manifested in various apparently external forms, the Buddha, through his understanding of the ultimate nature of phenomena and his boundless compassion, remained unruffled and attained enlightenment.

The demon of negative emotions generally becomes apparent to us that when it reaches a certain intensity: our anger explodes, jealousy eats away at us, or ignorance blinds us. But in reality it is an old enemy that we have unconsciously befriended and learned

* The tree (*ficus religiosa*) under which the Buddha attained enlightenment (Skt. *bodhi*).

259

to foster. It can even appear to be virtuous, reasonable, and logical, as in the case of hatred based on sectarian arguments.

When we start to progress on the spiritual path, and profound changes take place in us, those demon-obstacles manifest with greater force. As a teacher quipped, "The demons do not bother with those who neglect their practice." In any kind of business, great profit is accompanied by great risk. So it is unsurprising that, in our inner journey, we will come up against all kinds of forces that oppose our progress. Properly managed, these obstacles can be catalysts of realization, but they can also interrupt our practice or make us deviate from our goal.

Only the lucidity of wisdom, impartial altruism, trust in an authentic spiritual master, and the unwavering intention to attain enlightenment can overcome these obstacles, whether they be subtle or gross.

Machik Lapdrön

The source of the "demon" is our own mind.
When the mind apprehends phenomena and fixates on them,
It becomes the demon's prey.
When mind takes itself as an "object," it is spoiled.

Jatshön Nyingpo

ADVICE GIVEN BY PADMASAMBHAVA
TO NYANG BEN TINGZIN SANGPO*

If those who practice the Dharma are as numerous as the stars in the sky, those among them who are free from the obstacles of the

* Nyang Ben Tingzin Sangpo, one of the foremost disciples of Padmasambhava, the master who introduced Buddhism in Tibet, was a minister of the Tibetan king Trisong Detsen (eighth century).

demons are fewer than the sun and moon. Were it not for these obstacles, it would be easier to accomplish realization than it is to accumulate virtuous actions for one year. That is why these demons must be identified and outwitted.

At first, while you are imprisoned in the samsaric city of suffering, you may have some faith in the Dharma. This is soon carried away by the demon of laziness and by clinging to gross realities. By harboring hatred toward enemies, attachment to dear ones, maintaining an attitude of competitiveness, and being distracted by worldly affairs, you fail to keep death in mind, and, caught up in all kinds of other activities, you always postpone Dharma. That itself is the demon. In order to drive it away, search for a qualified guru, who is the root of unalterable faith, and reflect on death and impermanence, which is the root of unalterable diligence. Leaving lesser tasks behind, give yourself up to the great task of Dharma.

Then will come the demon of changing your mind. It may take the shape of intimates, family, or friends, who will say, "Don't practice the Dharma" and will create obstacles in all kinds of ways. At other times it may manifest as fear of enemies, or as competitiveness, or as wealth. In this way Dharma will always be postponed until tomorrow and the day after. A life filled with delusion soon runs out, and finally you will be plunged into the mire of samsara. In order to subdue this demon, trust only in the teacher and supreme objects of refuge. Decide for yourself and do not ask ordinary people's advice.

When you stay with your teacher, the demon of doubting him and considering him as an equal will arise. The signs of its presence are that you become blind to the teacher's qualities while noticing the slightest defect. You develop adverse views toward his actions and doubt whether they are endowed with wisdom, and you devote yourself to using religion to acquire wealth and food. Having set out on a spiritual journey, you will end up in hell.

This is really a demon. In order to thwart it, perceive the teacher as the Buddha.

Then will come the demon of reverting to worldly desires. The signs of its arrival are that, thinking about sex, money, and business, with dishonest dealings and greed, you give up religious robes, spiritual friends and brothers, and the practice of Dharma. Losing interest in listening to the Dharma, you pursue the attachments and hatreds of the world; you thirst for women and wine; you turn your back on the Buddha's teaching. In order to subdue this demon, develop unwavering determination to follow the supreme Dharma. Whichever profound teachings inspire you, persevere in them earnestly, keep far away from temptations, and avoid actions contrary to the Dharma, thinking of the lives of previous saints. This is important.

Taking a casual view of the teachings is the demon that appears next. The signs of its presence are that you conceitedly say that you have received this teaching and that teaching, when you haven't grasped the meaning, and it is all theory. Knowing one or two sentences, you broadcast the secret instructions in the marketplace. Whatever deep teachings are being given, you say, "I've already heard that." Certainty and understanding will never arise from this attitude. Such a failure to reach the ultimate point of the Dharma is the "demon" in person. In order to overcome it, reflect again and again upon the teachings that you have received, and immerse yourself in their meaning.

At this time the demon of your qualities giving birth to covetousness appears in the guise of patrons and disciples. Not devoting yourself to practice, convinced that you are very learned, you become infatuated with yourself and ambitious for wealth. This will create obstacles leading you away from the path of Dharma. In order to subdue this demon, vow to remain in mountain solitudes for a long time and discard all activities other than the Dharma.

The next demon to approach is that of metaphysical views. You discriminate in a partisan way between your own point of view and that of others, and the Dharma turns into the five poisons. In order to prevent this, abandon all doctrinal rivalry and train yourself to see the purity of everything without bias.

When, having disentangled yourself from that, you are meditating on voidness, there will arise the demon of emptiness itself as the enemy. "Everything is nonexistent," you will say, while inverting sin and virtue in your actions. You will have neither faith in the Three Jewels nor compassion for sentient beings. When this happens, cultivate virtue and purify sins. With fervent devotion train your mind to see all phenomena as pure and to understand dependent origination and the inseparability of emptiness and compassion.

Then there is the demon of compassion arising as an enemy. Without being liberated yourself, you will be impatient to work for the good of others, while postponing your own practice. When this happens, develop your aspiration bodhichitta and let the application bodhichitta wait for a while....

It is said that, until you reach buddhahood, the obstacles of the demons will follow endlessly one after another. But if, abandoning all distractions, you give yourself entirely to the practice of the path, no obstacles of any kind will ever find a way in to disturb you.

The Eight Great Chariots
of the Accomplishment Lineage
in Tibetan Buddhism

Although Buddhism reached Tibet as early as the fifth century of our era, it was only established there two centuries later, during the reign of Songtsen Gampo, and especially in the eighth and ninth centuries, when King Trisong Detsen invited the abbot Shantarakshita and Guru Padmasambhava, the "Lotus-Born Master." The latter completed the construction of Samye, Tibet's first monastery, gave Vajrayana empowerments to the king and many other disciples, and transmitted essential instructions concerning the nature of reality. Under his guidance, Tibetan translators accompanied by many Indian scholars translated into Tibetan the entire canon of the Buddha's teachings, known as the *Tripitaka*, literally the "Three Baskets," and countless volumes of tantras, with their ritual texts and related commentaries.

In retrospect, the followers of the teachings of this first period of translation came to be known as *Nyingmapas*, "the Ancients." They classified the Buddhist teachings into nine progressive "vehicles" (Skt. *yana*) covering all the various aspects of Buddhist philosophy and spiritual practice.

The term "vehicle" means an approach to achieving the goal of the spiritual path, perfect enlightenment. The multiplicity and progression of vehicles respond to the diversity of natural predispositions and capacities of different beings. Each vehicle is a step that integrates the previous vehicles. According to the tradition of the Nyingma, all vehicles lead up to the "luminous heart essence" of the Great Perfection, or

Dzogchen. "Perfection" means that mind, in its essential nature, naturally contains all the qualities of enlightenment. "Great" expresses the fact that this completeness naturally embraces all phenomena.

The three main modes of transmission of the Nyingma tradition are the long transmission of canonical texts (*kama*), the short transmission of spiritual treasures (*terma*), and the direct transmission of pure visions (*danang*).

In the eleventh century, there was a second phase of propagation of Buddhism, when translators brought new texts from India. This period, known as the New Translations, or New Tradition (*Sarmapa*), begins with the great translator Rinchen Sangpo (957–1055). The emergence of outstanding scholars and great saints gave rise to new schools of philosophy and spiritual lineages.

Tibetan Buddhism now has four main traditions known as Nyingma, Kagyu, Sakya, and Kadam-Gelug, which perpetuate the transmission of the rich philosophical and contemplative heritage of Tibet. There are four other lineages that have become less prominent: Shangpa Kagyu, Chö and Shi Che, Urgyen Nyendrub, and Kalachakra, which have mainly continued within one or other of the four main schools. These eight traditions are known as the Eight Great Chariots of the Accomplishment Lineage.

The lineage of Kadampa—or "supreme precepts"—was founded by Atisha Dipamkara (982–1054). It focuses on "training the mind" (*lojong*), which emphasizes mainly renunciation and compassion. Atisha was born in Bengal and studied with many spiritual masters. Following a prophecy he received, he went to Indonesia, where he studied for twelve years with the sage Serlingpa, whom he considered to be his principal teacher. Upon his return to India, he became the abbot of the great Buddhist university of Vikramashila. Then he was invited to Tibet by the kings Yeshe Ö and Changchub Ö. He remained there until his death. The most eminent of his countless disciples, Dromtönpa Gyalwe Jungne (1004–64), continued his work by propagating the gradual path taught by his master.

The Kadampa school later evolved into the Gelugpa—or "virtuous tradition"—which started at Ganden Monastery through the influence of an extraordinary master, Tsongkhapa Lobsang Trakpa (1357–1419). The latter was the instigator of a major reform that aimed to strengthen respect for monastic discipline and the study of texts. Among his many writings, *Lam Rim Chenmo*, "The Great Gradual Way," expresses with great clarity the fundamental steps of the basic vehicle (Hinayana) and the vehicle of the Bodhisattvas (Mahayana). His two chief disciples were Gyaltsap Je (1364–1432) and Khedrup Je (1385–1438). A reincarnation of the latter became the first Dalai Lama, whose lineage has profoundly marked the history of Tibet to the present day.

The Sakya tradition, based on the teachings of the Path and Fruit (*Lamdre*) of the great Indian master Virupa, was introduced to Tibet by the charismatic translator Drokmi Lotsawa (993–1077?). The spiritual lineage that passed on these instructions was called "Sakya," literally "Gray Earth" because of the color of the landscape that surrounds the monastic seat erected by the five founding masters: Kunga Nyingpo (1092–1158), Sonam Tsemo (1142–82), Jetsün Trakpa Gyaltsen (1147–1216), Sakya Pandita (1182–1251), and Chögyal Phakpa (1235–80).

Sakya Pandita, who was considered to be an incarnation of Manjushri, the bodhisattva of wisdom, became one of the most influential masters of his time. The ground on which the teachings of the path and the fruit is based is the metaphysical point of view that samsara and nirvana are fundamentally indivisible, the path is the maturing process of the four initiations, and the fruit is the development of the five wisdoms. The central theme of these teachings is "liberation from the four attachments" (to the concerns of this life, the cycle of rebirths, egocentric desires, and conceptual fixations).

The Kagyu or "oral instruction" lineage goes back to two of the *mahasiddhas* ("great accomplished masters") of India, Tilopa and his disciple Naropa. Marpa the Translator (1012–97) made the perilous journey from Tibet to India three times to receive the teaching of Naropa. Marpa submitted his heroic disciple Jetsün Milarepa (1040–1123) to severe trials before passing on to him all the empowerments and instructions that he had received. The extraordinary life of Milarepa, during which he lived a life of extraordinary asceticism in the mountains for twelve years, made him Tibet's most famous yogi. He transmitted his teachings in the form of beautiful spontaneous songs of realization, which remain a powerful source of inspiration to this day.

Among the many disciples of Milarepa, the foremost were Rechungpa (1084–1161) and Gampopa (1079–1153). The latter was the teacher of Phagmo Drupa (1110–70) and the first Karmapa, Dusum

Khyenpa (1110–93). The Kagyu school gave rise to four major lineages—Karma Kagyu, Drigung Kagyu, Drukpa Kagyu, and Taklung Kagyu—and eight minor lineages. The Kagyu teachings emphasize the Six Yogas of Naropa—inner fire, illusory body, dream, luminosity, bardo (the intermediate state between death and the next life), and transfer of consciousness at the time of death. The culmination of those teachings is Mahamudra, the "Great Seal," or "Great Symbol," a term meaning that when we have a stable recognition of the ultimate nature of mind, we realize that that nature embraces all phenomena, placing its "seal" on everything that we perceive.

The Shangpa school was founded by Khyungpo Naljor (born about 990). Although it has preserved its specificity to the present day through its eminent spiritual masters, it is intimately associated in its historical transmission with the Kagyu tradition.

The deep and complex tradition of the Kalachakra, "Wheel of Time," based on the Kalachakra tantra is still very much alive today. Transmitted and practiced by many followers of different traditions, it has inspired a vast literature. However it has never produced a distinct school that developed a set of specific practices.

The practice of Chö was introduced to Tibet by the yogini Machik Lapdrön (1055–1153), one of the most important female figures of Tibetan Buddhism. The word "chö" means "cutting," in this case cutting ego-clinging and other forms of dependence derived from it.

The practice of Shiche, or "pacification" (of suffering), was propagated by Padampa Sangye (d. 1117).

The tradition of mahasiddha Urgyenpa (1230–1309) owes its survival to the untiring efforts of Jamyang Khyentse Wangpo (1820–92) and Jamgön Kongtrul (1813–99), two great masters of the nineteenth century known as the "great beacons," who took on the task of collecting all the traditions still existing in Tibet. However, in practice, the tradition of mahasiddha Urgyenpa no longer exists as an autonomous spiritual lineage.

As the Fourteenth Dalai Lama has often pointed out, the Tibetan tradition harmoniously integrates three complementary and incremental levels of Buddhism, namely, Hinayana, Mahayana, and Vajrayana. These three vehicles correspond to three fundamental aspects of practice: renunciation, compassion, and pure vision.

Renunciation, foundation of the Basic Vehicle (Hinayana) and thus also of the two other vehicles, means the powerful aspiration to break free of the suffering of samsara.

Compassion, heart of the Great Vehicle (Mahayana), leads the practitioner to vow to attain enlightenment to liberate all beings wandering in samsara in the grip of ignorance.

Pure vision, the extraordinary perspective of the Diamond Vehicle (Vajrayana), is to recognize the buddha-nature present in all beings and the original purity of all phenomena.

Sources

Chapter 1. The Value of Human Existence

SHABKAR TSOGDRUK RANGDRÖL: Shabkar Tsogdruk Rangdröl, *Chos bshad gzhan phan nyi ma*, pp. 16–17.

SHECHEN GYALTSAP: p. 10, Shechen Gyaltsap, *Rdo rje theg pa'i thun mong gi sngon 'gro spyi la sbyor chog pa'i khrid yig kun mkhyen zhal lung rnam grol shing rta*, pp. 66–67. P. 12, ibid., p. 361. P. 17, Shechen Gyaltsap, *Rdo rje theg pa'i thun mong gi sngon 'gro spyi la sbyor chog pa'i khrid yig kun mkhyen zhal lung rnam grol shing rta*, pp. 77–78.

DILGO KHYENTSE RINPOCHE: Adapted from Dilgo Khyentse Rinpoche, *The Excellent Path to Enlightenment*.

JAMGÖN KONGTRUL LODRÖ THAYÉ, YONTEN GYATSO: Jamgön Kongtrul Lodrö Thayé, *Bla med nang rgyud sde gsum gyi rgyab chos padma'i zhal gdams lam rim ye snying 'grel pa ye shes snang ba*.

JIGME KHYENTSE RINPOCHE: Oral advice transcribed by the author.

MINLING TERCHEN GYURME DORJE: Minling Terchen Gyurme Dorje, *Smin gling gter chen rig 'dzin 'gyur med rdo rje'i gsung 'bum*, pp. 90–91. Translated at Yan-nga in the hills of western China, August 8, 1988.

Chapter 2. Reflections on Impermanence and Death

NAGARJUNA: Nagarjuna, *Nagarjuna's Letter to a Friend with Commentary by Kangyur Rinpoche*, verse 55.

PADMASAMBHAVA: p. 20, verse quoted in numerous Tibetan works. P. 22, quoted in Shechen Gyaltsap, *Theg pa chen po'i blo sbyong gi man ngag zab don sbrang rtsi'i bum bzang*.

DILGO KHYENTSE RINPOCHE: p. 21, Dilgo Khyentse Rinpoche, *The*

Heart Treasure of the Enlightened Ones, p. 157, and pp. 53–54. P. 22, ibid, p. 157.

SHECHEN GYALTSAP: Shechen Gyaltsap, *Byang chub kyi sems bsgom pa'i rim pa bdag 'dzin 'dzoms pa'i sman chen*, pp. 41–56.

GUNTHANG TENPAI DRÖNMÉ: Thubten Jinpa, *Songs of Spiritual Experience*, p. 35.

TENNYI LINGPA, PEMA TSEWANG GYALPO: Excerpts from *Kunzang Nyingthig* (*kun bzang snying thig*) quoted in Chögyal Ngakyi Wangpo, Ngawang Dargyé (chos rgyal ngag gi dbang po ngag dbang dar rgyas, 1736–1807), *Gter gsar rdzogs chen gyi khrid yig ma rig mun sel ye shes sgron me*, pp. 55–63.

SHAKYAMUNI BUDDHA: *Udanavarga (ched du mjod pa'i mtshoms)*.

THE SEVENTH DALAI LAMA, KELSANG GYATSO: The Seventh Dalai Lama, *Meditations to Transform the Mind*, p. 98.

GODRAGPA SONAM GYALTSEN: Tibetan text and translation in Stearns, *Hermit of Go Cliffs*, p. 153.

GAMPOPA: quoted orally by Dilgo Khyentse Rinpoche.

MILAREPA: extracted from Milarepa, *Mi la'i mgur 'bum* [Hundred Thousand Songs].

JIGME LINGPA: Jigme Lingpa, *Treasury of Precious Qualities*, p. 22.

PATRUL RINPOCHE: Story about Patrul Rinpoche told to the author by Nyoshul Khen Rinpoche.

Chapter 3. From Seed to Fruit, or the Law of Cause and Effect

SHANTIDEVA: Shantideva, *The Way of the Bodhisattva*, chap. 1, verse 28.

JETSÜN MINGYUR PALDRÖN: Jetsün Mingyur Paldrön, *Bka' gsang rdzogs pa chen po dkon mchog spyi 'dus khrid yig man ngag gsal sgron snying po*, pp. 17–18.

DILGO KHYENTSE RINPOCHE: Dilgo Khyentse Rinpoche, *The Heart of Compassion*, p. 90.

THE FOURTEENTH DALAI LAMA, TENZIN GYATSO: oral teachings given in Schvenedingen, Germany, 1998.

KANGYUR RINPOCHE: Nagarjuna, *Nagarjuna's Letter to a Friend with*

Commentary by Kangyur Rinpoche, Kangyur Rinpoche's commentary on verse 44.

Chapter 4. The Inherent Unsatisfactoriness of the World Conditioned by Ignorance

THE FOURTEENTH DALAI LAMA, TENZIN GYATSO: p. 39, oral teachings given in Schvenedingen, Germany, 1998. P. 42, teachings in Amaravati, India, 2005.

ASANGA: in Jamgön Kongtrul Lodrö Thayé, *Gdams ngag mdzod,* vol. 3, pp. 458–59.

DILGO KHYENTSE RINPOCHE: p. 40, Dilgo Khyentse Rinpoche, *The Heart of Compassion,* pp. 91–92. P. 41, Dilgo Khyentse Rinpoche, *The Heart Treasure of the Enlightened Ones,* pp. 117–18.

THE SEVENTH DALAI LAMA, KELSANG GYATSO: The Seventh Dalai Lama, *Meditations to Transform the Mind,* p. 233.

JIGME LINGPA: p. 42, *Treasury of Precious Qualities,* chap. 4, verses 3–5. P. 43, ibid., commentary on verse 5.

Chapter 5. Giving Up the Causes of Suffering

THE FOURTEENTH DALAI LAMA, TENZIN GYATSO: p. 46, oral teachings given in Schvenedingen, Germany, 1998. Author's translation. P. 48, oral teachings given in Toronto in 2004.

DILGO KHYENTSE RINPOCHE: *The Heart Treasure of the Enlightened Ones,* pp. 51–52.

NYOSHUL KHEN RINPOCHE: oral instruction given in Paro, Bhutan, in 1987, translated by the author.

SHABKAR: Shabkar Tsogdruk Rangdröl, *'Jam dbyangs sprul pa'i glegs bam,* pp. 404–5.

MILAREPA: Milarepa, *Mi la'i mgur 'bum.*

DRIGUNG JIGTEN GÖNPO: *Snying gtam gces bsdus.*

JAMGÖN KONGTRUL LODRÖ THAYÉ: Jamgön Kongtrul Lodrö Thayé, *Rgya chen bka' mdzod,* vol. 6, pp. 17–24.

PEMA LINGPA: Pema Lingpa, *Rig 'dzin padma gling pa yi zab gter chos*

mdzod, vol. 13 (PA), pp. 200–205. Translated at the monastery of Nyima-
lung in the home province of Pema Linpga, Bumthang, Bhutan, 1983.

PATRUL RINPOCHE: Story about Patrul Rinpoche told to the author by
Nyoshul Khen Rinpoche.

MILAREPA: Milarepa, *Mi la'i mgur 'bum*. Author's translation, conden-
sed from the Tibetan.

Chapter 6. Taking Refuge

THE FOURTEENTH DALAI LAMA, TENZIN GYATSO: oral teachings
given in Toronto in 2004.

PADMASAMBHAVA: Padmasambhava, *Dakini Teachings, a Collection of
Padmasambhava's Advice to the Dakini Yeshe Tsogyal*, pp. 11, 12, 20.

Chapter 7. Altruistic Love and Compassion

YONGEY MINGYUR RINPOCHE: Yongey Mingyur Rinpoche, *The Joy of
Living*, chap. 13, p. 178.

SHANTIDEVA: p. 79, Shantideva, *The Way of the Bodhisattva*, chap. 8,
verses 129–30. P. 85, ibid., chap. 3, verses 18–22.

THE FOURTEENTH DALAI LAMA, TENZIN GYATSO: p. 80, oral teachings given in Schvenedingen, Germany, 1998. P. 87, summarized and
adapted from Sa Sainteté Tenzin Gyatso, *Les voies spirituelles du bonheur*. English version: The Dalai Lama, *The Compassionate Life*.

NYOSHUL KHENPO RINPOCHE: oral teachings given in Paro, Bhutan,
in 1987, translated by the author.

SHABKAR: Shabkar, *The Life of Shabkar, the Autobiography of a Tibetan
Yogin*, pp. 422 and 501.

JIGME LINGPA: Jigme Lingpa, *Treasury of Precious Qualities*, chap. 7,
verses 4–7, pp. 59–60.

DILGO KHYENTSE RINPOCHE: p. 83, Dilgo Khyentse Rinpoche, *The
Heart Treasure of the Enlightened Ones*, pp. 2, 39, 45, and 66. P. 94, simpli-
fied from Dilgo Khyentse Rinpoche, *The Heart of Compassion*, pp. 107–12.

THE SEVENTH DALAI LAMA, KELSANG GYATSO: The Seventh Dalai
Lama, *Meditations to Transform the Mind*, p. 89.

KANGYUR RINPOCHE: Nagarjuna, *Nagarjuna's Letter to a Friend with Commentary by Kangyur Rinpoche.*

ATISHA: quoted in Shechen Gyaltsap, *Theg pa chen po'i blo sbyong gi man ngag zab don sbrang rtsi'i bum bzang,* pp. 340–41.

GYALSE THOGME: Excerpts from the biography of Gyalse Thogme by Palden Yeshe (dpal ldan ye shes), in the introduction to Dilgo Khyentse Rinpoche, *The Heart of Compassion.* Tibetan text: Gyalse Thogme, *Rgyal sras rin po che thogs med pa'i rnam thar bdud rtsi'i thigs pa.*

Chapter 8. The Six Perfections or Transcendent Virtues

SAKYA PANDITA: quoted in Shabkar, *Chos bshad gzhan phan zla ba,* pp. 578–79.

DRIGUNG DÖNDRUP CHÖGYAL: *Snying gtam gces bsdus,* p. 207.

JIGME LINGPA: p. 108, Jigme Lingpa, *Treasury of Precious Qualities,* verses 71–72, p. 87. P. 126, *Sgom phyogs dris len,* p. 5.

ATISHA: Atisha, *Mkha 'gdams kyi skyes bu dam pa rnams kyi gsung bgros thor bu ba rnams,* p. 4. Quoted in Patrul Rinpoche, *The Words of My Perfect Teacher.*

GESHE POTOWA RINCHEN SEL: extract from *Tshig lab ring mo* quoted in Shabkar, *O rgyan sprul pa'i glegs bam.*

DRIGUNG DONDRUP CHÖGYAL: *Snying gtam gces bsdus,* p. 196.

MIPHAM RINPOCHE: Mipham Rinpoche, *The Rdzong-gsar-prints of the Writings of 'Jam-mgon 'Ju Mi-pham-rgya-mtsho.*

KANGYUR RINPOCHE: p. III, Jigme Lingpa, *Treasury of Precious Qualities,* pp. 281–84. P. 113, ibid., pp. 319–21. P. 120, ibid, pp. 322–23. P. 122, ibid. pp. 324–29. P. 128, ibid., p. 335.

GAMPOPA: quote received orally.

CHENGAWA LODRÖ GYALTSEN: quoted in Shabkar, *Bka' gdams sprul pa'i glegs bam,* fol. 177b.

SHANTIDEVA: Shantideva, *The Way of the Bodhisattva,* chap. 5, verses 12–13, and chap. 6, verses 1–3, 10, 22, 41, 107–8.

SHECHEN GYALTSAP: Shechen Gyaltsap, *Theg pa chen po'i blo sbyong gi man ngag zab don sbrang rtsi'i bum bzang,* pp. 441–44.

PATRUL RINPOCHE: story about Patrul Rinpoche told to the author by Nyoshul Khen Rinpoche.

LANGRI THANGPA: p. 118, anecdotes told by Shabkar in his *Chos bshad gzhan phan zla ba*. P. 119, ibid.

SHAKYAMUNI BUDDHA: source not known.

MILAREPA: Milarepa, *Mi la'i mgur 'bum*.

DILGO KHYENTSE RINPOCHE: story told by Dilgo Khyentse Rinpoche.

GYALWA YANGÖNPA: oral quote collected by the author.

MILAREPA: Milarepa, *Mi la'i mgur 'bum*.

DZATRUL NGAWANG TENZIN NORBU: Dzatrul Ngawang Tenzin Norbu, *Rgyal sras lag len so bdun ma'i 'grel pa gzhung dang gdams ngag zung 'jug bdud rtsi'i bum bzang*, folio 87ff. English translation in appendix 3 of Dilgo Khyentse Rinpoche, *The Heart of Compassion*.

DRIGUNG JIGTEN GÖNPO: *Snying gtam gces bsdu*, p. 100.

RATNA LINGPA: Ratna Lingpa Rinchen Pal, *Chos rgyal ratna gling pa'i gter chos*, vol. 1 (Ka, *rnam thar*), p. 190.

Chapter 9. Purifying Obscurations and Acquiring Merit

DILGO KHYENTSE RINPOCHE: p. 132, adapted from Dilgo Khyentse Rinpoche, *The Heart Treasure of the Enlightened Ones*, pp. 68–70. P. 134, poem sent by Dilgo Khyentse Rinpoche to Chögyam Trungpa Rinpoche, translated by the Nalanda Translation Committee.

ANONYMOUS TEXT: *Nyon mongs pa lam du blangs pa'i chos*, in Jamgön Kongtrul Lodrö Thayé, *gdams sngags mdzod*, vol. 4, pp. 89–90.

JIGME LINGPA: *Sgom phyogs dris len*.

KANGYUR RINPOCHE: Jigme Lingpa, *Treasury of Precious Qualities*, p. 212.

Chapter 10. The Spiritual Master

KANGYUR RINPOCHE: p. 144, Jigme Lingpa, *Treasury of Precious Qualities*, pp. 191–97. P. 151, ibid., pp. 197–204.

DILGO KHYENTSE RINPOCHE: Dilgo Khyentse Rinpoche, *The Wish-Fulfilling Jewel*, p. 11.

JAMGÖN KONGTRUL LODRÖ THAYÉ: Jamgön Kongtrul Lodrö Thayé, *Bla med nang rgyud sde gsum gyi rgyab chos padma'i zhal gdams lam rim ye snying 'grel pa ye shes snang ba.*

DRIGUNG JIGTEN GÖNPO: This famous saying is quoted in numerous works, including Dilgo Khyentse Rinpoche, *The Wish-Fulfilling Jewel.*

SHABKAR: p. 149, Shabkar, *Bya btang tshogs drug rang grol gyis rang dang skal ldan gdul bya la mgrin pa gdams pa'i dang mdzod nas glu dbyangs dga' ston 'gyed pa rnams.* P. 150, Shabkar, *The Life of Shabkar,* chap. 10.

PATRUL RINPOCHE: Story about Patrul Rinpoche narrated to the author by Dilgo Khyentse Rinpoche.

Chapter 11. Understanding the Nature of the Mind

DILGO KHYENTSE RINPOCHE: p. 160, Dilgo Khyentse Rinpoche, *The Heart Treasure of the Enlightened Ones,* pp. 92–93. P. 161, ibid., pp. 107–9. P. 167, ibid., pp. 125–26. P. 169, Dilgo Khyentse Rinpoche, *The Heart of Compassion,* pp. 120, 132, 134. P. 171, Dilgo Khyentse Rinpoche, *The Heart Treasure of the Enlightened Ones,* commentary on verse 43, pp. 115–16. P. 173, Dilgo Khyentse Rinpoche, *The Hundred Verses of Advice,* extracts from commentaries on verses 51, 52, 53, 55, 56, and 74, pp. 96–97, 102, 131, 103, 104, 99.

MIPHAM RINPOCHE: p. 163, Mipham Rinpoche, *Cintamani,* p. 129. P. 168, Mipham Rinpoche, *Tshig gsum ngad kyi man ngag,* pp. 415–16.

NYENDRAK LUNGRIG NYIMA: Nyendrak Lungrig Nyima, *Sde gzhung sprul sku rin po che 'jam dbyangs kun dga' 'bstan pa'i rgyal mtshan la sog pa'i zhal gdams khag bzhugs,* pp. 67–68.

SHABKAR: p. 168, Shabkar, song 7 of *'od gsal rdzogs pa chen po'i khregs chod lta ba'i glu dbyangs sa lam ma lus myur du bgrod pa'i rtsal ldan mkha' lding gshog rlabs.* P. 171, Shabkar, *The Life of Shabkar,* p. 418.

MINLING TERCHEN GYURME DORJE: Minling Terchen Gyurme Dorje, *Smin gling gter chen rig 'dzin 'gyur med rdo rje'i gsung 'bum,* vol. 6 (Cha), p. 113. Translated at Yan-nga in the hills of western China, August 8, 1988.

GYALWA GOTSANGPA, GÖNPO DORJE: quoted by Shabkar in *O rgyan sprul pa'i glegs bam.*

PATRUL RINPOCHE: story about Patrul Rinpoche told to the translator by Nyoshul Khen Rinpoche. Translated from the Tibetan sound recording.

Chapter 12. The Hermit

SANGYE WÖN RE DHARMA SENGE: Sangye Wön Re Dharma Senge, *Byang chub dom du gnyer ba'i gcod yul ka rnams lam mkho ba'i ri chos rtsibs stong 'khor lo, in rtsib-ri spar-ma*, pp. 1–3.

GYALSE THOGME: Gyalse Thogme, *Rgyal sras thogs med kyi gsung thor bu.*

GODRAGPA SONAM GYALTSEN: Stearns, *Hermit of Go Cliffs*, p. 157.

GYALWA YANGÖNPA: Dudjom Rinpoche, *Ri chos bslab bya nyams len dmar khrid go bder brjod pa grub pa'i bcud len.*

JIGME LINGPA: *Sgom phyogs dris len*, p. 258.

DRIGUNG DÖNDRUP CHÖGYAL: *Snying gtam gces bsdus*, p. 194.

JETSÜN TRAKPA GYALTSEN: Jamgön Kongtrul Lodrö Thayé, *Gdams ngag mdzod*, vol. 6.

SHABKAR: p. 183, Shabkar, *The Life of Shabkar*, p. 55. P. 183, ibid, p. 49. P. 184, ibid., pp. 168–69. P. 184, ibid., p. 259.

RIGDZIN CHÖKYI TRAKPA: *Snying gtam gces bsdus*, p. 157.

LHATSÜN NAMKHAI JIGME: from manuscript copy, author's collection.

DUDJOM RINPOCHE: Dudjom Rinpoche, *Ri chos bslab bya nyams len dmar khrid go bder brjod pa grub pa'i bcud len.*

Chapter 13. Deepening Spiritual Practice

DRIGUNG DÖNDRUP CHÖGYAL: *Snying gtam gces bsdus*, p. 199.

PHAGMO DRUPA, DORJE GYALPO: *Snying gtam gces bsdus.*

KHYENTSE CHÖKYI LODRÖ: Khyentse Chökyi Lodrö, *The Complete Works of rdzong gsar mkhyen brtse rin po che 'jam dbyangs chos kyi blo gros*, vol. 2 (Kha), pp. 351–54. Translated at the monastery of Dzongsar Tashi Lhazé, eastern Tibet, 1988.

Chapter 14. View, Meditation, and Action

GYALWA LONGCHEN RABJAM: p. 195, Longchen Rabjam, *Man ngag rin po che'i mdzod* in *klong chen mdzod bdun*, p. 52. P. 198, Longchen Rabjam, *Ngang pa'i dri lan sprin gyi snying po*, vol. 1, pp. 351–52.

ATISHA: quoted in Shechen Gyaltsap, *Theg pa chen po'i blo sbyong gi man ngag zab don sbrang rtsi'i bum bzang*, vol. 6 (Cha), p. 397.

JETSÜN TARANATHA: Taranatha, *Rje btsun ta' ra na' tha'i zhal gdams mgur 'bum gyi skor*, vol. 1, p. 723.

THE FIFTH DALAI LAMA, NGAWANG LOBSANG GYATSO: quoted in Dilgo Khyentse Rinpoche, *The Heart of Compassion*.

DILGO KHYENTSE RINPOCHE: p. 197, modified from Dilgo Khyentse Rinpoche, *The Heart of Compassion*. P. 210, Dilgo Khyentse Rinpoche, *The Collected Works of Dilgo Khyentse*, vol. 3, commentary on Jigme Lingpa's *A Wondrous Ocean of Advice*, pp. 464, 473, 474, and 475.

GESHE CHAYULWA: Geshe Chayulwa, *Bka 'gdams kyi skyes bu dam pa rnams kyi gsung bgros thor bu ba rnams*, p. 89.

SHECHEN GYALTSAP: Selected verses of Shechen Gyaltsap in Shechen Rabjam, *The Great Medicine*. Tibetan text: Shechen Gyaltsap, *Byang chub kyi sems bsgom pa'i rim pa bdag 'dzin 'dzoms pa'i sman chen*, pp. 41–56.

DUDJOM RINPOCHE: p. 202, Dudjom Rinpoche, *Ri chos bslab bya nyams len dmar khrid go bder brjod pa grub pa'i bcud len*. P. 204, ibid. P. 212, ibid., pp. 23–33. P. 216, ibid.

RIGDZIN CHÖKYI TRAKPA: p. 202, *Snying gtam gces bsdus*, p. 157. P. 203, ibid., pp. 159–60.

THE SEVENTH DALAI LAMA, KELSANG GYATSO: The Seventh Dalai Lama, *Meditations to Transform the Mind*, p. 111.

DRIGUNG DÖNDRUP CHÖGYAL: *Snying gtam gces bsdus*, p. 207.

GAMPOPA: P. 206, quote taken orally. P. 210, *Blo ldan dga' ba'i rgya mtsho*. P. 221, quote taken orally.

MOKCHOKPA RINCHEN TSÖNDRU: Jamgön Kongtrul Lodrö Thayé, *Gdams ngag mdzod*, vol. 12, 499. These verses in English translation can be found in Jamgön Kongtrul, *Timeless Rapture*, pp. 91–93.

Mɪᴘʜᴀᴍ Rɪɴᴘᴏᴄʜᴇ: Mipham Rinpoche, *Cintamani*, p. 191.

Rᴀʜᴜʟᴀʙʜᴀᴅʀᴀ: from oral teachings of Khyentse Rinpoche based on Rahulabhadra, *Byang chub sems dpa'i spyod yul yongs su dag pa'i mdo'i don mdor bsdus pa*.

Pᴀᴛʀᴜʟ Rɪɴᴘᴏᴄʜᴇ: story about Patrul Rinpoche told to the author by Nyoshul Khen Rinpoche.

Sʜᴀʙᴋᴀʀ: Shabkar, *The Life of Shabkar*, pp. 535–36.

Rᴀɴɢʀɪɢ Rᴇᴘᴀ, Kᴜɴɢᴀ Lᴏᴅʀö: quoted in Shabkar, *O rgyan sprul pa'i glegs bam*, p. 421. See also *Rje btsun khyab bdag chen po rang rig ras chen gyi gsung 'gur dang zhal gdams 'chi med bdud rtsi'i rlabs 'phreng*.

Chapter 15. Exposing Faults

Dɪʟɢᴏ Kʜʏᴇɴᴛsᴇ Rɪɴᴘᴏᴄʜᴇ: Dilgo Khyentse Rinpoche, *The Heart Treasure of the Enlightened Ones*, p. 44.

Sʜᴀʙᴋᴀʀ: Shabkar, *The Life of Shabkar*, pp. 178–82.

Pᴀᴛʀᴜʟ Rɪɴᴘᴏᴄʜᴇ: p. 232, Patrul Rinpoche, *Dpal sprul o rgyan 'jigs med chos kyi dbang po'i gsung 'bum*, vol. 8 (Nya), p. 286. P. 235, ibid., p. 280. P. 246, ibid., p. 140.

Kᴀʟᴅᴇɴ Gʏᴀᴛsᴏ: Kalden Gyatso, *Yab rje bla ma skal ldan rgya mtsho'i gsung 'bum*, vol. 1, pp. 115–16.

Gᴜʀᴜ Cʜöᴋʏɪ Wᴀɴɢᴄʜᴜᴋ: Guru Chökyi Wangchuk, *Ma ni bka' 'bum chen mo*, pp. 54–56.

Rɪɴᴄʜᴇɴ Pʜᴜɴᴛsᴏᴋ: *Snying gtam gces bsdus*, p. 141.

Dᴏᴅʀᴜᴘ Tᴇɴᴘᴀɪ Nʏɪᴍᴀ: Dodrup Tenpai Nyima, *The Collected Works (gsung 'bum) of rdo grub chen 'Jigs-med-bstan-pa'i-nyi-ma*, vol. 3 (Ga), pp. 208–11.

Gʏᴀʟᴡᴀ Lᴏɴɢᴄʜᴇɴ Rᴀʙᴊᴀᴍ: Longchen Rabjam, *Klong-chen gsung thor bu*, vol. 2, p. 303.

Chapter 16. Overcoming Inner Demons

Mᴀᴄʜɪᴋ Lᴀᴘᴅʀöɴ: Machik Lapdrön, *Shes rab kyi pha rol tu phyin pa zab mo bcod kyi man ngag gi gzhung bka 'tshoms chen mo*, p. 7.

Jᴀᴛsʜöɴ Nʏɪɴɢᴘᴏ: Jatshön Nyingpo, *The Collected Revelations of rig 'dzin 'ja' tshon snying po*, pp. 307–35. Translated at the Palace of Great Bliss, Dechen Chöling Phodrang, in Bhutan, 1983. Translation published by Padmakara as *The Questions of Nyang Ben Tingzin Zangpo*.

Bibliography

Tibetan Language Sources

Anonymous. *Nyon mongs pa lam du blangs pa'i chos*. In Jamgön Kongtrul Lodrö Thayé, *Gdams ngag mdzod*.

Atisha. *Mkha 'gdams kyi skyes bu dam pa rnams kyi gsung bgros thor bu ba rnams* [Songs of the Kadampa masters]. 119 manuscript pages. In Kawaguchi's Collection, *bka' gdams kyi skyes bu dam pa rnams kyi gsung bgros thor bu ba rnams | dge slong blo bzang chos 'phel | (bka' gdams)*, call no.163, ref. no. 2243, folios 1a1–24a6.

Chögyal Ngakyi Wangpo, Ngawang Dargyé (chos rgyal ngag gi dbang po ngag dbang dar rgyas). *Gter gsar rdzogs chen gyi khrid yig ma rig mun sel ye shes sgron me*. Paro: Ngodrup Lama and Sherab Demy, 1979.

Dodrup Tenpai Nyima. *The Collected Works (gsung 'bum) of rdo grub chen 'Jigs-med-bstan-pa'i-nyi-ma*. Gangtok: Dodrub Chen Rinpoche, 1974–75.

Dudjom Rinpoche. *Ri chos bslab bya nyams len dmar khrid go bder brjod pa grub pa'i bcud len*. Originally translated and published by Konchog Tendzin (Matthieu Ricard). Ogyen Kunsang Chöling Monastery:1976. Revised for this collection.

Dzatrul Ngawang Tenzin Norbu (dza sprul ngag dbang bstan 'dzin nor bu). *Rgyal sras lag len so bdun ma'i 'grel pa gzhung dang gdams ngag zung 'jug bdud rtsi'i bum bzang* [Vase of amrita]. Woodblock edition. Thubten Chöling monastery, Solokhumbu, Nepal. A commentary on *The Thirty-Seven Practices of the Bodhisattvas*.

Gampopa. *Blo ldan dga' ba'i rgya mtsho.*

Geshe Chayulwa. *Bka 'gdams kyi skyes bu dam pa rnams kyi gsung bgros thor bu ba rnams* [Kadampa masters lyrics].

Guru Chökyi Wangchuk. *Ma ni bka' 'bum chen mo.* Thimphu: Kunsang Topgey, 1976.

Gyalse Thogme. *Rgyal sras rin po che thogs med pa'i rnam thar bdud rtsi'i thigs pa.* 23 folios. Thimphu: Kunzang Topgye.

———. *Rgyal sras thogs med kyi gsung thor bu* [Collection of the writings of Gyalse Thogme]. Thimphu: National Library of Bhutan, 1985.

Gyalwa Longchen Rabjam. *See* Longchen Rabjam.

Jamgön Kongtrul Lodrö Thayé, Yonten Gyatso ('jam mgon kong sprul blo gros mtha' yas, yon tan rgya mtsho). *Bla med nang rgyud sde gsum gyi rgyab chos padma'i zhal gdams lam rim ye snying 'grel pa ye shes snang ba,* Jamgön Kongtrul's commentary on the *Lam rim ye shes snying po,* included in the *Rin chen gter mdzod chen mo,* vol. 63. Paro: Sherab Ngodrup Drimey, 1976; and Delhi: Shechen Publications, new edition in press.

———. *Gdams ngag mdzod.* Delhi: Shechen Publications, 1999.

———. *Rgya chen bka 'mdzod.* Delhi: Shechen Publications, 2000.

Jatshön Nyingpo. *The Collected Revelations of rig 'dzin 'ja' tshon snying po.* In *'Ja' tshon pod drug.* Darjeeling: Taklung Tsetrul Pema Wangyal, 1979.

Jetsün Milarepa. *See* Milarepa.

Jetsün Mingyur Paldrön (mi 'gyur dpal sgron). *Bka' gsang rdzogs pa chen po dkon mchog spyi 'dus khrid yig man ngag gsal sgron snying po.* Mindroling Monastery, Clement Town, India: D. G. Khochen Tulku.

Jetsün Taranatha. *See* Taranatha.

Jigme Lingpa. *Sgom phyogs dris len.* Paro: Ngodrup and Sherab Drimay, 1976.

Kalden Gyatso. *Yab rje bla ma skal ldan rgya mtsho'i gsung 'bum.* 4 vols. China/Tibet: kan su'u mi rigs dpe skrun khang, 1999.

Khyentse Chökyi Lodrö. *The Complete Works of rdzong gsar mkhyen brtse rin po che 'jam dbyangs chos kyi blo gros.* Gangtok: 1981–85.

Longchen Rabjam. *Man ngag rin po che'i mdzod.* In *Klong chen mdzod bdun,* section Ka, vol. 3 (Ga) in the a' dzom chos sgar edition.

———. *Ngang pa'i dri lan sprin gyi snying po.* In *Klong-chen gsung thor bu by Klong chen Rab 'byams pa Dri-med 'od-zer, Printed from the A 'dzom chos sgar Blocks.* 2 vols. Delhi: Sanje Dorje, 1973.

Machik Lapdrön. *Shes rab kyi pha rol tu phyin pa zab mo bcod kyi man ngag gi gzhung bka 'tshoms chen mo.* In Jamgön Kongtrul, *gdams ngag mdzod,* vol. 13 (Pha).

Milarepa (btsun rje mi la ras pa). *Hundred Thousand Songs (mi la'i mgur 'bum).* Edited by Tsang Nyon Heruka (gtsang smyon he ru ka rus pa'i rgyan can). Gangtok: Sherab Gyaltshen, 1983.

Minling Terchen Gyurme Dorje (smin gling gter chen 'gyur med rdo rje). *Smin gling gter chen rig 'dzin 'gyur med rdo rje'i gsung 'bum.* Dehradun: Khochhen Tulku, 1998.

Mipham Rinpoche. *Cintamani.* Varanasi: Tarthang Tulku, 1967. A collection of instructions by Mipham Rinpoche.

———. *The Rdzong-gsar-prints of the Writings of 'Jam-mgon 'Ju Mipham-rgya-mtsho.* In *The Expanded Redaction of the Complete Works of 'Ju Mi-pham,* vol. 27. Delhi: Shechen Publications, 1984.

———. *Tshig gsum ngad kyi man ngag.* In *The Expanded Redaction of the Complete Works of 'Ju Mi pham,* vol. 19. Delhi: Lama Ngodrup and Sherab Drimey, Shechen Publications, 1993.

Nyendrak Lungrig Nyima. *Sde gzhung sprul sku rin po che 'jam dbyangs kun dga' 'bstan pa'i rgyal mtshan la sog pa'i zhal gdams khag bzhugs.* Kathmandu: Ven. Khenpo Apey.

Palden Yeshe (dpal ldan ye shes). *Rgyal sras rin po che thogs med pa'i rnam thar bdud rtsi'i thigs pa.* 23 folios. Thimphu: Kunzang Topgye.

Patrul Rinpoche. *Dpal sprul o rgyan 'jigs med chos kyi dbang po'i gsung 'bum.* 8 vols. Khren tu: Si khron mi rigs dpe skrun khang, 2009.

Pema Lingpa. *Rig 'dzin padma gling pa yi zab gter chos mdzod*, vol. 13 (Pa). Thimphu: Kunzang Tobgay, 1975–76.

Rahulabhadra. *Byang chub sems dpa'i spyod yul yongs su dag pa'i mdo'i don mdor bsdus pa (Bodhisattvagocaraparishuddhisutrarthasamgraha)*. In Golden Tenjur, vol. 120, ff.358r –361r (pp. 715–21). Tianjing Edition, 1988.

Rangrig Repa, Kunga Lodro. *Rje btsun khyab bdag chen po rang rig ras chen gyi gsung 'gur dang zhal gdams 'chi med bdud rtsi'i rlabs 'phreng* (Kha). New Delhi: Ugyen Dorje, 1976.

Ratna Lingpa Rinchen Pal (ratna gling pa rin chen dpal). *Chos rgyal ratna gling pa'i gter chos* [The Collected Rediscovered Teachings of Ratna gling pa]. Darjeeling: Taklung Tsetrul Pema Wangyal, 1977–79.

Sangye Wön Re Dharma Senge (sangs rgyas dbon ras dharma seng ge). *Byang chub dom du gnyer ba'i gcod yul ka rnams lam mkho ba'i ri chos rtsibs stong 'khor lo*. In *rtsib-ri spar-ma*, a collection of advice from the Kagyupa and Nyingmapa traditions (*dkar rnying gi skyes chen du ma'i phyag rdzogs kyi gdams ngag gnad bsdus nyer mkho rin po che'i gter mdzod rtsibs ri'i par ma*), vol. 23 (A).

Shabkar Tsogdruk Rangdröl (zhabs dkar tshogs drug rang grol). *Bka' gdams sprul pa'i glegs bam*.

———. *Bya btang tshogs drug rang grol gyis rang dang skal ldan gdul bya la mgrin pa gdams pa'i dang mdzod nas glu dbyangs dga' ston 'gyed pa rnams* [Songs of Shabkar], vols. 3–5. Delhi: Shechen Publications, 2003.

———. *Chos bshad gzhan phan nyi ma*, SH60. In *Zhabs dkar tshogs drug rang grol gyi bka' 'bum*, vol. 10 (Tha). Delhi: Shechen Publications, 2003.

———. *Chos bshad gzhan phan zla ba*. In *Zhabs dkar tshogs drug rang grol gyi bka' 'bum*, vol. 10 (Tha). Delhi: Shechen Publications, 2003.

———. *'Jam dbyangs sprul pa'i glegs bam*. In *Zhabs dkar tshogs drug rang grol gyi bka' 'bum*, vol. 8 (Nya). Delhi: Shechen Publications, 2003.

———. *O rgyan sprul pa'i glegs bam*. In *Zhabs dkar tshogs drug rang grol gyi bka' 'bum*, vol. 9. Delhi: Shechen Publications, 2003.

—. *'Od gsal rdzogs pa chen po'i khregs chod lta ba'i glu dbyangs sa lam ma lus myur du bgrod pa'i rtsal ldan mkha' lding gshog rlabs* [The Flight of the garuda]. In *Zhabs dkar tshogs drug rang grol gyi bka' 'bum*, vol. 13 (Pa). Delhi: Shechen Publications, 2003.

Shakyamuni Buddha. *Udanavarga (ched du mjod pa'i mtshoms)*. A collection of verses taken from the Buddhist canon compiled by Dharmatrata (early fourth century).

Shechen Gyaltsap. *Byang chub kyi sems bsgom pa'i rim pa bdag 'dzin 'dzoms pa'i sman chen*. In *The Collected Works of Zhe chen rgyal tshab padma rnam rgyal*, vol. 5 (Ca). Delhi: Shechen Publications, 1975–85.

—. *Rdo rje theg pa'i thun mong gi sngon 'gro spyi la sbyor chog pa'i khrid yig kun mkhyen zhal lung rnam grol shing rta*.

—. *Theg pa chen po'i blo sbyong gi man ngag zab don sbrang rtsi'i bum bzang*. In *The Collected Works of Zhe chen rgyal tshab padma rnam rgyal*, vol. 6 (Cha). Delhi: Shechen Publications, 1975–85.

—. *Zhabs dkar tshogs drug rang grol gyi bka' 'bum* [The chariot of complete liberation, oral transmissions of the omniscient ones, instructions for all the preliminary practices of Vajrayana]. In *The Collected Works of Zhe chen rgyal tshab padma rnam rgyal*, vol. 7. Paro: Khyentse Rinpoche, 1975–94.

Snying gtam gces bsdus. An anonymous compilation of pieces of advice published in India. Publisher unknown.

Taranatha. *Rje btsun ta' ra na' tha'i zhal gdams mgur 'bum gyi skor*. In *The Collected Works of Jo-nang rje-btsun Taranatha, sman rtsis shes rig dpe mdzod*. Leh, Ladakh: C. Namgyal and Tsewang Taru, 1982.

European Language Sources

The Dalai Lama. *The Compassionate Life*. Somerville, Mass.: Wisdom Publications, 2003.

Dilgo Khyentse Rinpoche. *The Collected Works of Dilgo Khyentse*. 3 vols. Boston: Shambhala Publications, 2010–11.

———. *The Excellent Path to Enlightenment: Oral Teachings on the Root Text of Jamyang Khyentse Wangpo*. Ithaca, N.Y.: Snow Lion, 1996.

———. *The Heart of Compassion: The Thirty-Seven Verses on the Practice of a Bodhisattva*. Boston: Shambhala Publications, 2007.

———. *The Heart Treasure of the Enlightened Ones*. Boston: Shambhala Publications, 1993.

———. *The Hundred Verses of Advice: Tibetan Buddhist Teachings on What Matters Most*. Translated by the Padmakara Translation Group. Boston: Shambhala Publications, 2002.

———. *The Wish-Fulfilling Jewel: The Practice of Guru Yoga according to the Longchen Nyingthig Tradition*. Boston: Shambhala Publications, 1999.

The Fourteenth Dalai Lama. *See* the Dalai Lama; Sa Sainteté Tenzin Gyatso.

Jamgön Kongtrul, comp. *Timeless Rapture: Inspired Verse from the Shangpa Masters*. Translated and introduced by Ngawang Zangpo. Ithaca, N.Y.: Snow Lion Publications, 2003.

Jigme Lingpa. *Treasury of Precious Qualities: Commentary by Longchen Yeshe Dorje, Kangyur Rinpoche*. Rev. ed. Boston: Shambhala Publications, 2010.

Nagarjuna. *Nagarjuna's Letter to a Friend with Commentary by Kangyur Rinpoche*. Translated by the Padmakara Translation Group. Ithaca, N.Y.: Snow Lion, 2005.

Padmasambhava. *Dakini Teachings, a Collection of Padmasambhava's Advice to the Dakini Yeshe Tsogyal*. Translated from the Tibetan by Erik Pema Kunsang. Hong Kong: Rangjung Yeshe Publications, 2004.

Patrul Rinpoche. *The Words of My Perfect Teacher*. Translated by the Padmakara Translation Group. Boston: Shambhala Publications, 1994.

Sa Sainteté Tenzin Gyatso. *Les voies spirituelles du bonheur*. Paris: Presses du Châtelet, 2002. English translation published as the Dalai Lama, *The Compassionate Life*, Somerville, Mass.: Wisdom Publications, 2003.

The Seventh Dalai Lama. *Meditations to Transform the Mind.* Edited and translated by Glenn H. Mullin. Ithaca. N.Y.: Snow Lion, 1999.

Shabkar. *The Life of Shabkar, the Autobiography of a Tibetan Yogin.* Translated by Matthieu Ricard. Ithaca, N.Y.: Snow Lion, 2001.

Shantideva. *The Way of the Bodhisattva: A Translation of the Bodhicharyāvatāra.* Translated by the Padmakara Translation Group. Boston: Shambhala Publications, 1997.

Shechen Rabjam. *The Great Medicine That Conquers Clinging to the Notion of Reality: Steps in Meditation on the Enlightened Mind.* Boston: Shambhala Publications, 2007. Root verses of Shechen Gyaltsap with commentary by Shechen Rabjam.

Stearns, Cyrus. *Hermit of Go Cliffs: Timeless Instructions from a Tibetan Mystic.* Boston: Wisdom Publications, 2000.

Tenzin Gyatso. *See* Sa Sainteté Tenzin Gyatso; The Dalai Lama.

Thubten Jinpa and Jaś Elsner, trans. *Songs of Spiritual Experience: Tibetan Buddhist Poems of Insight and Awakening.* Boston: Shambhala Publications, 2000.

Yeshe Tsogyal. *The Lotus-Born: The Life Story of Padmasambhava.* Translated by Erik Pema Kunsang. Hong Kong: Rangjung Yeshe Publications, 2004.

Yongey Mingyur Rinpoche. *The Joy of Living: Unlocking the Secret and Science of Happiness.* New York: Harmony Books, 2007.

————. *Joyful Wisdom: Embracing Change and Finding Freedom.* New York: Harmony Books, 2009.

Biographical Notes

ASANGA (thogs med, fourth century)—one of the greatest exponents of the teachings of the Great Vehicle; cofounder with his brother Vasubandhu of the Yogacara or Cittamatra philosophical school; and author of the *Five Teachings of Maitreya*, known as such because he is considered to have received them from Maitreya, the future Buddha. These works, which deal in particular with the buddha-nature present in all beings, are a core part of the higher studies of all the four schools of Tibetan Buddhism, although they are viewed somewhat differently by them, some considering these texts as expressing the real sense of the Buddha's understanding, and others the provisional, or interpretable meaning of his teaching.

ATISHA, also called Shri Jñana Dipamkara (982–1054)—scholar and Indian Buddhist master born into a royal family in Bengal. After studying in India with Vajrayana masters of the Diamond Vehicle, he went to Sumatra where he remained for twelve years with his principal teacher, whose teaching concentrated on the practice of bodhichitta, the "mind of enlightenment," and the techniques of mind-training, which Atisha made the heart of his practice and later teaching.

In 1040, at the invitation of a local king, he went to Tibet. He spent the rest of his life there, playing a key role in the second period of propagation of Buddhism, particularly in the transmission of teachings on mind-training. He also argued for a return to strict monastic discipline.

He is credited with more than two hundred volumes of original texts and translations. His most famous work is the *Lamp of the Path of*

Enlightenment (byang chub lam gyi sgron ma), which is the origin for the gradual path practiced by the Gelugpa school.

His chief disciple was Dromtönpa, the founder of the Kadampa school.

BUDDHA. *See* SHAKYAMUNI BUDDHA

CHENGAWA LODRÖ GYALTSEN (spyan snga ba blo gros rgyal mtshan, 1402–72).

CHÖKYI LODRÖ. *See* KHYENTSE CHÖKYI LODRÖ

DHARMA SENGE. *See* SANGYE WÖN RE DHARMA SENGE

DILGO KHYENTSE RINPOCHE (dil mgo mkhyen brtse rin po che bkra shis dpal 'byor, 1910–91)—one of the last representatives of a generation of great Tibetan masters who were educated and did their spiritual training exclusively in Tibet. He spent twenty-two years in solitary meditation retreat.

He was a discoverer of spiritual treasures hidden by Padmasambhava for future generations, and a leading master of Dzogchen, the Great Perfection. As an exemplary representative of the nonsectarian movement, he was renowned for his ability to transmit the teachings of each Buddhist lineage according to its own tradition. There are few contemporary lamas who have not received teachings from him, and very many of them, including His Holiness the Fourteenth Dalai Lama, revered him as one of their principal masters. Khyentse Rinpoche never ceased to inspire those who met him with his monumental presence, simplicity, dignity, and humor.

He was born in 1910 in the valley of Denkhok, in eastern Tibet. His father was a local dignitary. As a child, Rinpoche manifested a strong desire to devote himself entirely to spiritual life. His father, who had other ambitions for him, opposed it strongly. But when his son had a serious accident, his stubbornness ended since lamas he respected predicted that the child would not live long if he was not allowed to follow his aspiration.

At the age of eleven, Khyentse Rinpoche met his principal teacher,

Shechen Gyaltsap Pema Namgyal (see biographical notes), who recognized him as the reincarnation of the wisdom mind of the first Khyentse Rinpoche, Jamyang Khyentse Wangpo (1820–92). He also studied with some fifty other great masters.

From fifteen to twenty-eight, he spent almost all his time in silent retreat, meditating in caves and hermitages isolated in the mountains, sometimes simply in the shelter of an overhang.

Then he spent several years with Dzongsar Khyentse Chökyi Lodro (1896–1959), who was also a reincarnation of the first Khyentse. After receiving many empowerments from him, Rinpoche told him he wanted to spend the rest of his days in solitary meditation. But his master answered him, "The time has come for you to pass on to others all the precious teachings you have received." From then on Rinpoche worked constantly to benefit beings with the Khyentses' characteristic tireless energy.

After leaving Tibet because of the Chinese invasion, he sought refuge in Bhutan and from there, traveled throughout the Himalayas, India, Southeast Asia, and the West to transmit and explain the Dharma.

Wherever he was, he got up before dawn to pray and meditate for a few hours before embarking on an uninterrupted series of activities, late into the night. Every day he accomplished an impressive amount of work with complete peace of mind and apparently without any effort.

He was also a tireless builder and restorer of stupas, monasteries, and temples in Tibet, Bhutan, India, and Nepal. He became the most respected master of the Bhutanese, starting with the royal family. During the last years of his life, Rinpoche went three times to Tibet, where he participated in the restoration of over two hundred temples and monasteries, including Samye and Mindroling.

In Nepal, he transplanted the rich tradition of Shechen in its new home in exile, Shechen Tennyi Dargyeling, a magnificent monastery, now headed by Khyentse Rinpoche's grandson, Shechen Rabjam Rinpoche, and by Khyentse Rinpoche's own incarnation, Dilgo Khyentse Yangsi Rinpoche.

After the systematic destruction of books and libraries in Tibet, many books survived in only one or two copies. Rinpoche strove for many years to publish everything he could from Tibet's extraordinary legacy of Buddhist teachings, some four hundred titles in total.

In 1975, he went to the West for the first time, after which he returned regularly. He taught in many countries and especially in Dordogne, France, where he had established his headquarters.

In 1991, he showed the first signs of illness. After a final retreat of three and a half months, he visited some of his disciples, who were also in retreat, to remind them that the ultimate master is beyond birth, death, and any physical manifestation. Soon after, he showed new signs of sickness. On September 27, 1991, at nightfall, he asked his attendants to help him sit upright. In the early hours of the morning, his breathing stopped, and his mind merged with the absolute space.

His complete works include twenty-five volumes of spiritual treasures (termas), meditation texts, poems, and commentaries.

DODRUP TENPAI NYIMA (rdo grub chen 'jigs med bstan pa'i nyi ma, 1865–1926)—known from a young age as an emanation of the previous Dodrupchen, he was enthroned at the age of five and received many teachings, especially Shantideva's famous *The Way of the Bodhisattva*, which he received at Dzogchen Monastery from Patrul Rinpoche. At the age of eight, he gave this teaching himself before a large assembly of monks and laypeople. He studied with the greatest masters of his time and began to teach continually.

Suffering from poor health, he had to spend the last years of his life in solitary retreat, studying, practicing, and composing treatises highly praised by eminent scholars but only teaching his principal disciples. His brother, seeing how he went on studying relentlessly, asked him when he would stop. He replied, "When I have reached perfect enlightenment."

His contemporaries describe him as being almost childlike, very easygoing, without any pride. But as he had perfect control of his mind, all who entered his presence felt overwhelmed.

One day, without leaving his hermitage, he dedicated a stupa that was two days away on horseback. When he threw rice grains, as is done traditionally in this ritual, they landed on the stupa.

While he was writing an important commentary, he asked his assistant to wrap up the manuscript in progress and leave it on a shelf for his successor to complete the work. Then he became very ill and died, while extraordinary signs manifested around him.

Drigung Döndrup Chögyal ('bri gung don grub chos rgyal, 1668–1718) —the incarnation of Rigdzin Chökyi Trakpa.

Drigung Jigten Gönpo, Rinchen Pal ('bri gung 'jigs rten mgon po rin chen dpal, 1143–1217)—also known as Rinchen Pal, Jigten Sumgön, Drigung Kyöpa, and Drigung Palzin ('bri gung dpal 'dzin) was born in eastern Tibet, and from an early age showed signs of his exceptional abilities. At the age of eight, he saw in meditation that all phenomena of samsara and nirvana are appearances without substance, like reflections in a mirror.

Many people came to him to receive teachings. He heard one day of Phagmo Drupa and knew immediately that he was his master. He immediately made the long and difficult journey to central Tibet to see him, and remained with him for two and a half years. Phagmo Drupa transmitted all his teachings to him and designated him as his successor. When Phagmo Drupa left this world, all the disciples present saw a vajra light emanate from his heart and dissolve in the heart of Drigung Kyöpa. The latter then gave away everything he had and went to meditate in a cave for seven years. He later founded the monastery of Drigung Jang-chub Ling, the largest of the Drigung Kagyu school, and spent the rest of his life teaching there.

Dudjom Rinpoche, Jigdral Yeshe Dorje (bDud 'joms' jigs bral ye shes rdo rje, 1904–87)—a direct descendant of King Trisong Det-sen (seventh century), Dudjom Rinpoche was born while his previous incarnation was still alive. The first Dudjom, before he died, gave specific instructions to find his successor, specifying that he would arrive there before them. When his aides went to find the child, the latter, who was already three years old, recognized them and called them by name.

At the age of fourteen, he publicly gave the transmission of the *Collection of Precious Treasures,* which takes several months. A discoverer of spiritual treasures, he soon became famous as both a remarkable scholar and an extraordinary spiritual master. His original works and compilations of past texts run to more than fifty volumes. He also assumed the role of supreme authority of the Nyingma school. Another noteworthy detail for a Tibetan master of his rank was that he decided to spend the last years of his life in Dordogne, France, where he passed away in January 1987.

DZATRUL NGAWANG TENZIN NORBU (dza sprul ngag dbang bstan 'dzin nor bu, 1867–1940)—a great scholar and accomplished yogi of the Nyingma school from southwestern Tibet. He founded the monastery of Rongpu Do-Ngak Chöling near Mount Everest, which he made his residence, gradually attracting numerous men and women disciples. He also founded monasteries in the Sherpa country of Nepal.

With his great energy and acute intelligence, he became famous in the region, earning the nickname "the Buddha of Rongpu," and even impressed the members of the first expedition to Everest in 1924 and those of subsequent expeditions.

He composed many works, some of which were unfortunately destroyed by the Chinese invasion. Those that could be saved total nine volumes.

THE FIFTH DALAI LAMA, NGAWANG LOBSANG GYATSO (Ngag dbang blo bzang rgya mtsho, 1617–82)—The Fifth Dalai Lama, revered as the "Great Fifth," was not only a remarkable spiritual master but also an enlightened political leader. He became the spiritual mentor of the Mongol ruler Gushri Khan and helped unify the different parts of Tibet. Of all the Dalai Lamas, it is he who exercised the greatest political power. The structure that he provided for the Tibetan government remained more or less the same until the Chinese invasion in 1959.

In 1645, on a hill in Lhasa where there was a pavilion founded by King Songtsen Gampo (609 or 613–650), he built the huge Potala Palace, which became the center of the Tibetan government. He also established the Chakpori medical school that was active until its destruction by the Chinese army in 1959. He was a visionary master, who adopted a nonsectarian attitude toward the various Buddhist schools.

THE FOURTEENTH DALAI LAMA, TENZIN GYATSO (bstan 'dzin rgya mtsho, born 1935)—the present Dalai Lama was recognized when he was two years old as the successor to the Thirteenth Dalai Lama, Thubten Gyatso. At twenty-four, he fled Tibet after the Chinese invasion and the Lhasa rebellion. He is the first Dalai Lama who has been forced to spend most of his life outside his country.

Hosted by India, he finally settled in Dharamsala, where he immediately devoted himself to the preservation of the Tibetan spiritual and cultural heritage.

Universally respected by all traditions of Tibetan Buddhism, the Fourteenth Dalai Lama is a great unifier who strives to study, practice, and transmit the teachings of all schools of Tibetan Buddhism. He emphasizes the importance of selfless love and compassion and often says: "My religion is kindness." As spokesman for the Tibetan cause in the world, he describes his commitment as a fight for justice. He was the instigator of a democratic system for the Tibetan government in exile.

Over thirty years he has established a running dialogue with the scientific community, which has led in particular to research programs in neuroscience to study the short- and long-term effects of mind-training on the brain.

For his efforts to promote human brotherhood and world peace and a sense of universal responsibility and nonviolence, he was awarded the Nobel Peace Prize in 1989. He describes himself as "a simple Buddhist monk."

GAMPOPA SONAM RINCHEN (sgam po pa bsod nams rin chen, 1079–1153)—born in eastern Tibet, he was originally a doctor, married with two children, when an epidemic decimated his family. He vowed at the bedside of his dying wife to devote the rest of his life to the Dharma. At the age of twenty-six, he took monastic vows and began studying and practicing Buddhism with Kadampa masters, but he still could not recognize the nature of his mind.

At thirty-two, simply hearing the name of Milarepa filled him with such faith that he almost lost consciousness. His only wish was to meet that master and become his disciple. He received the highest teachings of Vajrayana from him, and putting them into practice for ten years, attained an advanced level of realization.

He spent the rest of his life guiding thousands of disciples and left as his testament *The Jewel Ornament of Liberation*. In this work, he combined the gradual path of the Kadampa tradition and the instructions that Milarepa had transmitted to him on Mahamudra, the Great Seal of ultimate reality. Among his chief disciples was Dusum Khyenpa (1110–93), who became the first Karmapa.

GESHE CHAYULWA (1075–1138).

GESHE POTOWA RINCHEN SEL (1031–1105).

GODRAGPA SONAM GYALTSEN (ko brag pa bsod nams rgyal mtshan 1170–1249)—a master of the Sakya school, born in Dingri, in Western Tibet, he also received teachings from other schools, particularly from the famous Bengali master Vibhutichandra. After five years of meditation at the foot of Mount Kailash, he attained the highest realization.

He founded the monastery of Godrag, from which is derived the name by which he became famous. He was best known for his mastery of meditation and specific methods to overcome obstacles to spiritual progress, which brought him a large number of disciples.

His songs of spiritual realization helped to spread his fame far beyond monastic circles, to Tibetan leaders, followers of all schools, and even the Mongol royal court. His poetry, in sober contrast to the traditional ornaments imposed by the canons of Indian poetry that served as a standard reference in Tibet, freely expresses his impressions of the majestic landscapes of the solitary regions where he spent most of his life. His most famous disciple, Yangönpa (yang dgon pa), founded a branch of the Drugpa Kagyu school and had a great influence on Tibetan Buddhism in general.

GUNTHANG TENPAI DRÖNMÉ (1762–1822).

GURU CHÖKYI WANGCHUK (gu ru chos kyi dbang phyug, 1212–70)—a great master and revealer of spiritual treasures of the Nyingma school, he was born in Lhodrag, in southern Tibet. At the age of thirteen, he discovered an inventory of the treasures that he was destined to reveal. He also became the first chronicler of the tradition of treasures. His spiritual consort, Jomo Menmo, was herself a treasure-revealer.

Among the many texts he discovered in this way is a cycle of practices that still provides the basis for sacred dance ceremonies in honor of Padmasambhava held every year in most monasteries of the Nyingma school.

GYALSE THOGME (rgyal sras thogs med, 1295–1369)—born in central Tibet, he showed from an early age signs of great compassion. The suffering of others always made him sad, and their happiness made him happy.

At the age of fourteen, realizing that the apparent pleasures of samsara were suffering, he took the vows of a novice and, from sixteen, he received teachings from many masters of all schools. With his brilliant mind and unparalleled determination, he very quickly mastered a large number of texts and made rapid progress in his inner practice. He began to teach and write commentaries clarifying the meaning of the teachings. On the basis of the great difficulties he encountered, he wrote a famous text entitled *Thirty-Seven Stanzas on the Practice of Bodhisattvas* that summarizes the bodhisattva path.

Thousands of people came to see him, attracted by his goodness and his perfect integrity and ability to teach students according to their particular needs.

Applying the conduct of the bodhisattva to perfection, he gave away everything he had without hesitation, until he had no more food to eat. He almost never lay down but would remain sitting, day and night. It became clear, on several occasions, that he could take the illnesses of others upon himself, and the mere fact of meeting him aroused faith, love, and compassion. Nobody ever heard him say a harsh word to anyone.

GYALWA GOTSANGPA, GÖNPO DORJE (rgod tshang pa mgon po rdo rje, 1189–1258)—one of the greatest yogis, hermits, and spiritual masters of the Drukpa Kagyu lineage. He spent much of his life in caves, particularly around Mount Kailash, and became famous for his attitude of complete renunciation. His writings on altruistic love, compassion, and pure vision are particularly inspiring.

In his youth he was a talented and seductive actor. He traveled the country with a troupe that performed music, song, and dance in the streets of towns and villages.

At sixteen, inspired by the devotion he witnessed during his visits to Lhasa, he felt a distaste for the ordinary activities of the world and wanted to get to know the teachings of Buddhism. He studied extensively and received teachings from many masters, especially of the Kadam, Kagyu, and Shi Che traditions.

When he heard the name of Tsangpa Gyare, the lama who was to become his principal teacher, he was overcome by deep devotion. When he finally met him, Tsangpa Gyare simply exclaimed: "Here you are! Wonderful!"

He spent many years in meditation in solitary places and was able to withstand the most extreme difficulties, refusing to consider obstacles as a problem. On the death of his master, he decided to apply his final advice to the letter: "Give up all ordinary concerns and remain in the solitude of the mountains." He spent many years meditating in caves, particularly around Mount Kailash. At Ralung, while he was practicing in a hut, a lake overflowed and water flooded into his shelter, but he remained in meditation, his body half submerged.

He spent the last years of his life establishing monasteries that attracted thousands of followers. He began the tradition of pilgrimage around Mount Kailash, for which he designated the route.

GYALWA LONGCHEN RABJAM. *See* LONGCHEN RABJAM

GYALWA YANGÖNPA (rgyal ba yang dgon pa, 1213–87).

JAMGÖN KONGTRUL LODRÖ THAYÉ ('jam mgon kong sprul blo gros mtha' yas yon tan rgya mtsho, 1813–99)—born in eastern Tibet into a family of the Bönpo tradition, he subsequently received a Buddhist education. From an early age, he showed signs of his extraordinary capacities.

His open-mindedness led him to study with masters of all schools, and his keen intelligence enabled him to quickly master many kinds of teaching, including those on medicine. He spent his whole life writing, meditating, and teaching. Flying in the face of custom, he refused to have servants despite his rank.

His major contribution to Buddhism was the "Ri-me" (*ris med*) or nonsectarian movement, which he created with Jamyang Khyentse Wangpo who was both his master and his student, to overcome the biased views that divided the various schools, while maintaining their distinct identities and the specific characteristics of their instructions.

His vast erudition enabled him to compose, among other works, the *Five Great Treasuries*, a veritable encyclopedia of Buddhism in more than ninety volumes that brings together the principal teachings of the major and minor lineages of Tibet.

JATSHÖN NYINGPO (rig 'dzin 'ja' tshon snying po, 1585–1656).

JETSÜN MILAREPA. *See* MILAREPA

JETSÜN MINGYUR PALDRÖN (mi 'gyur dpal sgron, 1699–1769).

JETSÜN TARANATHA. *See* TARANATHA

JETSÜN TRAKPA GYALTSEN. *See* TRAKPA GYALTSEN

JIGME KHYENTSE RINPOCHE ('jigs med mkhyen brtse rin po che nus ldan rdo rje, b. 1964)—the youngest son of Kangyur Rinpoche (see biographical notes), he was recognized as one of Khyentse Chökyi Lodrö's emanations. He was educated by his father and other contemporary masters like Dilgo Khyentse Rinpoche, Dudjom Rinpoche, and Trulshik Rinpoche. Fluent in English and French, respected for his profound teachings and his perfect humility, he travels the world tirelessly to guide his students on every continent.

JIGME LINGPA (rig 'dzin 'jigs med gling pa, 1729–98)—one of the greatest masters, writers, and discoverers of spiritual treasures of the Nyingma school. When very young, he remembered his previous lives. From the age of six, he took the vows of a novice and started to receive many teachings and transmissions. At thirteen, he met his principal teacher.

At twenty-six, he made a long retreat during which he studied the *Seven Treasures* of Longchenpa and felt an intense devotion to that master. In a second retreat, Longchenpa appeared to him in vision, whereupon Jigme Lingpa understood the meaning of *The Heart Essence of the Great Expanse (klong chen snying thig)*, the principal spiritual treasure that he was about to reveal and that later became one of the teachings most practiced by the Nyingma school. He then propagated this teaching, founded the monastery of Tsering Jong, and composed texts on many subjects, both religious and secular, most notably *The Treasury of Precious Qualities*, a brilliant presentation of the steps of the path according to the Nyingma school, accompanied by two autocommentaries.

KALDEN GYATSO (yab rje bla ma skal ldan rgya mtsho, 1607–77).

KANGYUR RINPOCHE (bka' 'gyur rin po che klong chen ye shes rdo rje, 1897–1975)—born in the province of Kham in eastern Tibet, he displayed amazing spiritual qualities from his earliest childhood. One day, accompanying a group of pilgrims, he visited the great Mipham Rinpoche, in his cave hermitage. "Who is this boy?" asked Mipham, pointing at him with his finger. "A young village boy," the monks replied. Mipham then made this reflection: "Certain boys become great masters."

At a young age, he entered the monastery of Riwoche, a vast center in which different traditions were practiced side by side. There he studied with his principal teacher, Jedrung Trinle Jampa Jungne, one of Jamyang Khyentse Wangpo's main disciples.

Upon completion of the monastic cycle of traditional studies, Kangyur Rinpoche undertook a nine-year meditation retreat on the borders of Kham. Then he walked to the monastery of Taklung in central Tibet, a journey of several months. There, during the summer retreat, the monks officially requested him to give the oral transmission of the *Kangyur*, the Tibetan translation of the Buddha's discourses, which comprises 103 volumes. The skill which he displayed in the recitation and explanation of those texts led to his being known as "Kangyur Rinpoche."

He was a revealer of spiritual treasures and composed a number of major texts including a commentary on Jigme Lingpa's *Treasury of Precious Qualities*.

In 1955, Kangyur Rinpoche foresaw the impending invasion of Tibet by the Chinese and decided to leave for India with his wife and their young children, taking with him by pack-mule his only wealth, hundreds of books. In 1960 he settled near Darjeeling where he lived until his death in 1975, constantly teaching. He had many Western disciples and was thus one of the first Tibetan masters to lay the foundations of Tibetan Buddhism in the West.

His sons and spiritual heirs, Taklung Tsetrul Pema Wangyal Rinpoche, Jigme Khyentse Rinpoche, and Rangdröl Rinpoche, perpetuate the transmission of his teachings in the world, particularly at the Centre d'Etudes de Chanteloube, in the Dordogne, France.

KELSANG GYATSO, THE SEVENTH DALAI LAMA. *See* THE SEVENTH DALAI LAMA, KELSANG GYATSO

KHYENTSE CHÖKYI LODRÖ ('jam dbyangs mkhyen brtse chos kyi blo gros, 1893–1959)—widely considered to be the lama from eastern Tibet who had the greatest influence on the Tibetan Buddhism of his time. Recognized as an emanation of the great Jamyang Khyentse Wangpo, he was enthroned at a young age at Katok monastery, where he began his studies. At fifteen, he was invited to direct Dzongsar Monastery. He studied under many great masters from different schools. He then tirelessly gave transmissions of the Tibetan Buddhist heritage to countless lamas from all schools, and particularly to those from the Nyingma and Sakya traditions, including one of his main Dharma heirs, Dilgo Khyentse Rinpoche.

In 1955, when he sensed that the conflicts generated by the Chinese invasion would cause great destruction in Tibet, Dzongsar left and went into exile in Sikkim. There he established his permanent residence and for the rest of his life continued to give extensive teachings.

LANGRI THANGPA (glang ri thang ba rdo rje seng ge, 1054–1123)—a renowned master of the Kadam tradition whose most famous work, *Eight Verses on Training the Mind*, is still practiced in all schools of Tibetan Buddhism.

He is also famous for his sadness at the endless sufferings of the beings that inhabit the illusory world of rebirth, and his attitude has become a model for beginners to measure the depth of their reflection on the faults of samsara. This characteristic earned him the nickname "gloomy face," because he was never seen to smile, except on one occasion, when he noticed a mouse trying to carry off a piece of turquoise placed on his altar. The mouse, unable to move the stone, called one of its fellows to come and help. The antics of the two animals struggling to move the turquoise made Langri Thangpa laugh.

LHATSÜN NAMKHAI JIGME (lha btsun nam mkha' 'jigs med, 1597–1650)—a great master and treasure-revealer born in southern Tibet, he began by studying for seventeen years with a master of the Great Perfection, then spent years meditating in the most remote places in the east and west of Tibet, perfecting the realization that he had acquired from his master. It was during these solitary retreats that he discovered his spiritual treasures, the most famous being *The Spontaneous Song of*

Clouds of the Adamantine Essence, regarded as the quintessence of the profound teachings contained in the treasures.

LONGCHEN RABJAM (klong chen rab 'byams dri med 'od zer, 1308–63)—the most brilliant teacher and scholar of the Nyingma tradition. He wrote more than 250 books on all types of teaching, both sutra and tantra, and particularly on the Great Perfection, and also on secular subjects such as history and literature. Among his most important works are the *Four Heart Essences (snying thig ya bzhi)*, the *Seven Treasures (mdzod bdun)*, and the *Trilogy of Finding Rest (ngal gso skor gsum)*.

After studying with great masters, he acquired an extraordinary perfect mastery of all teachings. He refined his inner experience through years of meditation in the most austere conditions, with only an old sack that served as clothing, bed, and meditation seat, thus achieving the highest possible realization.

His major contribution to Tibetan Buddhism was to compile, organize, and codify all the teachings and practices of the Nyingma school and, more particularly, to elucidate the teachings of the Great Perfection with unequaled clarity and brilliance.

MACHIK LAPDRÖN (ma gcig lab sgron, 1055–1153)—probably the most famous woman among the great teachers to have shaped Tibetan Buddhism. She was interested in the Dharma from her earliest youth. Her two main teachers, Dampa Sangye and Sonam Drakpa, emphasized the internalization of the meaning of the teaching through practice, rather than through mere intellectual understanding. Thus she came to the full realization of what her masters had passed on to her.

She continued to teach throughout her long life, at first living in the manner of a yogini, uniting with an Indian yogi with whom she had five children, then returning to a monastic life. She eventually settled in the cave Zangri Kangmar, where a community formed around her.

She is the origin of a large body of practices and teachings that had a great influence on all schools, especially the practice of Chö, which means cutting the attachment to a self. She also composed the melodies for this practice, which are still used in all schools of Tibetan Buddhism.

MILAREPA (rje btsun mi la ras pa, 1040–1123)—the most famous Tibetan yogi and poet and the main disciple of Marpa the translator, the originator of the Kagyu school.

Milarepa was born in western Tibet near the Nepal border. His father died when he was only seven years old, and the family properties were put in the charge of relatives who ill-treated him and his mother and sister. His mother, in despair, sent her son to learn black magic to avenge this injustice.

Using the techniques he had learned from a sorcerer, Milarepa first caused the death of thirty-five of his enemies and then caused a hailstorm that destroyed their grain harvest.

But he soon regretted his actions. Disgusted with his life, he sought a Buddhist teacher who would be able to help him purify the negative karma he had accumulated. He became a disciple of a master of the Nyingma school who, perceiving that he had a deep karmic connection with Marpa the Translator, sent him to see that teacher. Marpa had journeyed to India, risking his life, and brought back and translated the teachings of the Indian master Naropa, who had received them from Tilopa.

Marpa had the intuition that he had before him someone with an exceptional destiny who would be his successor. However, he did not show anything, and knowing the past misdeeds of Milarepa, he decided first to test his will and purify him of his crimes. It was thus that, to prepare Milarepa to receive the instructions and practices he intended for him, for six years he put him through very hard trials. Then he gave Milarepa all the teachings that he had himself received and sent him to practice in the solitude of the mountains.

For many years, Milarepa practiced in absolute poverty, wearing only a light cotton cloth (hence his name, meaning "cotton-clad Mila") and eating only wild nettles, until, as he says himself, his body took on a green tinge, as he is often depicted in paintings representing him.

He attained enlightenment in one lifetime, had many disciples, and became famous for his poetic songs, which were transcribed under the title *The Hundred Thousand Songs of Mila*. Among his most famous disciples were Gampopa (see biographical notes), the monk who became the lineage holder, and Rechungpa, who had himself transmitted teachings to Milarepa and who continued the tradition of lay yogis.

MINLING TERCHEN GYURME DORJE (smin gling gter chen 'gyur med rdo rje, 1646–1714)—a great teacher and spiritual treasure-revealer of the Nyingma school. He founded the monastery of Mindroling, one of the six major monasteries of the Nyingma school, and saved a lot of teachings that were about to disappear. They include the tantras of the ancient tradition in a first *Collection of Ancient Tantras* and an anthology of the most important spiritual treasures, which was to be the basis of the *Collection of Precious Treasures* of Jamgön Kongtrul Lodrö Thayé. His complete works include sixteen volumes.

He had a highly accomplished daughter, Mingyur Paldrön, who played an important role in the transmission of the teachings of the Mindroling tradition, one of the most influential of the Nyingma school, and was the first in a line of Jetsünmas, Mindroling holy women, of whom Khandro Rinpoche, born in 1969, is the current representative.

MIPHAM RINPOCHE (mi pham 'jam dbyangs rgya mtsho, 1846–1912)— Mipham Rinpoche, known as Mipham Chole Namgyal and also as Jampel Gyepe Dorje, was from Dzachuka, eastern Tibet. He displayed exceptional talents very early on, memorizing whole books at the age of six and becoming a renowned author at the age of ten.

He spent years in meditation retreat and showed many signs of realization.

Encouraged by Jamgön Kongtrul Lodrö Thayé and Jamyang Khyentse Wangpo, to whom he was very close, he composed brilliant treatises and commentaries on the philosophy and practices of the Nyingma tradition, and also on the sutras, the Kalachakra, and many other subjects. His knowledge was wide ranging, and he wrote on topics as diverse as medicine, painting, astrology, grammar, and poetics. His complete works fill thirty volumes.

MOKCHOKPA RINCHEN TSÖNDRU (rmog lcog pa rin chen brtson 'grus, 1110–70).

NAGARJUNA (klu grub, first and second century AD)—one of the foremost scholars of the Indian tradition of the Great Vehicle, he is also considered to be one of the eighty-four mahasiddhas, or fully accomplished masters, of India. He was a major exponent of the most profound teachings of the Buddha, especially concerning the Prajnaparamita, the Perfection of Wisdom. He is credited with many medical and philosophical texts. Among his most important works are *Root Verses of the Middle Way* and *Seventy Verses on Emptiness.*

NGAWANG LOBSANG GYATSO. *See* THE FIFTH DALAI LAMA, NGAWANG LOBSANG GYATSO

NYENDRAK LUNGRIG NYIMA (nineteenth century).

NYOSHUL KHEN RINPOCHE, JAMYANG DORJE (smyo shul mkhan po 'jam dbyangs rdo rje, 1932–99)—a master of the Nyingma tradition of eastern Tibet. Since childhood he felt a great interest in the Dharma. He studied with twenty-five masters and spent many years in meditation retreat. In particular, he received from his principal master, Shedrup Tenpe Nyima, the "great transmission of pith instructions of the Great Perfection," which he made the heart of his practice and teaching, and passed on to many disciples, including the great masters of his time.

In 1959 he narrowly managed to escape from Tibet and sought refuge in India, where he lived in extremely difficult conditions, begging in the streets of Calcutta in order to survive. Then he started teaching again, sometimes to other lamas, sometimes to large crowds, and great teachers invited him to come to their monasteries or study centers to transmit the special instructions that he held.

He spent much of the latter part of his life in the West, especially in France, teaching in the three-year retreat centers there and responding to invitations from other Western Buddhist groups.

PADMASAMBHAVA (eighth or ninth century?)—the great Indian master who played a key role in the first spread of Buddhism in Tibet, and especially that of the Vajrayana, the Diamond Vehicle. Simply called "Guru Rinpoche," "the Precious Master" or "the second Buddha" by Tibetans, he is the subject of countless "guru yoga" practices (in which devotees merge their mind with the wisdom mind of the master) and other practices of the Secret Mantra.

He was invited to Tibet in the eighth century by King Trisong Detsen. He opened the way for the real establishment of the teachings of

Buddhism and founded Tibet's first Buddhist monastery, Samye. He passed on a vast number of practices and teachings from the tantras and, in particular, hid thousands of spiritual treasures throughout the Himalayan region to be revealed in due course for the sake of future generations. Some of those treasures are still being discovered today by certain masters, called *tertön* (treasure-discoverers), who are regarded as the emanations of the main disciples of Padmasambhava.

The extraordinary life story of Padmasambhava, as recorded in several biographies, or rather hagiographies, does not obey the usual criteria of historical record and is often considered as legend. His many symbolic feats are in fact teachings in themselves, more of an opening the mind to an inner journey than a literal description of outer events.*

PATRUL RINPOCHE (Dpal sprul o rgyan 'jigs med chos kyi dbang po, 1808–87)—a renowned master of the Nyingma school from eastern Tibet, he owes his fame to his nonsectarian approach, his great compassion, and the extreme simplicity of his lifestyle. He spent most of his life, apart from a few years in the study center of Dzogchen Monastery, in caves, forests and remote hermitages. He usually traveled incognito, dressed like a nomad.

In his youth he learned most of the fundamental works by heart, even the vast *Seven Treasures* of Longchenpa. Thus, he could teach the most complex subjects for months without resorting to any written medium. At his death, he owned only a copy of *The Way of the Bodhisattva* and a begging bowl.

From childhood he already displayed a natural kindness and exceptional intellectual ability. He was recognized as the combined emanation of several great masters, including the great Indian master Shantideva, and was made head of his previous incarnation's monastery.

Soon after, he met his principal teacher, Jigme Gyalwai Nyugu, who had meditated for many years in solitude, on the snowline in the remote valley of Dzamalung. On the windswept slopes where he stayed, there was not even a cave for shelter. He lived in a depression in the ground and survived by eating wild plants. Over time, the fame of this

* See Yeshe Tsogyal, *The Lotus-Born*.

remarkable ascetic spread far and wide. The disciples flocked to him by hundreds, settling in tents. It was the perfect example of Dharma practitioners who lead a simple life and remain where they are until they reach enlightenment.

In addition to Jigme Gyalwe Nyugu, Patrul Rinpoche met most of the great lamas of his time and studied with them.

On the death of the nephew of his predecessor, who had been taking care of the monastery until then, Patrul Rinpoche decided to spend the rest of his days without home or possessions. Once he had settled the affairs of the monastery, he set off for a life of wandering.

In the rugged mountains and wooded valleys surrounding the monastery of Dzogchen there are shelters and overhangs where Patrul Rinpoche would often stay during the first period of his life, and where he often returned. He wrote many books, including the famous *Kunzang Lama'i Shelung* (*The Words of My Perfect Teacher*). He sometimes convinced robbers to abandon their life of crime and hunters not to kill animals.

When he taught, all those who listened were transformed. They felt naturally calm and could sit effortlessly, as if absorbed in contemplation. He expressed himself directly in a language that people could understand, giving advice that his listeners could immediately apply to their personal experience. His vast knowledge, the warmth of his blessings, and depth of his realization gave his teachings a unique quality.

All those who had spent some time with him said that he spoke only of the Dharma. He would teach or tell stories of the great teachers of the past, but no one ever heard him participating in ordinary gossip. He spoke little, and when he did, he was completely frank, and anyone hoping for flattery would be disappointed. His presence at first inspired awe and respect, and only those who really needed his spiritual guidance dared approach him. But all who had spent time with him were extremely loath to leave him.

This is how his servant, Sönam Tsering, described his last hours: "When the sun began to shine, he undressed, sat up straight, legs in the vajra position, and put his hands on his knees. Moments later, he looked straight ahead, snapped his fingers with both hands, rested his hands in the mudra of equanimity, and entered the spacious interior light of primordial purity, the perfect sublimation of death."

PEMA LINGPA (padma ling pa 1450–1521)—considered to be the emanation of Longchen Rabjam, he was one of the most influential masters of the history of Bhutan, where he founded many temples and
monastic communities and revealed and taught his spiritual treasures
over thirty years.

Some of his contemporaries doubted his authenticity as a revealer of
treasures. Some even considered him to be a crook. One day a rumor
spread that he was about to retrieve a treasure in a deep pool formed by
a river. The local governor, suspecting a hoax, sent a crowd of witnesses.
"If you really reveal a treasure, I will reward you. Otherwise I will pun-
ish you for organizing this deception in my district." The master replied
that he would plunge into the water with a lighted torch. If he was a true
revealer of the treasures of Padmasambhava, he would resurface with
the torch still lit. If not he would perish by drowning. He lit the torch
and plunged into the water. As time passed, the crowd began to mourn
the death of the master. The governor himself was ashamed of having
provoked the tragedy. But Pema Lingpa eventually emerged from the
waters with the torch still lit in one hand, and in the other, a statue and
a small box. From that day, no one had any doubts about Pema Lingpa.
The place was named Mebartso ("the lake of the lighted torch") and is
still a place of pilgrimage today. He had innumerable disciples, and his
fame spread beyond Bhutan throughout Tibet.

PHAGMO DRUPA, DORJE GYALPO (phag mo gru pa rdo rje rgyal po,
1110–70).

RAHULABHADRA (sixth century).

RANGRIG REPA, KUNGA LODRÖ (rang rig ras pa, 1619–83).

RATNA LINGPA RINCHEN PAL (ratna gling pa rin chen dpal, 1403–78)
—a master and discoverer of spiritual treasures of the Nyingma school,
Ratna Lingpa was born in Lhodrag in southern Tibet.

He was an incarnation of Langdro Lotsawa, one of the twenty-five
close disciples of Padmasambhava. A child prodigy, Ratna Lingpa
learned reading and writing effortlessly and had numerous pure visions
starting from the age of ten. When Ratna Lingpa was twenty-seven,

Guru Rinpoche appeared in person in front of him, in the form of a yogi dressed in yellow raw silk. He showed him three scrolls, a white, a red, and a blue one, and asked Ratna Lingpa to choose one of them. Ratna Lingpa answered that he wanted all three. Because of the auspicious connection created by his answer, Ratna Lingpa received all three inventories and revealed in a single lifetime the termas he would have otherwise revealed in three successive lives.

It is said that when he taught or practiced, extraordinary signs appeared around him. He collected the tantras of the Nyingma tradition in forty-two volumes. This work no longer exists but served as the basis for subsequent compilations.

His spiritual lineage was continued by his own children and great masters of the time such as the sixth Karmapa.

RIGDZIN CHÖKYI TRAKPA (rig 'dzin chos kyi grags pa, 1595–1659).

RINCHEN PHUNTSOK (rin chen phun tshogs, 1509–1602).

RINZIN JIGME LINGPA. *See* JIGME LINGPA

SAKYA PANDITA (sa skya pan di ta kun dga' rgyal mtshan, 1182–1251)— considered a manifestation of the bodhisattva Manjushri, he was one of the greatest scholars of Tibetan Buddhism.

He studied all the spiritual disciplines and secular knowledge of his day, including the arts, medicine, Sanskrit, and other languages.

This immense scholar and Sanskritist of the Sakya school played a key role in the transmission of traditional Indian sciences such as grammar, logic, medicine, astrology, etc., to the Tibetan tradition.

A prolific translator of Sanskrit texts, he was also the author of over a hundred original works, including a major explanation of the three kinds of vows, which had a great influence on Tibetan literature and gave rise to numerous commentaries.

His reputation and his spiritual authority earned him an invitation from the Mongol emperor Godan Khan, the grandson of Genghis Khan, accompanied by an implied threat of the invasion of Tibet if he refused. He became the emperor's spiritual mentor and also saved him from an incurable disease, at the same time saving Tibet from destruction and spreading his teachings in Mongolia and China.

SANGYE WÖN RE DHARMA SENGE (dhar ma seng ge sangs rgyas dbon, 1177–1237).

THE SEVENTH DALAI LAMA, KELSANG GYATSO (skal bzang rgya mtsho, 1708–57)—a great scholar, poet, and meditator whose simple life won the hearts of his contemporaries. The place where he was born was recognized by a famous prophetic poem of his predecessor, the Sixth Dalai Lama, Tsangyang Gyatso:

> White crane, lovely bird,
> Lend me your wings!
> I will not go far:
> One day I will return
> By the path of Lithang.

Deprived of political power by the conflict between the Mongols and Manchus, he devoted himself to spiritual practice and writing commentaries on the tantras. When he could return to Lhasa, he established the Kashag, the equivalent of a cabinet of ministers today.

SHABKAR TSOGDRUK RANGDRÖL (zhabs dkar tshogs drug rang grol, 1781–1851)—a wandering yogi and poet, originally from eastern Tibet, this great teacher of the Nyingma school reminds us of Milarepa—of whom he is considered to be an emanation—because he was the uneducated son of a nomad family and taught using songs of great poetic beauty that owed nothing to intellectual learning and everything to an extraordinary authentic inner experience.

He was famous for his humility and immense compassion. Wherever he went, in Tibet and Nepal, he bought domestic animals in order to free them and persuaded the people he met not to kill or hunt animals. He made a vow before the famous statue of Jowo Rinpoche in Lhasa to stop eating meat, a rarity among Tibetans. On many occasions, he calmed bloody feuds among the tribes of his region.

He was constantly on the move, finding shelter in caves, especially those where Milarepa had meditated on the slopes of the snowy mountains, and never staying long in one place, except on an island on Lake Kokonor where he spent several years in retreat.

He had innumerable disciples to whom he often spoke through poems sung in the manner of Milarepa. His complete works comprise fourteen volumes of teachings of great depth, in a very clear style.

SHAKYAMUNI BUDDHA (sangs rgyas sha kya thub pa, fifth century BCE)—the historical Buddha is not worshiped as a god or a saint, but as the ultimate sage and the expression of enlightenment, the realization of ultimate truth. His life is well known. Here it is in outline.

Shakyamuni was born Prince Siddhartha in the small kingdom of Shakya, whose capital was Kapilavastu, on the current border of India and Nepal. The sage Asita predicted that the child would be a great king or a great sage.

In his youth he led a life of pleasure. He married and had a son, Rahula. At the age of twenty-nine, Siddhartha saw a sick man, an old man, a corpse, and an ascetic, and clearly identified the real suffering that everyone undergoes. He renounced his title of prince to follow his spiritual quest as a wandering mendicant.

He studied with two famous masters of the time, but their teachings did not satisfy him. He devoted himself to an extreme asceticism for six years but found that the mortification of the body did not lead to inner freedom. Renouncing asceticism, Siddhartha Gautama sat down at the foot of the tree that became known as the Bodhi tree, in a place today known as Bodh Gaya in Bihar, and vowed not to leave that spot before reaching complete realization. At dawn, after overcoming the attacks of Mara, the demon who personifies ignorance and attachment to "I," he attained perfect enlightenment at the age of thirty-five and became the Buddha, "The Awakened One."

At the deer park of Sarnath, he gave his first teaching, on the four noble truths: suffering, the cause of suffering, the cessation of suffering, and the path leading to the cessation of suffering.

A group of wandering disciples gathered around him and then grew rapidly. From then on the Buddha taught continuously, both to laypeople and those who gave up everything to follow him.

When he was eighty-one, he gave his last teaching on impermanence of all things and passed into nirvana, the state beyond suffering.

The collection of his teaching stretches to 303 volumes in its Tibetan translation, the Kangyur.

SHANTIDEVA (zhi ba lha, 685–763)—one of the eighty-four Indian mahasiddhas. Born into a royal family in western India, he renounced the succession to his father's title and took monastic vows at the Buddhist university of Nalanda, where he became a hidden scholar, sleeping by day and working by night, and wrote in secret two treatises, the *Compendium of Instructions* and the *Compendium of Sutras*. Despised by his companions who thought he was an ignoramus, he was summoned to give a public discourse on a ridiculously high throne, with the sole purpose of ridiculing him and expelling him from the university. However, the teaching he gave stunned the entire audience. This was *The Way of the Bodhisattva*, which was to become renowned as his principal work and the most studied and most commented text in Tibet.

It is said that Shantideva then gave back his monastic vows and left the university of Nalanda to lead a life of a wandering yogi, debating with non-Buddhist masters and helping beings in all kinds of ways, including through miracles.

SHECHEN GYALTSAP PEMA NAMGYAL (zhe chen rgyal tshab padma rnam rgyal, 1871–1926)—this great scholar and spiritual master of the Nyingma school belonged to the second generation of propagators of the nonsectarian movement in Eastern Tibet. The founders of this movement, Jamyang Khyentse Wangpo, Jamgön Kongtrul, and especially Mipham Rinpoche, figured among his teachers. Recognized as the third emanation of the *gyaltsap*, or regents, of the monastery of Shechen Tennyi Dargyeling, he was installed on the throne of his predecessor at a young age.

He devoted over twenty years to the extensive study and practice of all aspects of the path of enlightenment. When he had accomplished the fruit of those practices, "the treasure of his wisdom flowed," as the Tibetan expression goes, and through the exceptional quality of his teachings, he became the teacher of the greatest masters of eastern Tibet, including Dzongsar Khyentse Chökyi Lodrö, the sixth Shechen Rabjam, and Dilgo Khyentse Rinpoche.

He spent most of his life at the hermitage of Pema Ösel Ling above the monastery of Shechen, where he wrote clear and profound commentaries on various aspects of Buddhist philosophy and practice.

His complete works, comprising thirteen volumes, is one of the most varied collections of Tibetan literature and includes clear and profound commentaries on various aspects of Buddhist philosophy and practice.

TARANATHA (ta ra na tha kun dga' snying po, 1575–1635)—this great master was born at Karak in central Tibet and was the reembodiment of another important teacher of the Jonang tradition, Jetsun Kunga Drolchok (rje btsun kun dga' grol mchog, 1507–66). Taranatha was one of the major proponents of the *zhentong* view that had been expounded in great depth by the Omniscient Dolpopa Sherab Gyaltsen (dol po pa shes rab rgyal mtshan, 1292–1361). He strove to refute erroneous opinions about this profound view of the essence of buddhahood (*tathagatagarbha*) and of ultimate reality. Among his many teachers was the great Indian master Buddhaguptanatha, who had traveled to Tibet and given him extensive teachings related to the Tantrayana.

Adopting a nonsectarian approach, Taranatha practiced and taught from various lineages, had countless visions, and achieved ultimate spiritual realization. He emphasized the practice of the Sakya teachings of *Lamdre* (*lam 'bras*) and the instructions of the Shangpa Kagyu and especially focused on the explication of the Kalachakra Tantra and the practice of its Six-Branch Yoga (*sbyor drug*). He was also one of the last great Tibetan translators of Sanskrit texts. His collected works fill twenty-three volumes.

The Jonang tradition is still practiced in the Dzamthang province of Eastern Tibet, as well as among the Tibetan refugee community in India.

TENNYI LINGPA, PEMA TSEWANG GYALPO (bstan gnyis gling pa padma tshe dbang rgyal po, 1480–1535).

TENZIN GYATSO. *See* THE FOURTEENTH DALAI LAMA, TENZIN GYATSO

TRAKPA GYALTSEN (rje btsun grags pa rgyal mtshan, 1147–1216)—a learned and accomplished master of the Sakya school.

From an early age he showed signs of great maturity and did not behave like other children. He had no attachment to food and other ordinary pleasures. When he could only just walk, he already liked to stay in quiet places to study.

At eight, he took the vows of a novice. At twelve, to general surprise, he commented on the Hevajra tantra before a vast assembly. From the age of thirteen and until his death, he was responsible for the Vajrayana teaching at Sakya monastery.

He unceasingly sought teachings from different masters and practiced with extraordinary diligence, only sleeping a few hours a night. Those who knew him remarked that he was never idle but always busy studying, practicing, or teaching.

He left a large number of texts in simple and elegant style, easily understood by everyone, and covering topics as diverse as tantra, meditative practices, history, astrology, and medicine. He was also a talented traditional artist and created mandalas, statues, and stupas.

Without attachment to worldly goods, he regularly gave away all his possessions to others. Although he received many gifts from his disciples, when he died his only possessions were his meditation cushion and monastic robes.

YONGEY MINGYUR RINPOCHE (yongs ge mi' gyur rdo rje, born in 1975)—belongs to the generation of *tulkus*, recognized as emanations of Tibetan masters of the past, who received all their training outside of Tibet due to the Chinese occupation. He was born in Nepal as the son of Tulku Urgyen Rinpoche, a great meditator who spent most of his life in hermitages. At the age of three, he was recognized as both an emanation of the discoverer of spiritual treasures Yongey Mingyur Dorje and of Kangyur Rinpoche (see biographical notes).

From an early age he was attracted to the contemplative life and at thirteen, on his own initiative, he undertook two consecutive retreats of three years each. He then became one of the most popular teachers of his generation for his humor and his ability to communicate the most subtle and difficult Buddhist concepts in a simple and direct way. He has been invited to teach all over the world and published two books of advice, the first of which also chronicles his own life and experience.* Recently he disappeared, taking nothing with him, but leaving detailed advice for his

* *The Joy of Living* and *Joyful Wisdom*.

many students, to anonymously follow the life of a wandering yogi, in the manner of Milarepa and Nyoshul Khenpo.

He has shown a particular interest in modern science, and especially research in neuroscience, to which he lent his support by participating, in 2002, in the experiments conducted by leading researchers such as Antoine Lutz whose goal was to determine the influence of meditation training on brain function. When he saw the results that Mingyur Rinpoche and a handful of other experienced meditators produced, the world-renowned neuroscientist Richard Davidson exclaimed, "We did not expect anything so spectacular."